UNDERSTANDING ORGANIZATIONAL BEHAVIOR

A CASEBOOK

UNDERSTANDING ORGANIZATIONAL BEHAVIOR
A CASEBOOK

HARRY R. KNUDSON
University of Washington

C. PATRICK FLEENOR
Seattle University

ROBERT E. CALLAHAN
Seattle University

Charles E. Merrill Publishing Company
A Bell & Howell Company
Columbus   Toronto   London   Sydney

To my father

To Wendy, Michelle, and Timothy

To the OB crowd at Case

Published by Charles E. Merrill Publishing Co.
A Bell & Howell Company
Columbus, Ohio 43216

This book was set in Univers
Production Editor: Mary Harlan
Cover Designer: Cathy Watterson
Text Designer: Cynthia Brunk

Library of Congress Catalog Card Number: 85–62479
International Standard Book Number: 0–675–20481–X
Printed in the United States of America
1 2 3 4 5 6 7 8 9—91 90 89 88 87 86

PREFACE

This book was written as a companion book to *Understanding Organizational Behavior: A Managerial Viewpoint*. That book is a comprehensive text in the field of organizational behavior and contains a great deal of conceptual material, applications from the real world of organizations, experiential exercises, and a limited number of cases. This book is designed to provide a relatively large number of cases for the instructor or reader who wishes to use the case method as a means of learning about organizational behavior. It can be used to augment the cases in the companion volume, or it can be used independently. How it is used will depend in large measure upon the feelings that the user has about the case method of instruction.

Each of us has had different experiences regarding learning by the case method. One of us has a background that includes almost total immersion in the case method at one of the pioneer and continued strong advocates of case learning, the Harvard Business School. Another comes from the opposite end of the continuum, with education and training that included few case situations. The third author has an educational experience that perhaps represents a middle ground—an emphasis on the case method about equal to that given other methods of learning. But we all feel that the case method is a powerful learning tool and have devoted considerable time in our extended teaching careers to the development, writing, and classroom use of cases. Indeed, we have been honored on occasion to have been asked to share our experiences with colleagues from other colleges and universities. So we present this material as strong supporters of the case method, yet realizing that the inefficiency of the method and the significant change in the typical role of the instructor is threatening to some. We believe that the effectiveness of the case method and the real learning on several levels that results is worth it!

Many of the cases in this book have been developed by us in the recent past and are published here for the first time. These cases come from a variety of sources, including students, former students, participants in executive development programs in which we have been involved, consulting clients, colleagues, and, in a number of situations, friends and neighbors. Other cases have been developed by colleagues. A few are old favorites—cases that we were raised on, so to speak.

We are particularly pleased with that group of cases dealing with the aspirations, problems, feelings, attitudes, and victories of young people relatively new to organizational life. These cases relate the experiences of many of our former graduate and undergraduate students, often experiences we had the opportunity to watch unfold. We feel these cases will have particular value in the classroom in that they present situations to which students can readily relate and which they will readily understand. These cases offer an opportunity for significant learning.

Those cases that we did not author were selected for the book after review of approximately three hundred cases from a variety of sources. The authors of these cases are acknowledged individually in a special section of the book.

In choosing cases for the book, both ours and those of others, we were guided by a few fundamental concepts. First, we wanted cases that dealt with organizational issues that were significant, yet relatively common. We didn't want the spectacular situation that occurs only once every fifty years or so. We also desired cases that had a great deal of information in them so that the student could do some significant analysis. But most importantly, we chose cases that stressed a managerial point of view and required that a decision be made and that some action be taken. We were not concerned with behavior in organizations from a clinical view but were interested in behavior from the viewpoint of the manager. Similarly, we wanted more from the cases than "understanding." We wanted understanding, of course, but further we wanted the student to have to wrestle with some significant issues and make some decisions. Often difficult decisions. From these decisions flows the necessity to develop action plans for implementing them.

All of the cases are from real situations, and all have been used extensively in a variety of classroom situations.

Many people have helped to make this book possible and we want to acknowledge their contributions. As noted, the authors of those cases that are not our own have been acknowledged individually. Their cooperation was of prime importance in this project. Those people who participated in our classes in which these cases were initially used also deserve our thanks. The many valuable suggestions for improvement altered the final form of many of the cases. Several of our colleagues were helpful in reviewing early drafts of the cases and providing many helpful comments.

Professor Karl Vesper of the Graduate School of Business, University of Washington, was especially understanding in scheduling classes in such a way that relatively large blocks of time were available for concentrated effort on the project.

Three research assistants provided invaluable help in writing the cases, being involved in almost all phases of this process. Ms. Caroline Holmes, while completing an M.B.A. degree, took charge of many of the early case writing activities in an extremely competent and professional manner. In the later phases of the book, Ms. Sara P. Knudson did innumerable revisions of the cases and organized much of the effort necessary to turn a concept into a completed manuscript. A great deal of the time involved in this activity was accomplished in addition to the regular responsibilities she holds in her position as a professional writer, and we appreciate her high level of interest and competence. Ms. Renee Catton became involved in the project during its final stages and provided some very valuable administrative assistance that assured its successful completion. Her efforts were completed at the same time that she was finishing an M.B.A. degree, and her ability to remain competently cheerful while under a great deal of pressure is very much appreciated.

Finally, an inadequate word of thanks to our families who have lived through yet another book. As they often tell us, we don't really appreciate the extent of their suffering while we are in the writing mode. In a feeble attempt to make amends, at least two of the authors have talked somewhat seriously about a glorious vacation at the seashore. It probably won't happen.

ACKNOWLEDGMENTS

We are delighted to acknowledge the cooperation of the following individuals and institutions who graciously permitted us to use their materials in this book.

POLAR STAR BEVERAGES COMPANY (A), (B), (C)
Anthony G. Athos
Author and Consultant

OUT OF THE FRYING PAN
George Eddy
University of Texas

ELECTRONIC SYSTEMS COMPANY
THE FOSTER CREEK POST OFFICE
NORTHEASTERN ELECTRIC LIGHT AND POWER CORPORATION
Alvar O. Elbing
Professor and Consultant

WATSON SIDING
Richard N. Farmer
Indiana University

DICK SPENCER
Margaret E. Fenn
University of Washington

THE BARREL OF LUG NUTS
Jerry L. Gray and
Frederick A. Starke
University of Manitoba

BIRKENFIELD FURNITURE MANUFACTURING COMPANY
Gerald Hampton and
Bruce Mullins
Seattle University

STANLEY LOWELL
O. Jeff Harris, Jr.
Louisiana State University

DASHMAN COMPANY
LAMSON COMPANY
The President and Fellows of Harvard College
Harvard University

JUDY SIMPSON
Robert D. Hay
University of Arkansas

SAVEMORE FOOD STORE 5116
John W. Hennessey
Dartmouth College

VILLAGE INN
Jay T. Knippen
University of South Florida

RONDELL DATA CORPORATION
John A. Seeger
Bentley College

TOO MANY PERSONAL CALLS
Sterling Shoen
Washington University

MOOSAJEES, LIMITED
"PERFECTLY PURE PEABODY'S"
Board of Trustees of the Leland Stanford Junior University
Stanford University/Graduate School of Business

METROCENTER POLICE DEPARTMENT
Charles E. Summer
University of Washington

CONSTRUCTION EQUIPMENT INTERNATIONAL, AG (A), (B), (C)
Charles E. Summer
University of Washington and IMEDE

THE UNITED CHEMICAL COMPANY
Andrew D. Szilagyi, Jr.
University of Houston

ASPEN COUNTY HIGH SCHOOL
Sherman Tingey
President, INCAP Group
Tempe, Arizona

MICHAEL SIMPSON
Michael Tushman
Columbia University

A MATTER OF PRIORITIES
Robert A. Ullrich
Vanderbilt University

ACME WHOLESALE DISTRIBUTING COMPANY
Gary G. Whitney
University of San Diego

CONTENTS

PART TWO
UNDERSTANDING INDIVIDUAL BEHAVIOR IN ORGANIZATIONS

PART THREE
INTERPERSONAL DYNAMICS

PART FOUR

THE INFLUENCE PROCESS

PART FIVE

CHANGE AND CONFLICT

PART SIX
HUMAN RESOURCE SYSTEMS

PART SEVEN
SPECIAL ISSUES IN ORGANIZATIONAL BEHAVIOR

INTRODUCTION

The cases in this book involve people in organizations. The situations are taken from a wide variety of organizations—private and public, profit and nonprofit—and an equally diverse range of activities—service, manufacturing, educational, health, high tech, and others. The overall objective of the book is to provide an opportunity for students to develop their abilities to analyze managerial problems and opportunities and to propose effective and responsible plans of action. In the process, students will experience some of the challenges of managing people in today's complex society and may begin to appreciate the even greater challenges of managing people in the more complex society of the future.

THE CASE METHOD OF STUDY

Although the case method of study has become a mainstay of business education throughout the world, those who have not had an opportunity to be involved in a program that uses the case method in a systematic fashion may ask, "What is a case?" A case is simply a written statement of an actual situation taken from a real organization. The situation may involve people at the lowest or the highest levels of the organization. It may relate to one or to several operating functions, or it may embrace the overall situation of an organization. It may focus on a unique situation or it may deal with broader issues.

Usually, a case describes a situation in which a manager has to make a decision and take action. As far as possible, the same information is furnished to the student as was available to the manager. Actually, the reader is at an advantage in that the material in the case is presented in a concise, readable format, whereas the manager may have had to go to considerable trouble and expense to acquire the same data.

But why bother with cases at all? Discussion of cases is a relatively time-consuming way in which to learn. Why doesn't the instructor simply tell the students what they need to know and save everyone a lot of time and bother? Perhaps some of the best answers to this question are contained in the classic article "Because Wisdom Can't Be Told," written by Charles I. Gragg, one of the pioneers of case teaching at the Harvard Business School:

> It can be said flatly that the mere act of listening to wise statements and sound advice does little for anyone. In the process of learning, the learner's dynamic coop-

eration is required. . . . The key to an understanding of the . . . case plan of teaching is to be found in the tact that this plan dignifies and dramatizes student life by opening the way for students to make positive contributions to thought and, by so doing, to prepare themselves for action.[1]

Gragg elaborates on the notion that the case method is a democratic method of instruction, as contrasted with the lecture method, which is seen as dictatorial or patriarchal. With the case method, all members of the academic group, teacher and students, are in possession of the same basic materials in light of which analyses are to be made and decisions taken. Thus, any member has the opportunity to make a real contribution toward an effective solution of the issue under consideration. And this is important, for the world of organizations is not exact, and a manager or prospective manager cannot simply memorize a list of "principles" and apply them at the appropriate times. Even with a memorized list, how would a manager decide what time was appropriate for any specific principle? Mature judgment is essential to managerial effectiveness, and the case method helps develop this kind of judgment. As the title of Gragg's article states, wisdom, or judgment, cannot be told; it must be developed through experience.

All the cases in this book are real. The situations actually happened in functioning organizations, and managers had to take action based on the information presented here. Many of the cases resulted from our own contacts with managers and were written by us or by research assistants under our direction. Others were selected for inclusion after an extensive survey of several hundred cases developed and written by others.

Because this book emphasizes the behavior of people in organizations, all of the cases have a strong human orientation and deal with typical situations that managers face. Although questions dealing with marketing, finance, and production activities appear, they are subordinate to the issues of people, how they behave, and what the manager might do to promote more effective behavior. While all of the cases have this strong human orientation, the cases do differ. Some cases are primarily descriptive and provide opportunities to understand particular kinds of situations. Others are rich in data and can sharpen analytical skills. A few contain relatively little data and require the student to develop a plan of action despite little information and little possibility of obtaining more. Most require you to assume the role of manager, to make a decision, and to develop a plan of action. Indeed, the two main thrusts of the book are *action* and *management,* and we have chosen materials that will force you to assume the role of a manager and take some action.

---

[1]Charles I. Gragg, "Because Wisdom Can't Be Told," *Harvard Alumni Bulletin,* October 19, 1940. Reprinted in *The Case Method at the Harvard Business School,* ed. Malcolm P. McNair (New York: McGraw-Hill, 1954), p. 6.

Benefits of the Case Method

What benefits do you get from spending time and effort in analyzing a case? Although the case method may be relatively inefficient, it is effective. You really do learn, and you can expect several positive things to happen, assuming that you do your part and carry out your responsibilities. (We'll talk more about these later.) Our goals in preparing this book, or when teaching Organizational Behavior using the case method, are as follows:

- ☐ *To provide you with the opportunity to experience many different types of organizational situations.* All organizations are not the same, and you will appreciate more fully their considerable differences as you work your way through this book.
- ☐ *To increase your ability to predict what will happen in organizations,* thus providing you with some valuable lead time during which you can develop appropriate plans of action that will let you take advantage of forthcoming opportunities and make future problems less onerous.
- ☐ *To increase your ability to develop alternative ways of handling a situation.* Too often managers seem to adopt the first plan of action that occurs to them, or the one that was successful the last time this kind of problem occurred, rather than systematically explore a range of feasible alternatives. The manager who always follows the same approach and plan of action will find it increasingly difficult to be effective as organizational issues become more complex.
- ☐ *To provide you with the opportunity to critically analyze the assumptions you have about people and how they behave in organizations.* Further, we encourage you to evaluate the effectiveness of those assumptions that form the basis for your behavior as a manager or a member of an organization. We do not have a particular set of assumptions that we advocate—assumptions that are "better" than others. Our purpose is to have you understand the assumptions you now hold and the impact of these assumptions.
- ☐ *To provide you with some managerial tools and approaches.* These tools and approaches have proven useful and can be applied to a situation, *if you choose,* without a great increase in resources, more skillful subordinates, a new boss, or changes in any of the other factors that are important to the situation. But note that *you* must decide whether to use them.
- ☐ *To integrate the concept of TRADEOFF in your managerial practice.* We continue to be amazed at the number of experienced managers who spend an inordinate amount of time looking for the "perfect" solution, one that will have nothing but positive outcomes. Although many textbooks indicate that such an outcome is possible, it simply isn't so! Any

solution has some positive and some negative aspects, and a manager should carefully weigh the benefits of a proposed action against its cost. We want you to understand this and to develop skill in framing the tradeoffs involved, so that you can better analyze costs and benefits rather than waste your physical, emotional, and intellectual energies searching for the perfect solution.

Although many of our students do not intend to become managers, we have found that accomplishing the kinds of objectives noted above makes them more effective organization *members.* A greater understanding of the forces that cause people to behave as they do in organizations can help these students determine their own courses of action.

Responsibilities of the Student

Learning by the case method differs significantly from the more traditional approaches of lecture or lecture and discussion. Some of these differences concern the amount of time required, the degree of involvement and enthusiasm developed, the amount of flexibility present, and the locus of control of the learning process. Perhaps the most significant differences, though, lie in the areas of the responsibility for the learning that takes place and the nature of the learning process.

In the case method, much of the responsibility for learning rests with the individual participant rather than with the instructor. Learning by lecture, or even by lecture and discussion, is much more passive in that the instructor assumes the responsibility of organizing and presenting the material in an effective way, and the student assumes the role of listening attentively and absorbing the information presented. In the case method, the student becomes much more involved in the learning process in many different ways. First, the student must do a great deal of preparation beyond simply reading and understanding factual material. The preparation often involves evaluating material, much of which may not be factual, and developing a plan of action based on this evaluation. Further, because any action plan is based on assumptions about organizational behavior that are peculiar to the individual, the student literally invests a part of himself or herself in the learning process. Finally, a great deal of the responsibility for learning actually rests with the student. The instructor plays a multifaceted role, guiding discussion, asking questions, providing perspectives, summarizing comments—but rarely providing answers. It is the responsibility of the individual students to reach conclusions that are meaningful to them and that will increase their ability to deal effectively with organizational situations.

The Group Process

The learning process also differs in that much of the learning takes place through active group discussion and interaction rather than through a passive relationship between an instructor and an individual student.

The group environment substantially affects the learning process. Each student not only must analyze the case information and develop an effective action plan but also must be able to present the plan to the group members in such a way that they also agree that it is effective. This is not a passive process. A student's ability to persuade and influence others in the group is as significant as the ability to analyze a situation. Indeed, mediocre plans are sometimes received enthusiastically because of the persuasive abilities of the presenter— just as in organizations. Conversely, wonderful action plans are not adopted because those who designed the plans are unable to persuade those in power to adopt them. Just as in the organizational world.

Remember, though, that the class *is* an organization, and you can learn much about organizations by observing the ways in which individuals in the class behave and by noting the various stages through which the class progresses during the academic term. In the case method, the class becomes part of the learning process rather than an administrative vehicle of the university.

Case discussions provide an excellent opportunity for you to learn from others in the class. Invariably, a group of twenty persons will have at least twenty different approaches to a case. This is to be expected because each person brings to his or her analysis a different set of experiences, assumptions, interests, and levels of analytical ability. While the lack of consensus in group discussions can prove frustrating, it provides a rich opportunity to learn from the other members of the group. Indeed, one of the first major benefits of the case method may be simply the realization that each person involved will approach the same situation differently, and the question "What problem, if any, is present in this situation?" will elicit a very wide range of responses. The proposed action plans are usually similarly diverse. But the important consideration is that the group and the group processes inherent in the case method become an invaluable part of the learning process.

Stages of Progress

It is not unusual for a student to go through three distinct stages of development during the experience of the case method.

The first stage is the discovery that no one student will think of everything. While the challenge and responsibility of original thought can be exhilarating at first, often a feeling of disillusionment or frustration develops. After you have spent considerable time preparing a case and developing creative action plans, it can be disconcerting to discover that others in the group have considered factors, arguments, and approaches that had not occurred to you, and that they have developed what seem to be perfectly feasible action plans based on these considerations. It may appear that you are the only person in the entire world who doesn't understand the problem!

The second stage is the realization that no one person has a monopoly on good analyses or creative solutions. In this stage, the student recognizes the need for cooperative assistance and accepts it easily and naturally. As time goes on, students learn to draw from one another's ideas and use them in building their own analytical skills.

The third stage is the realization that even professors don't know all the "right" answers, and even if they might, each person in the group is welcome to present and preserve his or her own views. At this point, the student is operating as a truly responsible person, accepting help as appropriate but making decisions with confidence, not seeking approval from an authority figure.

Progress through these phases takes time and is not accomplished without effort and frustration. But successful progress culminating in the ability to make effective decisions and develop effective action plans is the essence of the case method.

(Almost) Risk-Free Learning

One valuable aspect of this learning process is that you can experiment with different analyses and action plans at considerably less risk than in a real organization. In group discussion, for example, a student might say, "I'm not certain about this plan of action, but I think that it would be reasonable to do. . . .What do you think?" In this way the student can test a solution by inviting comment from fellow class members and evaluating their reactions. While some risk is involved in this approach—you may feel somewhat foolish if everyone else thinks your solution is inadequate or inappropriate or just plain dumb—it is a different kind of risk than if you had actually tried your solution in a real situation. Failure in those circumstances could have very unpleasant consequences for your career! And in the classroom situation, you can explore why your contemporaries didn't like your plan. Did you make some unrealistic assumptions? Did you analyze the data inappropriately? Was your plan of action consistent with your objectives? Did you have any objectives? Was it feasible in terms of the current culture of the organization? Exploration of these kinds of questions can provide meaningful learning experiences.

ANALYZING A CASE

There is no perfect way to analyze a case. Different authors advocate different approaches, each with its advantages and disadvantages. A careful look at these approaches, however, reveals certain areas of uniformity. The following procedure takes into account those areas of uniformity. While the result still doesn't achieve perfection, it should help you in your preparation of cases.

Whenever you are assigned a case, you will be expected to do three distinct things—except in unusual circumstances in which your instructor may give you very special instructions.

> ☐ *STUDY* Read the case thoroughly and be sure you understand all data. While a great deal of information in the case may not be "fact," you should understand that information as well.

☐ *ANALYZE* Isolate, break down, synthesize, compare, evaluate, and prioritize the data. You may find some of the analytical models in the field of organizational behavior useful. We'll talk more about this later.

☐ *DECIDE* Make a commitment. Choose one course of action and develop a plan of implementation.

The following specific steps should help you accomplish the tasks of studying, analyzing, and deciding.

1. Read the first few paragraphs of the case, then continue almost as fast as you can read, asking yourself, What is this case all about? What kinds of information am I being given to analyze?

2. Read the case again very carefully, underlining or noting key bits of information. Write no more than one or two short paragraphs that describe the situation and identify the salient issues. Writing forces you to be more specific.

3. Think about the case for a day or two! We realize the many demands upon a student's time, but our experience strongly suggests that if you first read a case a few days before the class discussion is scheduled you will do a much stronger analysis than if you read it just before class. The process of "mulling over" the data seems to be very valuable and will usually result in a much more effective action plan.

4. Do some analysis. Look for the significant components of the case—problems, opportunities, issues that must be considered, decisions that must be made. You should consider using some of the theoretical constructs from the field of organizational behavior in this analysis. For example, if you are trying to understand why certain individuals in the case behaved as they did, an application of need-reward theory or expectancy theory would be useful. If you are dealing with a situation involving change, you might find force field analysis useful.

5. Identify the major problems in the case. Be certain that you are dealing with the real problems rather than merely *symptoms* of the problems. For instance, a case might relate that a significant number of people regularly come to work late. In all probability, their tardiness is a symptom of a deeper problem. It might be that the psychological rewards they get from coming to work are so meager that they can hardly drag themselves in the door. Or it may be that the city transportation system can't handle all the traffic at that hour. But the important thing is to look beyond the symptoms to see whether you can discover the underlying cause.

   Remember that the description of a problem may depend greatly on the perspectives of the people describing it. A problem as seen from one point of view may not be considered a problem at all by others who have a different viewpoint.

6. Identify data from the case that confirm your description of problems (or opportunities). Is something a problem simply because you say it is, or do you have data to support your conclusion? Students sometimes complain about the lack of data in a case when they have not used appropriately the data available.

7. List the problems (opportunities) in order of priority. Which are the most important, the next most important, and the least important? Don't forget that rankings of priorities will differ according to one's perspective, just as descriptions of problems will. Why did you make the rankings you did?

8. Develop two or three feasible action plans for each of the major problems (opportunities). Each alternative action plan should include
   a. the specific actions to be taken
   b. who should take which actions
   c. the purpose or objective of taking the actions
   d. a time frame specifying when the actions will be taken
   e. any additional or different resources that might be needed to carry out the action plan and how these will be obtained
   f. the tradeoffs that are being made in the proposed action plan
   g. the predicted outcome of the plan

9. Select from the alternative plans the one you will follow. Why did one alternative make more sense to you than the others? Upon what analysis is your choice based?

If this procedure sounds like a large order and a lot of work, it is! But it's exactly the same process that a manager goes through, or should go through, in making decisions. And your task is simpler. In the organizational world, no one presents a manager with the data nicely arranged in a case form.

Remember that the primary purpose of case analysis is to give you the opportunity to make decisions and to develop plans of action to implement the decisions. This is a demanding task, which will not be successfully accomplished without considerable effort on your part, in cooperation with your classmates and instructor.

Common Errors In Case Analysis

While there is no one "best" or "correct" solution to a case, some solutions are better than others. The better ones avoid the following common errors in analyzing cases.

1. Unrecognized or inappropriate assumptions. All of us make assumptions all of the time. You will very legitimately make assumptions in analyzing cases. Recognize, though, that action plans should be based on analysis rather than on assumptions. You should clearly identify your assumptions so that others in the group can be aware of

what you are doing. Often, decisions are based on assumptions of which even the decision maker is unaware.

2. Generalizations. Such statements as "All of the employees dislike the boss" or "No one in the factory is very interested in increasing productivity" are inappropriate. Be specific! Don't make general statements when they are not accurate.

3. Clichés. Such comments as "The problem is one of poor communications" or "The problem is due to lack of motivation" are not helpful.

4. Overemphasizing one aspect. Don't spend all your time and effort looking at one small part of the situation. You may be ignoring other, perhaps more important, considerations.

5. Miracle cures. If your plan of action consists of hiring a consultant to solve the problem, your instructor will probably say, "OK, assume *you* are the consultant, what would you do?"

6. Placing blame. The question "Why did this problem arise?" is useful and can help you design a creative plan of action. "Who is to blame for this situation?" will probably not lead to a productive discussion.

7. Being unrealistic. Recommending a course of action that is not appropriate to the organization's situation is not useful. If your solution requires the purchase of three new factories in a period of depression, you should not expect critical acclaim from your classmates. Similarly, if the success of your action plan depends upon the CEO voluntarily resigning, we would predict difficulty. Likewise if the working capital you need must come from winning the state lottery!

8. Seeing things as "either—or." Don't assume that either this must happen or those consequences will result. Almost always another outcome or alternative is possible. You should continually ask yourself "What other possibilities are there in this situation?"

9. Mistaking opinions and assumptions for facts. You must discriminate between facts, opinions, and assumptions and treat them differently. To know for a fact that production is down should not be confused with someone's opinion that production is down. That people oppose the new policy is different from someone's assumption that people will oppose the new policy.

10. Hedging. Enumerating five or six things that a manager might do without recommending what should be done is inappropriate. Avoid the "on the other hand" syndrome. Make a specific recommendation.

Although it's unlikely that you will never make one or more of these errors, try to keep this list in mind as errors to avoid.

Participation in Class Discussions

We have mentioned before the dynamics of the class discussion that are so essential to the case method of learning, and we have used the word "participation" in describing these dynamics. Participation covers a broad range of classroom behaviors, including:

1. Listening and absorbing. An essentially passive student may learn something but misses out on the opportunity to challenge the analyses of others or offer ideas for discussion. Further, the passive individual contributes only in a very minor way to the development of the total class.

2. Emotional input. In this instance, a student contributes only by relating personal feelings about a certain situation or general opinions on a subject. Often, but not always, this input is based on immediate reaction rather than analysis.

3. Reactive input. Such comments as "I agree (or disagree) with that last comment" or "Right on!" indicate that the individual is essentially reacting to the comments of other class members rather than contributing to the discussion.

In early class sessions these kinds of behavior may be marginally acceptable because one of the instructor's goals may be simply to encourage any type of participation. As the class becomes more experienced, however, participation of the following kinds is more desirable—and usually more highly rewarded.

4. Analytical input. In this kind of participation, a student might state "Here are my conclusions and here is the analysis upon which they are based." Note the great difference between analytical input and the emotional input described earlier. In this situation the class is in a position to evaluate the analysis upon which the conclusions were based, challenge and test assumptions, and compare the analytical framework with other methods of analysis that might have been used. This kind of participation is very positive and extremely useful in helping the class move from conclusions based on opinion to conclusions based on analysis.

5. Synergistic input. In this instance, a student builds upon the contributions of others in the class by enlarging, amplifying, or expanding them, or by looking at them from a different perspective, or by combining ideas from several sources. This kind of participation is exciting and can help the class reach a new level of understanding.

6. Process input. In this kind of participation, a class member provides focus to the discussion by changing direction, adding emphasis, or drawing different people into the deliberations. Process participation is indicated by a statement such as "We've spent a great deal of time exploring this aspect of the case, are there other aspects we should examine?" (Perhaps the class member will suggest another area that merits consideration.) Or, "It seems that only a few of us have been ac-

tively participating. What do you folks who have been quiet so far think?" Or, "We've spent a lot of time talking about why the problem has arisen, and we seem to be in agreement. Should we consider what we might do about it?" Statements like these demonstrate concern with the *process* of the class discussion rather than the *content,* with developing an effective pattern of discussion rather than with what is being discussed.

Often, especially in the early sessions, your instructor will play the major process role. As the group matures, other individuals may take a more active part in determining what the group will do. Some of these attempts by fellow students to control the process will be readily accepted while others will be quickly rejected. To highlight this kind of process participation, your instructor may assign some members of the class to observe the class discussion and interaction and report their observations to the rest of the class. These reports can be very useful in helping you to learn how your organization is behaving.

In our judgment, analytical input, synergistic input, and process input are higher levels of input and more useful to the overall development of the class than are the others. We encourage our students to attempt these kinds of inputs and try to help them develop the kinds of skills they need to do so.

A FINAL COMMENT

Learning by the case method is exciting! At times it may seem frustrating—probably because of something that's happening, or not happening, in the group discussion, and you may wish that you were in a conventional lecture situation where you didn't have to invest so much of yourself in the learning process. At other times you may feel that studying cases is too demanding; every time you look at the case it seems to change. What is really fact and what is not? And every time you discuss it with a classmate it grows more complex. You may feel your instructor is not giving you enough support, much less any concrete answers. What's more, you have to think all the time and analyze everything, including your own value system!

But isn't that excitement! If your experience is similar to that of the many, many students who have had the opportunity to learn by the case method, these challenges will be stimulating, and you will respond positively to the fundamental assumption that the case method makes about you: that you are a mature person who can think independently, who can analyze and draw conclusions, and who has something of value to contribute to the learning process. If you are willing to do your part, you should discover that you are learning on both the conceptual and behavioral levels. This learning should stay with you for a long time and provide a foundation on which you can build successful behavior patterns, either as a manager or as an effective member of an organization. We wish you the best of good fortune as you undertake this unique, difficult, frustrating, challenging, and highly rewarding experience.

PART ONE
The Organization as a Whole

Dashman Company

The Dashman Company was a large concern making many types of equipment for the armed forces of the United States. It had more than twenty plants, located in the central part of the country, whose purchasing procedures had never been completely coordinated. In fact, the head office of the company had encouraged the plant managers to operate with their staffs as separate, independent units in most matters. When it began to appear that the company would face increasing difficulty in securing certain essential raw materials, Mr. Manson, the company's president, appointed an experienced purchasing executive, Mr. Post, as vice-president in charge of purchasing, a position especially created for him. Manson gave Post wide latitude in organizing his job, and he assigned Mr. Larson as Post's assistant. Larson had served the company in a variety of capacities for many years and knew most of the plant executives personally. Post's appointment was announced through the formal channels usual in the company, including a notice in the house organ which was published monthly by the Dashman Company.

One of Post's first decisions was to begin immediately to centralize the company's purchasing procedure. As a first step, he decided that he would require each of the executives who handled purchasing in the individual plants to clear with the head office all purchase contracts they made that were in excess of $10,000. He felt that if the head office was to do any coordinating in a way that would be helpful to each plant and to the company as a whole, he must be notified that the contracts were being prepared at least a week before they were to be signed. He talked his proposal over with Manson, who presented it to the board of directors. They approved the plan.

Although the company made purchases throughout the year, the beginning of its peak buying season was only three weeks away at the time this new plan was adopted. Post prepared a letter to be sent to the twenty purchasing executives of the company. The letter follows:

Dear _____ :

The board of directors of our company has recently authorized a change in our purchasing procedures. Hereafter, each of the purchasing executives in the several plants of the company will notify the vice-president in charge of purchasing of all contracts in excess of $10,000 that they are negotiating, at least a week in advance of the date on which they are to be signed.

I am sure you will understand that this step is necessary to coordinate the purchasing requirements of the company in these times when we are facing increasing difficulty in securing essential supplies. This procedure should give us in the central office the information we need to see that each plant secures the optimum supply of materials. In this way the interest of each plant and of the company as a whole will best be served.

Yours very truly,

Post showed the letter to Larson and invited his comments. Larson thought the letter an excellent one, but suggested that since Post had not met more than a few of the purchasing executives, he might like to visit all of them and take the matter up with each of them personally. Post dismissed the idea at once because, as he said, he had so many things to do at the head office that he could not get away for a trip. Consequently, he had the letters sent out over his signature.

During the following two weeks, replies came in from all except a few plants. Although a few executives wrote at greater length, the following reply was typical:

Dear Mr. Post:

Your recent recommendation in regard to notifying the head office one week in advance of our intention to sign contracts has been received. This suggestion seems a most practical one. We want to assure you that you can count on our cooperation.

Yours very truly,

During the next six weeks the head office received no notices from any plant that contracts were being negotiated. Executives in other departments, who made frequent trips to the plants, reported that the plants were busy and the usual routines for that time of year were being followed.

Jennifer Warren

In the five years following Jennifer Warren's graduation from the M.B.A. program, she has worked in a variety of capacities. Her education was paid for by a large Northwest corporation, to which she did not return; at graduation, she was hired by another large company in the same industry. Two years later, she took a job with a small consulting firm for approximately six months. Next, she worked as an independent consultant for a year. This work involved a single large contract, and when it ended, Jennifer again turned to employment within a company. Although she has been employed at her present job just over a year, Jennifer, now 37, is considering another job offer. However, her focus at this point has significantly changed: rather than attempting to climb the corporate ladder, she seeks a stable, well-paying job that will allow her to accumulate enough capital to start her own business.

Looking back at her erratic employment history, Jennifer sees two central features emerging. First, she realizes her career plans were both overly ambitious and idealistic, even though she considered herself more sophisticated in assessing her expectations than most graduating M.B.A.s. Second, although her experiences over the past years have been difficult and disheartening at times, through them she has been able to better define her career goals. As these two realizations emerge, she identifies a simultaneous personal growth:

There are a whole lot of things that have happened to me over this period, especially in the last year, that are not external. It's like saying "aha" and every other day there is some new "aha." I'm healthier now than I've ever been, more physically active. I feel I'm more capable—I really feel comfortable with myself. I like myself more than I ever have.

Jennifer was sent to graduate school mainly because of her own personal drive and ambition. She had worked for Hillside Corporation, a large national company, for several years, beginning as a clerical worker in the corporate personnel department. She became an assistant manager in that department, a job she described as a "good and fairly responsible" position. She realized, however, that if she wanted to move into more interesting jobs in other areas of the company, she would need five or six more years of experience or an M.B.A. degree.

She began attending school part-time, even though this meant it would take her six years to get her degree, by which time her personnel experience would make it difficult to break into a new field.

Her immediate supervisor, although warmly commending her work, thought she possessed few analytical skills and little potential—traits he felt she held in common with most women. However, his superiors had been her constant supporters throughout her tenure with the company. Rather than initiate a conflict that would only be damaging to all concerned, Jennifer sought a way out. The solution was to attend graduate school full time.

The way big companies typically handle a sensitive problem like mine is to try to make it go away, i.e., throw some money at it, rather than try to solve it. That's what they did. I wanted to go to school—in fact, I probably suggested they send me. The education program was already set up; other people had done it. And it was a way out.

So they sent me to school. I knew at the time that the vice president who was my mentor was going to retire before I graduated. I also knew chances were pretty slim that they would take me back. This program was a way to ease people out the door (they had used it in this way with others), so I wasn't all that surprised when there wasn't a job waiting for me when I finished.

She qualifies this statement:

Intellectually, I knew there was little chance I would go back to Hillside, but I wasn't prepared emotionally to "leave the nest." I knew I wouldn't go back, yet never imagined not, if that makes sense. I shouldn't have been as devastated as I was when they filled a job I felt should have been rightfully mine, or should have at least been offered to me.

Jennifer completed her M.B.A. with very high grades. She felt she had sacrificed so much to go to school that "every point I got less than a 4.0 meant I hadn't taken an opportunity to learn." She had set out to prove that those who said she had no analytical skills were wrong: not only could she do it, but she could do it well.

In addition, because she was completing her degree during the same time she was finalizing a long, drawn-out divorce, she admits she felt "cocky and ready to conquer the world," although her experience might have warned her otherwise.

It seems there are two kinds of people who go after an M.B.A. There are the younger people, who do it because it's a stepping stone to entry level jobs. And there are the relatively older people, who are interested in becoming more well-rounded and in learning the business aspects of their career.

I knew my younger classmates had expectations that were much too high, and that they were going to be shot down. Yet, my own expectations were high—I was earning good money when I went into the program, and I expected my salary would go up considerably when I came out. It didn't very much.

I felt I really wanted a career-type job—I wanted to stay with a firm. I felt I'd done my job-changing already, and I wanted to be stable. Of course, I knew M.B.A.s change jobs, but I felt may age was a stabilizing factor, and I think the people I eventually went to work for thought so too.

Jennifer was hired by another major firm in the same industry, and within six months was transferred to another part of the state. The move came sooner than she had anticipated, but was not unexpected. "I didn't really want to go, but I felt I had to. It was part of my career, and I had made that commitment." Again, she felt socially uprooted, having just adjusted to being single and having established a new circle of friends from school.

The first nine months following her transfer gave Jennifer "the best management experience a person could ever have, along with a sense of independence." She even bought a house. Soon, however, there was a change in managers, and the situation turned into one of the "unhappiest of my life." It ended with Jennifer being fired less than a year after her transfer.

I was fired because I was looking for another job. The reason I was looking was partly because I was bored—I was ready for promotion and for more responsibility. They weren't quite ready for me to move, and I wasn't getting along with the new manager.

Ken had been the assistant manager for six years when I came in, and from the first we hadn't gotten along. Here comes this hotshot M.B.A. as administrative manager—the next in line of responsibility after him—with six months' experience, who wants more responsibility. He was very insecure, and we were having all kinds of problems.

In those days, I was fairly confrontational, and that was part of it. I was pretty open about how I felt. Part of my job was credit manager, which is never a popular position because sales and the bottom line run the whole operation. The market was starting to get bad, and some of our customers had started getting late on their payments—we were having collection problems. On the one hand, I had the area credit manager telling me not to extend credit; on the other, I had the branch and sales managers telling me they needed the sales. I couldn't win. Whichever way I turned, it was wrong. That whole period was fairly traumatic.

The situation was finally brought to a head by a performance report in which Ken said he wouldn't consider recommending me for promotion until I had worked for him a year. That would have meant almost two years—and the agreement had been a year and a half at the most, including a transfer back.

I was very upfront about looking for other work; I wanted to be honest. I tried to get counseling from the employment manager with whom I had interviewed when they hired me. I told him I was looking and he explored some alternatives, but I could tell his heart wasn't really in it. I think they had decided I was a troublemaker, and didn't care to bother with me. They were looking for things inside the company for me, but suggested I look outside as well. I agreed, but asked for assurance that I wouldn't be fired prematurely because of my honesty. They said I would stay as long as my performance continued up to par. One week later, I got canned.

Certainly, part of the company's position was directly related to a severe market decline then beginning in the industry. Several stores that the company had anticipated opening in the area of Jennifer's choice never materialized, so their promise to bring her back could not easily be fulfilled.

Furthermore, Jennifer had chosen "a very macho business," so support from within took on particular importance. This became all the more evident because she had benefited from support in both her work experiences, and she had suffered from its absence in both situations as well.

As a woman administrative manager, she found it was often difficult to gain the respect of the customers, but felt she succeeded—in large part due to the support of her original manager.

Before, if someone complained of a problem with me, my manager would talk to me and get my side of the story before he resolved it. He would tell me if he thought I had screwed up, and he would tell me what he thought I should do to recover. If I was right, he stood up for me. When he left, all that support was gone—the change was obvious.

She comments:

I would much rather find out someone didn't like me or want me around because of my personality or performance than because I'm a woman. At least then it would be something personal they are reacting to—not just some mindless prejudice. Looking back, I think many opportunities have been limited, or things have happened because I am a woman.

I finally left because I realized the futility: why beat my head against a brick wall—life is tough enough! There's enough competition in just an ordinary situation; why make it worse by trying to succeed in a strongly male industry? If they didn't want to have women around, that was their problem; I was tired of crusading.

She speculates on how different things might have been had management support remained:

You talk to anyone who works in a big company, and depending on who they work for, it's either wonderful or terrible. I think your immediate boss, or maybe the department a couple of levels up, has a tremendous impact on your life. When you go to work for a company, you put your whole life in their hands. If my manager had not been transferred, my career with the company probably would have been a lot different.

The same thing holds true at Hillside. If the vice-president I worked for hadn't retired, I would have gone back. He would have wanted me and had a job waiting for me. The fact that he chose to leave changed not only my life, but the lives of a lot of people. Most of those who worked for him are no longer there. It's like the government: a change of administration and half the people are out of jobs.

Yet, when you go to work for someone, how can you know what's going to happen to them? Obviously, you have absolutely no way of knowing. We all have to put our lives under someone else's control at some time.

By analyzing this control issue, Jennifer has gained a clearer perspective and also has been able to establish a set of priorities relative to her own career goals. But she did not realize how important the control issue was for her until six months later.

Being fired was a traumatic experience for Jennifer, and she became insecure about being able to find another job.

I was burnt-out and tired. I had spent a lot of years going through a lot of trauma and hard work. In the last six years I'd gone through a fairly unhappy marriage, a very emotional divorce, school, two major relocations, and rejection by two major companies.

My thoughts at the time were "typically female": I can't possibly be marketable. God, I was lucky to get that job—they must be the only company in the world that would even consider

me—so now what am I going to do? Even worse, I was so tired I couldn't even think of anything I really wanted to do.

She took the first job that came along, a position with a small consulting firm. The work was enjoyable and consulting seemed a good thing to do. The job itself was not altogether exciting, but Jennifer found it suited her needs.

Six months later, she was laid off. As the newest member of an office staffed by six people, she was the expendable person when the company's biggest client cut its contract due to business slack. Feeling lost, Jennifer returned to the university, looking for a job idea. It was at this time that she began to address her need for control. When a former professor suggested she would "never be happy working for someone else," suddenly things became clear.

Son of a gun, I never thought of that! I mean, I went through the whole M.B.A. program without even thinking of being an entrepreneur or of being the boss—it didn't even occur to me. And while I had always thought the entrepreneurship class would be fun to take, I found room in my schedule for other classes, never that.

In particular, she recalls her earlier desire to be part of the business planning group at Hillside.

I'm not sure I knew what I wanted to do, or even what planning was, but I knew the people who worked there dealt with interesting problems. They were sort of the crown princes who eventually got to run things. So that's what I wanted to do. I really didn't know much about it, but I knew I wanted to run things. It's interesting that I never made the connection between running things for someone else and running things for myself. But I never did.

Her plans began to crystallize. She sold her home and planned to use the proceeds to buy a business. She and some friends made an offer on a jewelry manufacturing business, but because gold prices were at their height, their offer was rejected as too low. Meanwhile, she set herself up as a consultant, supplementing her financial needs with unemployment compensation. After a few weeks, she got a contract for work that lasted almost a year.

I got the contract through someone I knew socially, who worked for the company. I had given him my resume to pass around, and he told me his company controller was looking for someone with a background similar to mine. He set up an appointment for me to talk with the controller, and within a few weeks the contract was mine.

I was helping implement a computer system and didn't expect it to last more than three months—it really shouldn't have—but they dragged it out. They didn't make particularly effective use of my time, but I didn't care. The money was good, I loved working downtown, and I loved being independent. If I didn't want to work, I didn't have to. I just told them what I was going to do and what I wasn't going to do. I can't say I didn't have to answer to anybody, but I felt I was in control. That experience convinced me that I really wanted my own company or business.

When that contract ended, Jennifer was again forced to make a decision. Markets were slow all over, and there were no other contracts in sight. Plus, when the other principals from the jewelry business idea had gone their separate ways, and Jennifer hadn't identified any other business opportunities, she purchased another house—a decision that has cost her in several ways:

This house is somewhat more than I could afford, yet somehow still not what I wanted. It makes me feel very insecure. It certainly straightens out your priorities when you have to come to terms with mortgage payments! On the other hand, it's a terrific tax shelter.

Thus, for financial considerations, and because she was still uncertain about where she belonged, Jennifer once again went to work for someone else.

I felt I really didn't have enough to offer as an independent consultant, at least, not enough to compete with the C.P.A. and established consulting firms. I had neither the resources nor a technical speciality.

There were contract opportunities, but I felt it would be fairly uncertain whether I would get paid or not. I couldn't afford to take that kind of financial risk, even though I wanted to. Buying the house put economic pressures on me, and I felt I had to opt for security and the paycheck. And that's what I did.

Then, too, I felt a certain loneliness as an independent consultant. I wasn't part of a company, and yet I needed someone to bounce ideas off of, or sometimes just to commiserate with. I would have been more encouraged to stay independent if I had had a roommate, because I would have at least been able to get some of the frustrations off my chest. I guess when I recognized I was willing to make a trade-off—control for security and company—I felt "so old and wise." It's a heavy—I don't want to be that wise!

So, once again, Jennifer finds herself in an unsatisfactory job environment, in a fairly unchallenging position, with too few growth opportunities. She received two job offers, and chose the one she thought more promising.

It turned out exactly the opposite of what I had expected. I knew I had made the wrong decision after the first week. Although my immediate inclination was to see if the other job was still open, I'm such a moralist I had to give it a month to work out. By then, the other job was gone.

The company she now works for is a high-tech electronics manufacturer that has just gone through a super-growth phase. This period has been characterized by a great deal of political infighting, of which Jennifer was initially unaware. Her first assignment as a financial analyst was to a division whose management did not want any support. After three months in that division, Jennifer moved into a different position. It was one vacated by someone who had started work at the same time as Jennifer, but who had by now been promoted. She believes that her having started in such a hostile environment is one of the main reasons she has not yet been promoted to manager.

Three of us started at the same time; the other two have been promoted. I was pretty naive about the political situation at first. Actually, all I wanted to do was some interesting work, collect a paycheck, and keep my eyes open for my own business.

Most of the jobs in this company are in engineering, as befits a high-tech corporation. The other non-financial arena is production management, and Jennifer is in the process of obtaining certification through a series of examinations. Although she does not really want to climb the corporate ladder, she feels compelled to join the competitive environment. At the same time she feels stymied because she doesn't fit. Her working relationship is good, but the job is less than challenging.

Right now the division production manager's job is open. I asked the V.P. if he would consider me, as I've done significant work in that area. He said he needed someone who was APICS certified (American Production and Inventory Control Society), although he admitted I could certainly do the job. He said management was requiring certain things of him—to hire someone with a certain background. . .Well, I guess I don't believe him. I haven't done anything, or maybe I haven't cared enough, to make an issue out of it. I guess I don't want to make any issues until I'm ready to

leave. I think I'm a little insecure about making issues; I've learned it doesn't pay.

Her age is also a factor in her dissatisfaction: at 37, she is one of the few members of the finance staff over 30.

If I were 25 I might be willing to fight for promotions, but what I want now is just to be left alone to do a good job and to be recognized for it by being paid well. I guess that's not really different from what I've always been after, but here I've tried all these different paths, and none has worked for me. What else am I going to do? How long am I going to fight? How long am I going to be willing to be a financial analyst for a company run by people who are barely out of diapers?

She feels being a woman is also a factor in this situation, although she is not alone this time. Spontaneous meetings of women in management have been followed by the firing of two women personnel managers. Furthermore, there are only eight or nine women managers out of 100 women employees, and no women in high management positions. Jennifer, however, remains distant from that movement.

I don't know if making noise will do any good. I try to stay apart from it because I really don't believe that a woman's career is helped by being associated with feminist causes.

Part of this distancing clearly comes from her changing sense of direction. She is currently biding her time, casually looking at other opportunities. However, she does not yet feel financially or emotionally ready to start her own business. Her intent is instead to work at developing the necessary skills for running an independent business, while at the same time accumulating savings from a regular salary. Currently, she is interviewing for a job as business manager for a local law firm; she labels considering such a move as ''semiretirement for someone like me, who always has been after challenge and excitement." On the other hand, it would be "lucrative, not too hard, and would provide me with some useful experience."

What I want is to finish rounding out skills that would be useful if I had my own business. That's one reason the manufacturing materials management area is a good one to pursue. It may get me something in this company, but if it doesn't, I can use it later for myself. I think that's my focus, and I think that's been my focus for a while.

Maybe part of it's getting older, or "growing up," or coming to terms with what I am. I'm never going to be president of Hillside, or president of this company, no matter what I do or how good I am.

I don't think I'm capable of attracting a mentor who is strong enough to support a big move for me in this company. I think I have a lot to offer any company—I'm bright and capable of doing a great deal. But why should I beat my brains out for someone else, and get paid a salary that's peanuts compared to what the officers take home? Hell, if I'm going to work 12 to 18 hours a day, I want rewards! On my own, if I'm good I'll have substantial rewards, and if I'm average, the rewards will be mediocre. In any case, I'll be the determining factor!

I've realized you can't have control of everything, so maybe you have to choose what you are willing to let someone else control. And how important is that to you? When I was working for myself, I was horribly lonely and decided I didn't want to work alone. I was willing to give up control for companionship.

A move to business manager of a law firm would also remove some of the frustrations Jennifer presently feels. She explains:

I don't want to have to compete, and I don't want to be in a position where, educated as I am, I'm missing some requirement. I don't want to be a lawyer; as long as I can reconcile myself

to the fact that I don't want to be what they are, or that I don't want to play their game, then I'm okay. I can get along pretty well in that kind of situation. It's when I want to be one of the guys, and am not accepted for whatever reason—I don't know the right thing, haven't had the right experience, dress too well, am overeducated, am a woman, am too aggressive, whatever—it's then I start having problems.

Finally, another factor that has greatly influenced Jennifer's attitude toward her career direction is having found someone with whom to share her life at present.

Having a man in my life makes a big difference! It makes the rest of my life a lot more fun. I spend less time worrying about my career than I did six months ago. It's not less important now, but before it was all I had.

She is able to put her past five or six years in perspective: being rejected by Hillside, being fired twice, relocating twice, reestablishing relationships after her divorce, and redirecting her career goals. She says of Hillside:

I have so much to thank them for! If it wasn't for them, I would never have had the money to buy a house in the first place. I wouldn't have my M.B.A. God knows what I'd be doing. Certainly, they pushed me out of the nest, but with the tools I needed to take care of myself.

Of her personal development, she says:

I've learned how to be independent. I've learned how to live for me, to set a goal and strategies to achieve that goal. I feel I've finally taken control of my life, figured out what I want. I recognize I can't have it all right now, and that's okay. I've made some bad decisions, but I've also made some good ones—and I'm sure I'll make more of both kinds. But my career goal won't change, and I'll continue to do the things I think will get me there.

Center City Engineering Department

The Engineering Department of Center City employed approximately 1,000 people, all of whom worked under the provisions of the Civil Service System. Of these employees, about 100 worked in the Design Division. Parker Nolton, an Associate Engineer, had been employed in the Design Division for 19 years and was known personally by virtually everyone in the division, if not in Center City itself. Nolton had held the position of Associate Engineer for seven years on a provisional basis only, for he had never been able to pass the required civil service examinations to gain permanent appointment to this grade, although he had taken them often. Many of his coworkers felt that his lack of formal engineering education prevented him from passing the examinations, but Nolton felt that his failures were the result of his tendency to "tighten up" when taking an examination. Off the job, Nolton was extremely active in civic affairs and city sponsored recreational programs. During the past year, for example, he had been president of the High School Parent Teacher's Association, captain of the bowling team sponsored by the Engineering Department in the Municipal Bowling League, and a member of the Managing Committee of the Center City Little League.

As Center City grew and the activities of the Engineering Department expanded to keep pace with this growth, younger men were hired into the Department in relatively large numbers. Among those hired were Ralph Boyer and Doug Worth. Both of these young men were graduate engineers, and had accepted the positions with the Engineering Department after fulfilling their military obligations. Ralph Boyer had been an officer in the Army Corps of Engineers. In order to give the new men opportunities to achieve permanent status in the Civil Service System, examinations were scheduled with greater frequency than they had been in the past. Nolton's performance on the examinations continued to be unsatisfactory. The new men, however, passed the exams for successively higher positions with flying colors. Ralph Boyer in particular experienced marked success in these examinations and advanced rapidly. Three years after his initial employment he was in charge of a design group within the design division. Parker Nolton, in the meantime, had been shifted from the position of a project engineer to that of the purchase order coordinator. The position of purchase order coordinator was more limited in scope than that of a project engineer, although the responsibilities of the position were great. He continued to be classified as an Associate Engineer, however.

Ralph Boyer continued his successful career and soon qualified for the position of Senior Engineer. A new administrative group that had been created to meet the problems that arose in the Design Division because of the expanding activities of the Engineering Department was placed under his direction. Doug Worth, too, was successful in his examinations and was shortly promoted to the grade of Associate Engineer and transferred into the administrative group headed by Ralph Boyer.

One of the functions under the new administrative group was that of purchase order coordination. This relationship required that Parker Nolton report to Ralph Boyer. Nolton, however, chose to ignore the new organizational structure and dealt directly with the Chief Engineer, an arrangement which received the latter's tacit approval. Nolton was given a semiprivate office and the services of a Junior Engineer to assist him in his activities. His assistant, John Palmer, soon requested a transfer on the grounds that he had nothing to do and there was no need for anyone in this position. Nolton, on the other hand, always appeared to be extremely busy and was continually requesting additional manpower and assistance to help him with the coordination of purchase orders.

Some four months after the organizational changes noted above had taken place, the Chief Engineer left the Company and his replacement, Stan Matson, was appointed from within the division. Matson was the logical successor to the position; his appointment came as no surprise and was well received by all the employees. His appointment was shortly followed by the assignment of Ralph Boyer to a special position which took him completely out of the Design Division. Doug Worth was assigned to the position thus vacated, Supervisor of the Administrative Group, and consequently inherited the supervision of Parker Nolton's activities. This assignment, initially made on a provisional basis, was soon made permanent when Worth passed the required examinations and was awarded the grade of Senior Engineer. Doug Worth had never worked closely with Parker Nolton but

had been on cordial terms with him since his arrival in the Engineering Department. He had had contact with Nolton in several recreational activities in which they both had participated.

During the months which followed, Parker Nolton continued his direct reporting relationship with the Chief Engineer, now in the person of Stan Matson, and never consulted or advised Doug Worth regarding the progress of his activities as purchase order coordinator. His former assistant, John Palmer, had been transferred and had been replaced by an engineering aide. Both the aide and Nolton appeared to be busy most of the time, and Nolton was still requesting more manpower for his activity through formal channels. When occasions arose which required that Doug Worth check on Nolton's activities, he was always forced to go to Nolton's office for information. Nolton always claimed to be too busy to leave his own office. During the conversations which occurred when Worth visited Nolton, Nolton frequently gave the impression that he regarded Worth's activities and interest as superfluous. Several times he suggested that in future situations Worth just send the inquiring party directly to him if questions arose about his activities. He often made the comment that he knew everyone in the department and often it was better to handle many situations informally rather than through channels.

Doug Worth was concerned with Nolton's attitude, for he did not feel that he could effectively carry out his responsibilities as Supervisor of the Administrative Group if he did not know the current status of activities in all of the functions under his control. Consequently, he attempted to gain more cooperation from Nolton by approaching the subject at times when the two men were engaged in common off-hours recreational activities. These attempts were uniformly unsuccessful. Nolton always quickly brought the conversation around to the standing of the bowling team, the progress of the P.T.A., or any other unrelated subject close at hand.

After several attempts to talk with Nolton in a friendly way off the job, Worth concluded that the situation as it currently stood was intolerable. While he realized he must do something, Worth felt he understood Nolton's attitude and reactions and was sympathetic. After all, Nolton had been in the department for years and had been relatively successful. He knew all the "ropes" and had many friends. Worth reflected that it must be a blow to a man like Nolton to have to report to young, relatively inexperienced men. Worth had faced similar problems during his military career, when he had had more experienced men many years his senior under his command. After much thought, he decided his best approach would be to appeal to Nolton in a very direct manner for a greater degree of cooperation. Thus, Worth approached Nolton on the job and suggested that they have a talk in his private office where they would not be disturbed by all the activity in Nolton's office. Nolton protested that he could not take time away from his duties. Worth was firm, however, and Nolton reluctantly agreed to come to Worth's office, protesting all the way that he really could not spare the time.

During his opening remarks to what Worth had planned as a sympathetic discussion of the situation, Worth referred to "the normal relationship between a man and his superior." Nolton's reaction was violent. He stated that he didn't regard any young upstart as a "superior," especially his. He told Worth to run his own office and to let him, Nolton, run his. He concluded by stating "if you haven't anything

more to say I would like to get back to my office where important work is being neglected." Worth, realizing that nothing more could be accomplished in the atmosphere which prevailed, watched in silence as Nolton left.

Doug Worth subsequently reported his latest conversation with Nolton to Stan Matson, the Chief Engineer. He also related the events which had led to this conversation. In concluding his remarks, he stated that he could no longer take responsibility for Nolton's actions because Nolton would neither accept his guidance nor advise him of the state of his work. Matson's reply to his last statement was "yes, I know." This was the only comment Matson made during the interview, although he listened intently to Worth's analysis of the situation.

At the next meeting of the Supervisory Staff of which Worth was a member but Nolton was not, Worth proposed that Nolton be transferred to the position of Design Drafting Engineer, in effect a demotion. As Worth was explaining the reasons for his proposed action regarding Nolton, one of the other members of the Supervisory Staff interrupted to proclaim very heatedly that Nolton was "one of the pillars of the entire Engineering Department" and that he would be violently opposed to the demotion of "so fine a man." Following this interruption, a very heated, emotional discussion ensued concerning the desirability of demoting Nolton.

During this discussion Stan Matson remained silent; yet he reflected that he should probably take some action during the meeting regarding the Nolton situation.

Stanley Lowell

Business at Rainbow Sporting Goods Manufacturers has been booming since the day some five years ago when the decision was made to diversify the company's products into areas other than the long-established line of fishing equipment. For more than fifteen years, Rainbow had been satisfied with the role of being one of the leading fishing tackle manufacturers. The company's products were recognized throughout the States for their quality and workmanship. At the time, Rainbow's business was steady but volume was not great.

Five years ago Rainbow's management obtained new patents for golfing and tennis equipment and enlarged their activities rather extensively to begin manufacturing many new products. Several of the new items were an instant success. As a result, many new employees had to be added to meet the flood of orders that arrived. Business continues to be strong, and the company is constantly looking for new products to manufacture.

In the days when Rainbow's emphasis was strictly on fishing equipment, the work force was small and manager-worker relations were excellent. Company policies were liberal and vacation time, sick leave, and other benefits were flexible to fit workers' needs. A profit-sharing plan was developed that gave workers a small share of company profits at the end of each year. A retirement program was estab-

Reprinted by permission of Professor O. Jeff Harris, Jr., Louisiana State University.

lished in which the company put up a small amount of money each year for workers who had been with the company fifteen years or more and remained until age sixty-five. Employees were required to put 4 percent of their weekly earnings into the retirement program. If an employee left the company before retirement, he got back his contributions with interest but did not get any of the money contributed by the company. This arrangement seemed satisfactory to most of the employees.

Rainbow has always shown a sincere interest in the welfare of its employees. During the years before expansion, no effort was ever made by the company's employees to form a union. Even in more recent years, interest in unionization has continued at a very low level.

However, a major problem is now facing Rainbow's managers. There appears to be a deep and widening gap between the older, long-time employees of Rainbow and the younger employees who have been newly hired. The differences between the groups appeared to be minor at first but now have become rather serious.

The labor force at Rainbow is unique in that there are very few people currently employed who are in the thirty-five to fifty year age category. Almost all of the workers who were with the company before diversification are now above fifty years of age. Turnover in pre-expansion days was always low, and the steady, nonincreasing rate of business provided little room for hiring of new workers. When the expansion began, most of the new workers hired were in their twenties.

The underlying problem precipitating the conflict between the two age groups appears to be based upon differing interests and job demands. Most of the older workers are in positions of responsibility and are working in skilled and semiskilled positions. Because of their nearness to retirement, the company's program of retirement benefits is especially important to the older workers. The younger workers for the most part are in nonsupervisory positions, and many fill semiskilled or unskilled positions. The younger set has made known the importance of more money needed for immediate purchasing power.

No one seems capable of explaining how the rift between the younger and the older workers really began. In the early stages, it was noticed that the two groups rarely mixed during work breaks or lunch hours. Very little after-work socializing was enjoyed by the separate groups. Gradually cooperation on jobs began to decline. Young workers would do no more than the letter of the law required when working with older workers and vice versa. Casual name-calling gave way to serious verbal abuse. Two or three fights have been rumored between members of the two groups after work hours. Two weeks ago more than one-half the younger workers staged a half-day walkout to protest the promotion of one of the older nonsupervisory workers to a supervisory post. The younger workers felt that one of their group had been entitled to the position. In handing out penalties for the walkout, management stripped one day's earnings from the participating workers' salaries and warned them all that they would be fired for further similar actions.

Immediately following the walkout, Luke Cowpar, who is general manager of Rainbow, had a conference with Stanley Lowell, personnel manager, and gave Lowell the responsibility for investigating the division among workers and reporting a list of recommendations to resolve the problem. Cowpar gave Lowell three weeks to prepare and submit his proposals.

Lowell had prided himself on his close rapport with the workers. He had always practiced an open-door policy and had attempted to mix with the workers as much as possible. In the weeks prior to the assignment from Cowpar, however, Lowell had been unable to get much information from any of the workers about their hostilities toward one another. The older workers typically stated that "the young Turks were out to get their jobs" and otherwise made unreasonable demands of them. The younger workers said that their seniors were standing in the way of progress and had little interest in their welfare. Beyond these rather broad generalizations, most workers were reluctant to discuss specific details.

Lowell felt that because of his lack of information and knowledge on the subject, he must spend whatever time was available the first week after receiving the assignment attempting to identify more of the underlying problems through personal conversations with as many of the workers as he could talk with. He anticipated that he would form a committee representing different factions, which would meet early in the second week to help him formulate recommendations to be prepared and forwarded to Cowpar sometime before the deadline.

During the first week, Lowell was busy with many other matters but managed to find time to speak at length with twenty or more workers of different ranks, responsibilities, and ages. Lowell could sense the tension that existed as he talked with each worker. While some were still reluctant to discuss the matter, Lowell concluded that the main issues on the minds of the young workers were a desire for greater immediate income with less emphasis on retirement benefits, a desire for greater responsibility and more challenging assignments, and a desire to see merit stressed as the basis for promotions rather than seniority. Younger workers generally felt that the company emphasized the older workers at the expense of the younger ones. They felt that management was insensitive to and unconcerned with them. The older workers had become their enemy—the aggressor who received all of the breaks.

Older workers tended to express the belief that the younger workers were expecting too much too soon. They felt entitled to a certain amount of privileged treatment as a result of their long, devoted efforts for the company. Each of the senior employees indicated a keen interest in an even stronger retirement program. The present income level was fairly satisfactory to most of them. The younger workers were viewed as a threat to their security.

At the end of the week, Lowell realized that the workers were far apart in their ideas, and he hoped that a committee might establish grounds for a better mutual understanding and might also be able to develop some recommendations to help management cope with existing problems. With this in mind, Lowell selected seven workers on a representative basis and called a meeting for two o'clock the following Tuesday. The seven workers selected were:

Troy Levy, head of the Maintenance Department, age 56

Johnny Cafferty, tool and die maker, age 59

Sloan Broussard, foreman in the Fishing Equipment Section, age 50

Ralph Hansard, assistant accountant, age 39

Max Efurd, foreman in the Golf Equipment Section, age 31

Joanne Wobcott, assembly section worker, age 24

Scottie McBee, forklift operator, age 28

Lowell sent each of the workers a memorandum to inform them of the assignment and waited for Tuesday to arrive. (See Exhibit 1 for a copy of the memorandum.) When the workers arrived at the meeting the following week, Lowell introduced everyone and tried to establish a friendly rapport. Reactions were courteous but restrained. Lowell then began to explain the predicament of the company as he saw it and the role of the committee in making recommendations to the general manager. After a few questions, he reiterated the proposed agenda and suggested that the full discussion begin. The following illustrates the course of the conversation in committee:

LOWELL: The first item for close inspection is the company retirement program and related employee benefits. In my brief survey last week, I noted a wide difference of opinion among workers based largely along age lines. The older workers all appeared satisfied with the existing program. Some wanted even more. Most of the younger people thought we were doing too much. What are your opinions and suggestions on what we should do?

LEVY: (after a brief moment of silence) This is a topic you learn to appreciate more as you draw nearer to retirement. I know I probably once shared the attitudes of many of you younger people but, with nine years left, some security in years after retirement has gotten very important to me. If you people were in our shoes, I think you would feel the same way.

EFURD: We don't doubt that retirement is important to you, but that's the whole problem. Everything that is important to you gets taken care of. Things that are important to those of us who were hired within the last few years always get swept under the rug. I know

EXHIBIT 1
Memorandum to Special Committee Members

TO: Committee Members Levy, Cafferty, Broussard, Hansard,
           Efurd, Webcott and McBee

FROM: Stanley Lowell, Personnel Manager

SUBJECT: Special Committee Meeting to Discuss Employee Problems
           and Opinions

As all of you are quite aware, our company has experienced some
problems with differences of opinion between older and younger
members of our work force. Hostilities in recent days have served to
point out the severity of these problems. Mr. Cowpar, our general manager, has requested that I study the factors which are contributing to
existing differences of opinion and make recommendations for
solving these problems. I'm asking your help in doing this.

You and the other six people listed above are being assigned to a special task force committee to meet with me next Tuesday at 2:00 to discuss the causes of our internal differences and to prepare recommendations to go to Mr. Cowpar. The meeting time has been cleared with
your superior so that you can be free to attend.

In my preliminary research, I have identified some areas which I
would like for us to discuss specifically. Please be prepared to share
your comments on each of these topics as well as other factors which
you believe are important. Our agenda for the meeting will be as follows:

1. Our company retirement program and other benefits

2. Promotion policies

3. Assignment of responsibility to workers

4. Other contributing problem areas; and

5. Solutions to problems

I look forward to hearing your opinions and recommendations.

Stanley Lowell

---

that I speak for myself and most of the people in my department when I say that what we would prefer would be to take home more money each month and have less money go into some of these benefit programs that are not too urgent for us.

WEBCOTT: I'll second what Max has just said. Speaking as the only woman in this group, I'd like to say that money put into retirement and a lot of these other benefits is money wasted so far as I'm concerned. Don't forget, there are quite a few women working at this place, and most of those who work here are married and are trying to supplement the family income and bring in a little extra cash. There are some exceptions, of course. Most of us are depending on our husbands' retirement programs or Social Security to take care of us when the time comes.

CAFFERTY: Don't forget that most of the men around here are married and have families who depend upon their retirement program when their time comes, too.

LOWELL: May I remind you, Joanne, that the money you put in now will be returned to you if you should leave the company in a few years, or even in a few months. You're not losing any of the money you put into the retirement program in the long run.

WEBCOTT: You're missing the point. I need the money now, not when I quit! I would even go further by saying that I wish the company would pay me directly rather than diverting its own funds into retirement programs, insurance benefits, and that kind of thing.

BROUSSARD: You're overlooking the fact that most other companies have the same type of program we have here. We've got to keep this up to be competitive.

MCBEE: Just because other companies do certain things is no basis for this company's decisions. I've got a friend working over at Bloomfield Corporation, and he tells me that they are experimenting with some kind of program that gives them an option on whether to participate in things like retirement programs or to take the money home with them each week. That's what I'd like to see this company do.

LEVY: That program just won't work. Everyone has to contribute or there won't be enough funds to keep the plan working. It takes a lot of money to meet the obligations of this program.

EFURD: You see, that's just what I was talking about a moment ago! This organization is run for the benefit of the older workers!

LEVY: I don't see how you can say that. You're making a good salary, and so is everybody else who works around here.

MCBEE: Man, you don't know what you're talking about. I make so little that my wife has had to go to work to help support our family, and lots of people around here make a lot less than I do.

And so the conversation went. At five o'clock the group was still discussing the retirement plan and other benefit programs. Hostility had erupted several times. No solutions were in view. Lowell closed the meeting by saying that he believed the workers on each side had learned more about the problems of their fellow workers, and he appealed for unity. He announced another meeting for two o'clock on Thursday, at which time promotions and job responsibilities would be discussed before considering recommendations.

The Thursday meeting turned out to be more of the same rather hostile discussion. After two hours of conversation, it became obvious to Lowell that no consensus of ideas was possible. He thanked the group for their efforts, requested their future efforts to cooperate, and indicated that he might be calling on their help again before submitting his report to Cowpar.

After everyone has left the conference room Lowell has stayed behind to ponder his next actions. He has only a little more than a week to prepare his recommendations, and he is almost as far from a solution now as he was in the beginning.

Too Many Personal Calls

John Dixon, vice president of operations for Consolidated Stores, Inc., is responsible for the Springdale region. Forty-four retail clothing stores and outlets in four midwestern states are in the region, which is divided into three districts. Each district is supervised by a district manager and an assistant district manager. Managerial, accounting, merchandising, and advertising activities serving the stores are carried on in the Springdale regional office. A common clerical group in the Springdale office serves all managers and supervisors and is located on the second and fourth floors of the company building. A spacious, well-appointed lounge, used by office personnel, is located on the third floor along with the cafeteria and restrooms.

At the time of this case, John Dixon had over thirty-five years of service with the company. During his five years as regional manager in Springdale, he had been very successful in meeting the problems created by shortages of facilities and by an increase of nearly 40 percent in store sales. Service and operating results for the region were above average for several years, and the current year had shown improvement over the corresponding months of the previous year.

In addition to the district managers and their assistants, a number of other managers

Reprinted from R. L. Hilgert, P. M. Towle, and S. Shoen, *Cases and Policies in Personnel/Human Resources Management,* 4th ed., p. 56. Copyright © 1982 by Houghton Mifflin Company. Used by permission. Places and names have been disguised.

and supervisors maintain offices in the Springdale building. A controller, a merchandise manager, and an advertising director each have private office space. Although a number of clerical employees work directly for the various managers and supervisors at Springdale, many employees report directly to several office supervisors who in turn report to the office manager, Harriet Black.

Since most managers and supervisors travel frequently to the stores, all clerical employees are responsible to Ms. Black for office procedures, practices, and discipline. Harriet Black is an experienced manager who has been in the Springdale office for over fifteen years. She generally is recognized as being exceptionally capable, and other supervisors and managers often consult with her for help on various problems. All other office supervisors are former clerical employees who have been promoted and trained during the last five years.

The Personal Calls Problem

John Dixon devoted some time each week to operating and personnel problems within the Springdale office. Sometimes he observed various office activities jointly with one or more of the managers and supervisors, but he also made it a frequent practice to observe certain operations by himself.

Over a period of weeks, Dixon became increasingly aware that a number of personal telephone calls were being made by the office supervisors and certain clerical employees at their desks. He noticed that this was not peculiar to any one unit but seemed to be a general practice. On several occasions when he was in the various offices, he had to wait for supervisors to finish their personal calls before he could discuss business matters with them. One morning, as he was observing activities alone, he noted a supervisor's telephone was tied up for almost an hour with two successive calls that Dixon believed to be personal in nature. He was not always sure that he was able to distinguish a personal from a business call, but it was obvious that company telephones were often used for other than business communications.

Company policy was not to prohibit personal calls, but such calls were to be strictly limited so that the telephone lines would be available for calls from stores, suppliers, customers, and other business people needing to communicate with the regional office. Several complaints from store managers had been received by Dixon to the effect that it was difficult "to get through" to the regional office by telephone. Consequently, on two different occasions earlier in the year, Dixon had discussed the policy on personal calls in regular meetings with his management personnel, and he believed the policy was generally understood. Further, Dixon felt that the office supervisors and managers through their own observations should have been aware of the excessive number of personal calls currently being made by their people.

The New Policy

It seemed apparent to Dixon that the corrective action—if any—that had been taken by the managers and office supervisors had not been effective. He decided that prompt personal action on his part was needed.

To dispose quickly of the problem, as was his usual practice, Dixon issued the following memo, a copy of which was distributed to every person in the Springdale office: "To keep our telephone lines available for business calls, all personal calls by supervisors and employees should be made from the telephones that have been placed in the lounge." Dixon then arranged for four additional telephones to be connected in the lounge the same afternoon.

Problems

During his observations the following week, Dixon did not discern any personal calls. However, early one morning about two weeks after he had issued the directive regarding telephone calls, Dixon received a call from Janet Smythe, one of the most reliable stenographers in the secretarial pool. He invited her to come right up to his office. Ms. Smythe had been a "Class 1" stenographer for three years; she frequently was called on for special assignments because she was popular and well liked by everyone. As she walked into his office, Dixon noticed that she seemed to be quite upset.

Ms. Smythe, in her usual low voice, commenced by saying, "I would like to question the fairness of your ruling on personal telephone calls." She went on to cite her own experience on the day before. She had been informed of an overtime assignment by Ms. Black, late in the afternoon. Feeling obligated to let her family know that she would be late, she started for the lounge to call home, when Ms. Black questioned her as to why she would be leaving her desk since she had already taken her afternoon coffee break. After explaining her reason for leaving, she was told by Ms. Black that the only time personal calls were allowed was during the normal rest period.

Dixon promptly told Ms. Smythe that the directive had been issued for the purpose of stopping excessive calling from the supervisors' and employees' desks, and he had not intended it to be interpreted as it had been in her case. He told her that he would like to investigate this incident and that he would get in touch with her later.

Several days later Dixon discussed the situation at a regular meeting of his managers and supervisors. He found that the supervisors and managers were unanimous in disagreeing with his directive. They pointed out that the instructions permitted no flexibility and were too severe. Dixon apologized to the group for not discussing the problem with them prior to issuing the directive, and he asked for their suggestions.

A supervisor in accounting was emphatic and insisted that the directive should be rescinded in its entirety. She said, "Really, Mr. Dixon, if you expect an order like that to be enforced by us, you should have let us give the instructions to the people ourselves!" The advertising department director commented, "This whole matter is ridiculous; it's a waste of time! Why not let employees make personal calls? To stop excessive calls would cost more than they are worth!" One of the assistant managers suggested that the employees should be allowed to make personal calls only with the approval of their supervisors. Several members of the group immediately disagreed with this suggestion, stating that the responsibility for policing personal telephone calls should not be placed on supervisors who are trying to motivate their people positively.

After a prolonged discussion of the telephone-call problem and other matters, Dixon adjourned the meeting stating that they would hear from him or the district managers at a later date about the problem of personal calls.

As he returned to his office, Dixon wondered what alternate procedures could be used to reduce successfully the time wasted and the expense of excessive personal telephone calls. In addition, he began to speculate on what method of communications or supervisory practices could be used to help him obtain a better reception of management policies and decisions.

National Lumber Company

Frank Jensen was general manager of the Fabricated Components Division of the National Lumber Company. Located in Trenton, New Jersey, the Fabricated Components Division manufactured and sold a line of prefabricated components such as walls, floors, and roofing systems to building contractors on the Eastern seaboard. By utilizing the products of the Fabricated Components Division contractors could, under certain circumstances, achieve great economy in construction of their projects.

The Fabricated Components Division was significantly different from the other operations of the National Lumber Company. National Lumber Company manufactured and sold a wide range of lumber products from a series of plants and wholesaling points throughout the United States. The National Lumber Company was a large, successful organization that had been in business for over 75 years. The Fabricated Components Division had been started on an experimental basis, as the management of the National Lumber Company felt that prefabricated components offered real promise in the construction industry, and it wished to be aware of the problems and opportunities in the field. By establishing this division, management felt that valuable experience and insights could be gained and that the National Lumber Company would be in a good position to capitalize on the expected boom in components.

A large modern plant, more than adequate for the expected level of immediate operations, was erected in Trenton. Mr. Jensen, who had a great deal of experience in the fabricated components business as manager of one of the small independent organizations that were engaged in this type of activity, was hired to supervise the construction of the plant and to head the operations of Fabricated Components Division after the plant was completed. He was considered a very capable administrator by executives of National Lumber Company.

During the first year of operation many diverse things had to be done: building an organization to both manufacture and sell products, staffing the office force, working at production and control difficulties, and establishing a market for what was basically a new, relatively untested concept in the building industry. Many problems were encountered, but at the end of the first year the Fabricated Components Division had shown a profit of $12,000 on sales of $400,000 and an investment of $250,000.

The second year was, according to Mr. Jensen, a continuation of the "shakedown period." Changes in both the product and the organization were made, additional capital was invested in the plant, and advertising and selling expenditures were increased. The product line seemed to be gaining the approval of many contractors, although competition with the more traditional methods of construction was severe. At the end of the second year the operating statements showed a net loss of $4,000 on sales of $350,000 and a net investment of $300,000.

The third and fourth years of the life of Fabricated Components Division were, in Mr. Jensen's words, "a madhouse." Several new products were introduced, the plant was again expanded, advertising expenditures were increased still more, and a great number of people were added to the organization to handle the increased volume of business. Sales for the third year totaled almost $1 million. However, a net loss of $63,000 was realized. Mr. Jensen stated:

It was mass confusion and things just got away from us. We had too many things to do and too many people involved. When we lived through the third year without going under, we expected things to go very well from then on, but we had not expected problems with some of our people quitting. We also lost a lot of money on a big government order, partly because we didn't have good enough control of our operations. During the fourth year of operations we lost $80,000 on the big job and overall $127,000. But I felt that we were learning through our mistakes and that we still had great potential in this part of the business. We had pretty well perfected our manufacturing operations in Trenton, had added some new equipment, and had our organizational problems pretty well worked out.

I was concerned about the increasing pressure I was subjected to from National Lumber, however. Naturally, I didn't expect top management to be overjoyed by our performance. When we started, both they and I knew that we would have some difficult times, but neither of us expected our financial picture to be quite so bleak. Although we were doing some very good work and were by far the most outstanding outfit in this part of the business, we did not seem to be able to make any money.

Pressures from above increased greatly during the fifth year. At one time or another Mr. Jensen was called on by literally every member of the top management of National Lumber, including the chairman of the board of directors. According to Mr. Jensen, these visits were relatively pleasant, but unproductive and prevented him from attending to what he considered at that time to be the most important part of his job—getting sufficient sales so that the large plant could be operated on a profitable basis. Mr. Jensen stated:

We were like Grand Central Station! I couldn't get anything done, and the constant stream of top-level visitors was upsetting to our plant and office people. They knew that we hadn't yet proved ourselves financially, and all the top brass made them nervous.

Some of our visitors were quite candid. One man told me he had no faith in the basic ideas of our organization and he stopped by just "to see the rathole we're pouring all our money down." And when I found out many of our visitors were charging the expenses of their visits to our operations and we were getting billed for them through interdivisional charges, I really got pretty angry.

But the main thing was that we got little realistic advice or help from these people. Several suggested we "do better," but didn't tell us how we might. There were several things that I felt they could have done—but I got nowhere. Everyone had a gloomy attitude except me. I knew what our capabilities were and had great hopes. I didn't feel that many people understood the differences between running an old established business such as National Lumber and a new, struggling business such as Fabricated Components Division.

During the fifth year Mr. Jensen was under considerable pressure from his immediate superior, Avery Randell, Eastern Regional Manager for the parent company. Mr. Randell sent Mr. Jensen a "confidential memo" about every other week in which he commented upon events that had occurred or decisions that Mr. Jensen had made that did not meet with his approval. Mr. Jensen regularly ignored these memos. He kept them locked in his desk—to which only he had the key—as he did not want their contents known to his subordinates for fear of the effect upon their morale. Mr. Randell also frequently asked Mr. Jensen to have lunch in New York City, where Mr. Randell's office was located, so that he could keep in closer touch with the activities at Fabricated Components Division. Often Mr. Jensen would decline these invitations, but he did have lunch with Mr. Randell in New York about every two weeks. In an effort to satisfy Randell's demands for information, Mr. Jensen started to send him a weekly report on the activities of Fabricated Components Division. The information that went into this report was carefully screened by Mr. Jensen so that nothing that would upset Randell or increase his demands on Jensen's time was included. According to Jensen, "The sole purpose of these reports was to keep him off my back."

Mr. Jensen made the following comments about his relationship with Mr. Randell:

Avery's O.K., but he's quite nervous about our operations. His division almost runs itself. His people are experienced and well trained, and he really doesn't have too much to do. He plays golf a lot and cruises on his boat for long weekends, while I'm at the plant seven days a week and most evenings. He doesn't know much about what we're trying to do and this makes him uncomfortable. We're a thorn in his side and the only "disreputable" part of his division financially. He inherited us because we're geographically close to him, but he doesn't have much sympathy for or understanding of what we're trying to do and the problems we face. I keep telling him that I'll take all the blame for our operations, but with all the attention we're getting from top management he's very much inter-ested in taking part in many of our decisions—even though he doesn't know what is going on and is technically incompetent to assist in managing Fabricated Components Division. Personally, I like him and enjoy his company. Our meetings are very pleasant and we go to some very nice places for lunch. Avery does give us some kinds of help, too. For example, we've had some minor legal problems which he has gotten off our hands. But, in general, he is more of a hindrance than a help. He doesn't know enough about our operation to really help us, and the things he could do, he doesn't. I've wanted to hire another salesman for a long time, but I can't get Avery to approve it. It would cost us about $1,000 a month, but we need more sales and a good man would pay for himself in no time. But Avery's so upset about our losses that he won't let me hire anyone else without his approval, and he won't give it. I spend 30 percent of my time either dealing with Avery or worrying about our relationship. I've told him that if I answered all of his memos, I wouldn't have time for anything else. He's been a real problem to me, and it keeps me from doing the really important things. I'd like to hire some kid to do all of that kind of thing so I would have time to run the business.

About two months before the end of the fifth year of operations, a meeting of top management of the National Lumber Company was held in New York to decide the future of Fabricated Components Division. Mr. Jensen was not asked to attend this meeting, which irritated him considerably. He was asked to submit his plans for next year's operations, as well as several alternative plans and a capital and expense budget for the coming year. He spent a great deal of time preparing this information and submitted alternative plans ranging from considerable expansion of operations to shutting down the plant completely and going out of business. In the letter submitting this information, he requested that he be permitted to attend the meeting. He received no reply to this request.

Two weeks after the meeting had been held, Mr. Jensen had not been informed of what decision, if any, had been made. As he had had no information to the contrary, he assumed that operations for the next year would continue about as they had in the past. About three weeks after the meeting, Mr. Jensen began to hear rumors that the Fabricated Components Division would be shut down at the end of the year. These rumors came from sources both within and outside the company. On hearing these rumors, Mr. Jensen called Mr. Randell who told him, "Things are still undecided, but don't spend any more money than you have to." Mr. Jensen then called the chairman of the board of directors, who informed him that the company had decided to shut down the Fabricated Components Division and go out of that part of the business. Shortly thereafter, Mr. Jensen received a letter from the president of the National Lumber Company confirming this information. Mr. Jensen then began making plans for closing down the Fabricated Components Division. He felt that a poor decision had been made, but that it would be useless to attempt to have the decision reversed.

During these last few weeks of operation Mr. Jensen was faced with several unique problems: He was not sure what, if anything, to tell his employees—or what the timing should be. He was not greatly concerned about the fifty men in the plant, for they were skilled workers who could easily find other employment without suffering financial losses. He was especially concerned about the future of the production manager, the sales manager, and the office manager, all of whom had been with him since the start of Fabricated Components Division. Because none of these people had been with the National Lumber Company for very long, they would get little severance pay and, though capable people, could well be faced with a pe-

riod of unemployment until they found other jobs. He wanted to give these people adequate time to find new positions, yet felt that if the news was out, efficiency would drop considerably and the Fabricated Components Division would have an even greater loss than anticipated for its fifth—and last—year of operation.

Mr. Jensen also faced another kind of problem. He still had great faith in the kind of thing that the Fabricated Components Division was doing and had often considered the advantages of operating his own company in this field. When he had learned that the Fabricated Components Division was to be shut down, he had quietly explored the possibilities of buying the business and had found that he could arrange adequate financing without too much difficulty. Much of the equipment was specialized and not readily saleable. He didn't know of anyone—other than himself—who might want to buy the Fabricated Components Division and felt that he could get everything that he needed to operate with at a reasonable price. Thus, if the Fabricated Components Division showed a great loss for the year, this might discourage any other prospective buyers, as well as increase National Lumber Company's desire to get out of an unprofitable venture for any kind of recovered investment, thus driving down the price he might have to pay.

Along these same lines, Mr. Jensen was undecided about what action, if any, should be taken regarding several large sales that were in the closing stages. It would be quite easy to defer action on these sales until after he had purchased the operations and thus start on his own with a considerable order file. If the sales were closed now, the customers would probably revert to conventional construction techniques when they learned that Fabricated Components Division was not going to be in business. Or it was possible that these orders would be farmed out to small independents by National Lumber Company before Mr. Jensen could get operating on his own.

In reflecting upon the history of the Fabricated Components Division, Mr. Jensen observed that this was an excellent example of a good idea that had been defeated because of lack of support and meddling on the part of top management.

They bought the idea of the Fabricated Components Division in theory but refused, or were literally unable, to recognize the kinds of problems that would arise. When these problems did arise—and almost any new operation faces the same kinds of problems—they wouldn't leave me alone long enough to solve them. Certainly, I must take a great share of the blame for our poor record, but I sincerely believe that if we hadn't had so many visitors and so much attention from top management, we would have had a respectable, if not spectacular, financial success.

Avery Randell made the following comments regarding the Fabricated Components Division:

Frank Jensen is a very capable man, but we never really got him to operate as part of the company. He ran the Fabricated Components Division as if it were an independent organization and never really accepted or respected our advice. This past year in particular we had the very definite feeling that Frank wanted no part of us, even though several of our top management people went considerably out of their way to help him. Frank has not yet learned how to live in a relatively large organization and because of his inability to accommodate the organization creates a lot of problems for himself and detracts considerably from his excellent technical skills. He probably knows more about prefabricated components than anyone in the country, but because of his inability to adjust to the organization he has been an unsuccessful manager for us.

PART TWO
Understanding Individual Behavior in Organizations

Robert and Sylvia Fitzgerald

For both Robert and Sylvia Fitzgerald, entering the M.B.A. program represented a major change in their respective career directions. Robert had earned his degree before their marriage, while Sylvia subsequently finished her program. They had each been married previously, and together their marriage gave them a family of five children. They are an attractive couple; both are competitive, highly motivated, and successful in their endeavors. While they each were strongly oriented toward financial investments in their training, their careers have taken them on substantially different paths. In the past, Robert has been the primary risk-taker, with heavy involvements in venture investments; now, as he expresses interest in more secure enterprises, Sylvia sees her opportunity to shed her financially conservative background.

Robert Fitzgerald was raised on the East Coast, in the Boston area. He went to prep school and college in Vermont, and he was first married during his sophomore year in college. His first child was born when he was a senior, his second about a year and half later, and his third about four years after that. Immediately following his graduation, he and his family drove out to the West Coast where he had been accepted into a graduate school of oceanography. After two years in the program, he "went through one of those crises in your life when you are doing well, things are going fine, but you don't want to do it anymore—and I decided to change my direction."

It was a question of finding myself with which I had trouble for a while. When I entered the business field [as he did at this point], my whole world opened up. I did not want to work in a laboratory. I had spent a summer in the Arctic doing oceanographic research, and during that trip I realized I just did not want to do that. I really like to control and manage things, I wanted more interactions with people, I like to drive toward objectives, I really like to negotiate—it's just the natural flow of the day-to-day activities that either turn you on or don't. I call it the chemistry: all of a sudden the chemistry starts cracking—something just drives you in another direction. I don't know what it is but it happened to me. It has happened to me a couple of times.

Sylvia identifies this feeling too. She had worked for two years after having earned her undergraduate degree in psychology at the University of Pennsylvania. She left the work force to raise her two children. The death of her first husband shortly thereafter left Sylvia confronting major responsibilities and career decisions. It was at this point the "chemistry happened to me, too."

I can remember wondering what I was going to do with my life, feeling that I had to start getting back into gear again. I remember reading in the New York Times at the first of the year about what things liberal arts graduates like me were doing with themselves and that most of the op-

portunities were in business. Everything just clicked—I had never thought of that, even though I had a lot of interest in investments. All of a sudden a door was opened that I didn't think was there because of my background, and it was clear what I was going to do. I didn't really have a clear understanding at that point of what steps were involved other than thinking I had better get a graduate degree and get some credentials behind me with the feeling, "Hey, I want to do well in business!" There was still a big lack of understanding of what it took to get from one place to the next.

At that point, my direction was a combination of things: one, having to be a widow and managing my own money, and two, hopefully getting involved in running a business—things like that—very general.

Sylvia decided to move her family out west and pursue her graduate degree. It was during her program that she met Robert, now divorced and on a business trip. Coincidentally, they discovered they had grown up about half a mile from each other and had quite a bit of common background. She transferred to another M.B.A. program to be with Robert, and they were married. Robert adopted her two children; two of his own children live with them, and frequently the third does as well.

Robert's career change had not precipitated the divorce, in fact he says his first wife had been supportive, nor were there overriding financial difficulties. It was in the years immediately following graduate school, when Robert became involved in various entrepreneurial activities, that they grew apart. Robert characterizes this as "a classic growing apart from the way we were as childhood sweethearts in terms of desires and goals." He identifies the divorce as the most discouraging aspect of his career.

It was, I think, the entrepreneurial activities at a young age, from 28 to 33 or 34, with lots of things happening on her side of the fence, that contributed to our divorce, although not solely.

That's a very trying, totally absorbing enterprise to be involved in; I'm still involved in it, and have been involved in it up until right now. I am not an operating officer, I'm a controlling shareholder and director, but it's still very absorbing. Sylvia has felt the impact of entrepreneuring on our life, and I have felt a tremendous change in the desire of direction to go. Whereas I was in the entrepreneuring aspects earlier in my life, my responsibilities in marrying Sylvia, adopting her two children, plus my own saturation with that sort of thing, I now desire a more stable environment. I am now 41, not over the hill, but you look at life a little differently than you did when you felt you could do anything.

Robert had not sought the M.B.A. with the specific intent of getting into venture investments. Upon leaving the school of oceanography, he went downtown and applied to several brokerage houses with the thought of getting into selling securities. When he was in fact offered a job, he reconsidered his preparation: "At the last minute I thought, well, my training up until now has been sciences and so forth—when you do something you're prepared, you know the fundamentals—and here I was going to go out and sell securities. That doesn't make sense; even though they give you a training program, it is not an in-depth program." It was this attitude that led him to the M.B.A. program, where he concentrated his studies in finance and accounting. He manifests his belief that rigorous training in fundamentals is essential prior to any undertaking in many areas of his life, including extracurricular activities.

As an example, during graduate school he worked with professional dog trainers training Labrador retrievers as hunting dogs. As his children became interested in dogs, "I found it hard doing the dog thing without doing it right."

So we got a dog and I started introducing them to what you do in training and so on. Then we got another dog (I'm looking for a really good one now), and we'll keep going until we find two really good ones. Then we'll go and run trials together.

I don't like to do things half way. The dog thing I didn't want to get into until we could afford it; right now we have a dog locally with a trainer; he is the top guy on the west coast—he is the most winning guy. You look for the guy who can win, and then you go with him. And that costs a few dollars to have that hobby, but that's one of the dividends of all our work.

Now that their daughter is getting into horses, they are looking around at stables and horse trainers with much the same commitment.

When Robert graduated from business school, he went to work for a small investment firm, which within months was bought by a large national investment house. He worked there for four years, the last two as sales manager of the local office. It was at this time he got involved in venture investing.

I got involved in a very small way on borrowed money—the classic case of getting very highly leveraged to "strike it rich," so to speak (which I don't recommend)—and I was involved in doing those activities which led to more interest in that area. I left the investment firm to be involved with two of the companies that I had become involved with over a space of several years. I also had the opportunity to work as a turnaround manager in a company that we acquired when it was very sick, and to play a variety of roles which you do in entrepreneurial situations. For about five years thereafter I was in an entrepreneurial venture capital type of environment.

Then I sold the business we were involved in and for about a year worked as a consultant. I did some work for the company I'm presently employed by over the space of about a year, did some consulting work, and worked for the Small Business Administration as well. I'm now with Tilson Supply Company as vice president in charge of marketing and sales. It has grown from

about $5 million in sales to about $25 million in six years.

Upon her graduation, Sylvia chose a more traditional pathway: "I didn't have the entrepreneurial urge like Robert starting out; for one thing, because of my background, I wasn't ready." Robert did have some influence on her direction.

I just suggested to her that if she were going for an M.B.A., she take all the finance and accounting that she could. The rest you can learn on the job—learn the fundamentals, just like in physics. I think she took the advice and appreciated it; in the work she does now, she is ahead of some of the people. She is doing a lot of marketing applications, but financially based.

Sylvia had limited her job search to the local area; together they had decided not to move at least until the children were out of school. The custody agreements in Robert's divorce were a large part of that decision. Sylvia recalls the job search process and her acceptance of employment with one of the largest local corporations with some misgivings.

Toward the end of my program I thought I wanted to work for a bank. I also thought that if I couldn't work for a bank, it would be really neat to sell commercial real estate. The desire to get into commercial real estate development really hasn't gone away. I toy with it off and on all the time. I like the tangible aspects. I thought that either through a bank, through the real estate investment department of a bank or through a large commercial development company, I could get into that field. I really tried, and in the process I let a couple of good jobs go by because I felt I knew what I wanted to do—I didn't want to settle for anything. Then I got to the point where I almost got a job in the field, except I did not impress them with having a strong selling background. (Indeed, I had none!)

And then the job with Logan Industries came up. I had gone to school with Logan employees who were getting their M.B.A.s, and I had a perception of a fine company, well-managed, certainly something that wouldn't harm me—and I thought I had better start doing something. The job was in human resource management, which I had some interest in along with my psychology background, even though my M.B.A. was in finance and investments. The combination worked out really well. And Logan did a first-class job of handling me.

For example, I told them right from the start that at least for a period of time I would not be available to move around in my career. They were very frank in admitting this could substantially interfere with my career. But one thing I will say about Logan: if I were needed at home, it would not be looked upon negatively. If my child were sick at home and more than our caretaker could handle, I would get up and leave—and that to me is very important. In fact, I would have to say it's probably one of my top priorities in any job. I love to work—I'd rather work than be at home—but I want the ability to be there if my family needs me.

Yet Sylvia continues describing her misgivings:

I have looked back at the job offers I passed up. I think if I were doing it again I would ask, first, what would I gain in terms of a learning experience—not that it will necessarily be where I end up; second, am I going generally in the direction I want to go without closing any doors. Even though it's very desirable from the employer's point of view to have somebody who is very directed, from a personal point of view you could be limiting yourself later.

Now I feel it would be a good job to work for one of the big eight accounting firms where you get a broad-based experience that you can use later on. Even if they pay you much less, that background would be very beneficial. I think all of us were overly concerned with what that first job paid. The things you learn on the first job—how to get things done effectively, communicating, understanding how to solve

problems—are things you could get in a variety of places.

Not only did Robert and Sylvia differ in establishing their respective career paths, but they also differ significantly in their attitudes and goals within the work environment. To Sylvia "it's not that important what product you're in, but it's whether you're challenged, doing the things you want to do, satisfied in your job, and progressing." Robert disagrees:

The financial rewards are far more important in my mind. My job has to be firmly in place; that's the way she can be more flexible in her approach. I also feel it's important what business I'm in, what products I'm selling, because if you are riding a winner, you do well financially and personally—there is a direct linkage. I look at it as an investment of my time and my personal energy. You can't be fooling around; you only have so long to do it and you have got to get a return on it now.

Dollars are very important. I negotiate very hard for those because I think you have got to have them now. I don't want promises. That's very important because I'm thinking about the family.

In fact, they both view his job as the higher priority, at least for the moment. They feel that trying to compete on an equal level would result in working against each other.

On the other hand, both incomes go into the household account out of which the living expenses are paid. Separate from that are their individual estates that consist basically of the money they each had prior to their marriage. As a result both feel the responsibilities as wage-earners, yet each maintains management of the individual accounts. This financial arrangement allows each considerable freedom; they do, however, consult each other before making major financial commitments. Robert enthusiastically recalls a time when

Sylvia wanted to invest in a Sun Valley condominium:

> I did not at that time want to be involved. I had other commitments, as well as some apprehensions about this particular investment. I had some questions about the numbers and we discussed it fairly thoroughly. She went ahead, and it turned out to be one of the best investments I have ever seen! It has been a super investment and a total source of enjoyment for the family.

Yet their attitude toward living expenses is enormously different. They do not, for example, engage any household help, even though they both work long hours. Partially this is because they are protective of their family time together, but as Robert puts it, both with pride and in jest: "The fact is that I'm too tight to pay them anyway. I don't care how much money we've got!"

Their day starts at 5:30. Robert leaves an hour later, and Sylvia shortly thereafter to catch a company van which gets her to work by 8:00. She does not usually see her daughter before school; this is of some concern. Robert will sometimes share in picking their children up from school, especially when doctor's appointments are scheduled. Robert believes the children learn to be part of a team, seeing their parents working about the house after having spent a full day at work. And they describe spending a lot of personal time with the children, being outdoors and engaging in hunting, jogging, and skiing. Sylvia confesses that the two areas which suffer as a result of their hectic schedules are personal time and social engagements. Time alone is rare.

There are occasional moments, when the children seem especially needy of attention, that Sylvia becomes vulnerable to criticisms of their life-style. She can be particularly sensitive to comments from her own parents, but then, in weighing the alternative of staying home, she quickly resolves any feelings of guilt.

> I look at my next-door neighbor and see what she has become: I think I'll keep doing what I'm doing! The fact is that I like to work and the kids seem to be doing all right without me there all the time.

Robert emphasizes, "They are doing great!"

> She is the best mother I've ever seen. She gives a tremendous amount of love to all those kids. They are the biggest and happiest part of our lives. All I know is this marriage has been awfully good for them.

While supportive of one another as parents, they recognize that problems have arisen at home in handling their competitive spirit.

> We are both take-charge persons; we are both controlling; we both tend to manage; we both tend to delegate.

In response to those problems, they identify and carve out their own special areas, using care "around the edges."

They work together well as a team in terms of personal investments. Both of them being in business allows them to communicate fully about financial risks and gives an added dimension to their marriage. The excitement and success they have achieved from this teamwork approach derives partly from their complementary personal skills and partly from being at complementary points along their respective career paths.

For example, Sylvia believes she projects an image of competence at work and is highly oriented to strong interpersonal skills. Robert, on the other hand, who from the start has centered himself in very aggressive, high-growth businesses, believes his image is that of a person who is fueling the growth rate in that demanding environment. In pooling her analytical strengths and his entrepreneurial drive, they structure their team advantage. And they both feel more freedom in that they both work. Robert describes their most current investment decision:

Both of us feel comfortable enough together, working as a team, to assume a certain amount of interest-rate risk right now in acquiring a new home in this market. We bought it from a builder on contract, and we were able to negotiate an interesting payment schedule. We felt that, at the price, we were willing to undertake that interest rate risk and to refinance because we really wanted this for the family. Part of that is based on the fact that she is working. She is pulling on the oars just as hard as I am.

While they have indeed talked about going into business together, they view the prospect of working with one another on a daily basis in an operating capacity as threatening. They fear that the excitement of the investment decision would be diminished.

At this time, in fact, they are facing personal career decisions which may change the nature and style of this team relationship. Until now the timing of their careers has been an advantageous mix: Sylvia describes herself as the financial conservative, Robert as the risk taker. Now with two children in college, two in prep school, and the last about to enter prep school, Robert is becoming wary of "running off the deep end with a new fledgling company that is under-capitalized." Sylvia defines her readiness to accept risk as "even to the point of a career change."

Her job as business analyst for Logan Industries is to provide analytical reports and planning appraisals through which she exercises a large influence on the decision-making process. It is a position which is generally used to progress through the company, and Sylvia admits it has been a rewarding learning opportunity. Her major disappointment has been that career paths are not clearly defined within the company. Without that framework

she has found it difficult to gauge where she is in the company hierarchy; further, they provide little feedback, so she finds it frustrating to measure her performance abilities. No one has spoken to her concerning long-term career potentials.

She has, nevertheless, developed a loyalty toward her employer. Six months after she had accepted their job offer, Sylvia received another offer from a bank mortgage company by which she was very tempted. Logan put substantial effort into retaining her at that time. She remains impressed by the interest they displayed in redirecting her job to help satisfy her career goals, and as a result she is less inclined to look outside the company currently.

And yet, while Sylvia's eagerness to confront risk becomes somewhat unclear, Robert's resolve to stabilize his career and venture enthusiasm is even less certain. He appears somewhat hesitant to disclose the exact nature of his current business obligations. He admits to holding essentially two fulltime jobs, while venture capital is a personal interest beyond those. In this latter category, he is heavily involved in two large entrepreneurial companies, each with about $10 million in sales.

I attend board meetings; I am chairman of the executive committee (and chairman of the board in one); I run the board meetings. As chairman of the executive committee, I am involved in the appropriate capital expenditures, dividend policy, and approval of plans before they go to the board. I spend some significant amount of time (over time I would like to have that reduced and move it in a direction where investments are 100 percent controlled by me or very few partners) in these endeavors.

Again, I am moving away from those environments because it's time in my life cycle; it's time in the maturity of those investments for a change. I have a desire to concentrate more on building the company I'm involved with right

now; we are going through some pretty dra
matic growth steps there as well.

As an operating manager at Tilson Supply
Company, I have all the marketing and sales
functions. I have two sales managers, a product
manager, an advertising manager, and a custom
graphics manager all reporting to me. I am really
busy there and I travel some. I would like to have
my workday activities concentrated there for the
next two years. I can't see much further beyond
that anyway.

Sometimes the pressure gets to me. For a
while it was too much, and I had to restructure
things a little. I would like to see the intensity
ease for a while, I really would. I'm not saying I
won't get involved in more things, but it will be
on more of a 100 percent control type basis. I
probably will get involved in some commercial
real estate because that ties in with tax shelter
goals and overall financial planning. I might acquire an interest in a going business. . . .

Still, the Fitzgeralds clearly perceive themselves as confronting some changes in style.
Whether experimenting with new attitudes
will effect a major redirection is less convinc-
ing. In a light-hearted exchange about their extracurricular dog training activities, they express a fundamental theme of their
relationship:

SYLVIA: I'm not into dog training to the extent that Robert is.

ROBERT: [grins knowingly] Wait until you've
won that first field trial.

SYLVIA: [pauses, then slowly and thought-
fully] I do like winning.

Janet Brown

Since earning her M.B.A. almost two and a half years ago, Janet has been employed by Southeast Coca-Cola Bottling Company. Now, 34 years old and single, Janet feels she is presently at "a kind of plateau" professionally, although she does see long-term potential.

Things aren't working out as well as I'd originally planned. At this point, I don't see the potential for immediate future mobility, and that's giving me some personal pause right now. I'm not actively looking for another job, but I am paying more attention to what's available, and what's going on in the marketplace.

Janet's academic interests during her M.B.A. program were in administrative organization and operations management. She also took extensive electives in other areas since, by virtue of being a business undergraduate, she was able to waive many core course requirements. She financed her graduate education by, and now continues in, what she terms an unusual living arrangement: she works as a resident housekeeper for a retired widower and thus pays no room or board. In return, she does the shopping and cooking. Her employer is away three months out of the year as well as most summer weekends, so Janet sees her time commitment to him as "really quite flexible."

This arrangement was an unusual opportunity. I'd gone to school in the fall of 1975 to finish my undergraduate degree; the following spring, a sorority sister asked if I'd like a house-sitting job that summer. Given the choice between that and the dormitories, I was persuaded even before I saw the place. I didn't foresee staying this long, but on the whole it's worked out well, although I pay a high social cost because of the extra obligations.

Janet had interrupted her undergraduate work and moved out of state following an unpleasant divorce from an early marriage. Originally, she had hoped to finish her degree in California but was discouraged by the prospect of losing credits in the transfer between universities. At this point, she went to work for a California winery as a secretary to the Director of Compliance. Her duties at Gallo were largely oriented toward meeting the legal requirements of the Bureau of Tobacco, Alcohol and Firearms, such as calculating taxes, preparing samples, authorizing shipments, and keeping files as specified by federal and state regulations.

Returning to Savannah to finish her undergraduate degree, Janet used this secretarial experience to find employment at the university, working in a variety of departments. The opportunity to house-sit, however, allowed her more freedom to pursue her studies. Because of her living situation, she did not feel the immediate need to find work.

If it hadn't been for my living circumstances, I probably wouldn't have gotten my M.B.A. When I originally went back to school, I had savings enough only to finish my degree flat broke, but with my "free" living situation, I was financially able to go into the M.B.A. program. It was "the thing to do" at the time, and I'm very glad I did it. It opened doors for me that would have never been opened any other way.

Her return to Savannah was motivated not only by academic considerations but also by the fact she enjoyed living in the area. She elaborates:

I've invested a lot of time developing a network of friends and a life-style that's comfortable. I like the people I deal with, and while I'm thinking I probably could become as comfortable wherever I lived, you'd have to pay me a hell of a lot to make me seriously consider moving to Los Angeles, for example. On the other hand, I was more pleasantly surprised at receiving an Atlanta job offer than I'd ever thought I would be—especially in terms of the quality of life I found in the Atlanta metropolitan area.

Mostly, money isn't everything. Taking a job that perhaps offers less money but does provide congenial surroundings and a comfortable life-style makes a lot of difference to me.

As a graduate student, Janet had taken part in the campus interview system.

I'd gone to the high technology companies because I wanted to become involved with a manufacturing firm. I really wanted line supervision, and I think that's where I'd like to be again in the near future. The fact that I didn't have an engineering degree made them very reluctant to hire me. I think they just didn't feel I fit the traditional mold of what they expected in an employee.

If I had to do it again, I think I might do some things differently. My present job is not quite what I'd predicted. I didn't interview when Coke came to campus. I was very surprised when I heard about the opportunity and went about getting more information on it. I'd had some background working for the winery, so being in a

bottling plant was not all that unfamiliar. Plus, the fact that I'm a woman helped their EEO numbers and probably tipped the scale in my favor.

Coca-Cola offers a training program which Janet describes as "very, very good."

I spent six weeks rotating through every functional area in the company: quality control, production, sales, delivery, accounting, computer room, corporate office, the works. It was very good.

Her most rewarding positions have been line experiences:

If you have line responsibility, the feedback is much more obvious. You know if you're doing a good job sooner than if you're doing a staff project where the results may or may not be implemented, may not be evaluated, or may not be known for some time. That's exactly what's been happening in a project I'm currently involved with. It's a very slow thing to get going. I don't have control over all the players involved, at least not to the same extent as I would with a staff that reported to me at a branch.

In fact, she labels her two biggest frustrations with her job as "very little evaluation, very little feedback."

While Janet's present job title varies from "operations analyst" to "market analyst," she believes functional definitions are more important.

Partially, I'm a major account manager. This means I call on grocery chains, try to get them to book ads, increase sales in those chain stores. I'm partially a staff assistant to a division manager, who is also vice president of the company. And I'm partially a market analyst.

As a matter of fact, I just asked my boss "My operations analyst cards have almost run out; when I reorder my business cards, what kind of title do you want me to put on them?"

I presently have certain minimal responsibilities in several areas. I have responsibilities for recycling for six distributions centers. Our long-haul transports bring empty two-liter plastic bottles across state to service a central collection point at Southeast Recycling. While the recycling market hasn't yet developed very much, it is increasing. Our recycling efforts are basically in support of independent recycling centers. Because these centers serve as collection points for cans, plastics, and glass, as well as papers, we believe they are able to serve the public's environmental concerns more completely than, say, passage of "bottle bills," legislation aimed primarily at eliminating soft-drink cans through heavy taxation. Of course, the company has considerable financial interest in taking a stand against such bills, but we also feel the litter issue is better addressed by taking a broader approach. Presently, we are trying to work out some of our record-keeping, along with a few other details that will really get the program going.

I also used to do a quarterly company newsletter, but thankfully I got rid of that task. I have responsibilities for one of the convenience food store chains, as well as for non-chain convenience stores—not the big chains, but the medium-sized independents and the "Mom and Pop" neighborhood types of stores.

I have some responsibilities in terms of staff projects and in computing internal rates of return on a particular cooler refurbishment program. (And I haven't done internal rates of return since school!)

In carrying out these responsibilities, Janet views her relationship to her superiors as fairly distant, "a lot more distant than I'm really comfortable with. It's given me some concern."

Three weeks after I started, the man who hired me left to become president and general manager of one of six Atlanta-owned operations. So early on, I was a "corporate orphan." Yet, because of what was happening in the company at the time, I had some really interesting experiences. We were going through a major acquisition, divestiture, and reorganization program

within those first eighteen months. We acquired three independent franchise bottlers, divested one franchise territory, and merged two distribution centers. We also had several people taking jobs in areas that were new to them; we combined two divisions—there was a lot of activity going on. And that presented some good opportunities but, unfortunately, my new superior felt "a woman's place was in the home," not behind a manager's desk.

Janet's perception of this difficulty has been reinforced by the one other professional woman working in her office.

Rita faces similar biases; however, she is married, and the fact that her husband plays basketball with the company president smoothes their working relationship. I really feel that the fact that I am a single woman working with a bunch of married men makes a difference. I do face challenges in this regard, because the company is largely oriented toward men.

Janet describes these feelings, recalling a recent trip with the company president and the corporate director of marketing, during which she felt excluded from "99 percent of the conversation." Upon arrival at the distribution center, the manager presented corsages to all the wives of employees—and to Janet. Janet saw this as a subtle threat to her professional status but was unsure how to press the issue.

A similar situation also occurred within her own office soon after. When the group secretary left the company, Janet felt they would be better off hiring a "mature and stable person," one with experience. The rest of the staff decided to hire a young, good-looking and outgoing candidate with untested job skills. Subsequent performance proved "good looks" was a poor selection criterion.

Still, Janet describes her working relationship with her peers as reasonably good.

I try to learn from their direct sales experience, and I try to give them the benefit of my educational background as it applies to this business.

I have spent an awful lot of professional and personal time trying to make some bridges to the people I have to work with. I definitely think being a woman in this particular company is a challenge. I suspect anyone working for a company traditionally staffed by male employees would face a similar challenge. It's a little bit different in a bank, perhaps, because that has become a "clean" industry. Here, however, I've worn the uniforms, I've been on the production line, I've done some things that are physically pretty demanding—and I'm glad I don't have to do those things for a living every day of the week. But my thinking is: if I've done it enough to know what those who do that kind of work every day have to face, and if I've done it enough so I can appreciate what they do, then I'll have a greater sensitivity to the challenges they face.

Early in her career with Coca-Cola, Janet acquired a reputation as a "hatchet lady." One of her first assignments was to close out a small franchise bottler in Georgia, which corporate Coca-Cola viewed as a "nuisance" operation. The owner had filed suit against the company over franchise territory issues (eventually reaching the Supreme Court), but he was now ready to retire. This operation was managed by the Georgia company from Atlanta; their operations analyst had reported to corporate headquarters that his experience there as a plant manager had been extremely rewarding. Because of his positive report suggesting other operations analysts be given a similar opportunity, and because he and Janet were graduates of the same business program, Janet was given a temporary assignment there. It was viewed within the company as an opportunity to appreciate the scope of plant activity from a managerial standpoint, one with relatively few complexities because of its small size. Janet did in effect shut the plant down, and Coca-Cola bought out the franchise operator.

I had the keys to the plant and the combination to the safe; I had to take care of payroll for the two people who worked there. One was from Thailand, and the other was a 21-year-old woman with health problems, who worked to support her two young children. This employee didn't like working for a woman, so I drove the routes almost half-time. It was a very interesting experience; I had to either do everything myself or get the cooperation of the two other people. I did marketing, administration, finance, accounts payable, accounts receivable; the whole thing in a unit small enough to let me see all aspects of it and try to put it all together. Very, very, very valuable.

After I had been to Taft and shut that down, I went to Hinesville and shut that down; and when I was next sent to Valdosta, I'm sure everyone was thinking they were either about to be shut down or sold. That was my reputation. Circumstance.

But I did have fun. I saved accounts from going to competition. I got to work with the salespeople and, through a remarkable individual who is now 71 or 72 years old and had owned the Hinesville franchise, I learned how to drive a forklift! I got to do a lot of things I'd never had a chance to do before. When a worker came in to ask if there were any jobs, this former owner of the franchise nodded to me, a young woman, and said, "Talk to the boss."

However, this was not the typical pattern of Janet's other Coca-Cola experiences.

I have a theory that men and women do things just a little bit differently. I personally am not comfortable staying in a motel, and I will go out of my way to make my surroundings pleasant. I don't enjoy sitting around a hotel cocktail lounge; it's not comfortable for me, particularly in a strange community where, simply because of circumstances and other people's preconceived notions, what I am and what I intend are probably not congruent with their expectations.

When our division manager, who is black, brought me to Hinesville, he took me out to dinner the first evening. Going back to the same restaurant the next night, I had the feeling there had been a lot of gossip. The whole situation was not what most people there consider normal.

Thus, when Janet was sent to Valdosta as acting branch manager, she elected to stay with an aunt living there. This decision was based on her own comfort, but she felt the saved motel expense would also be to the company's advantage. When she didn't send motel bills into headquarters for reimbursement but rather sent receipts for groceries and other minimal living expenses, Janet encountered some disapproval. She was ultimately reimbursed but believes she is still receiving the subtle message that her expense account is not being used to its fullest.

Janet sees her greatest challenge as trying to gain acceptance within the company, and her greatest deficiency as lack of direct sales experience. These two areas, however, have not presented insurmountable difficulties. As an acting manager, Janet's branch was awarded the company's sales trophy, a traveling silver bowl inscribed with the branch name.

I was an acting branch manager for two months, which was about two and a half months longer than anyone expected. If I'd expressed interest in having that job permanently, I'm quite certain I would have gotten it. But, for personal reasons and lot of professional indecision, I didn't want to move to Valdosta permanently. Plus, as far as my personal life goes, it was a poor time for me to take on that kind of challenge.

I think I did fairly well at the time by simply drawing on my classroom experience in administrative organization, as well as using a lot of common sense. I simply told my staff "I have a leadership role here; there are certain things I don't want you to do because I don't think it's effective for your jobs. Your job is to get out and sell; mine is to do anything I can to help you sell more. I depend a lot on you because of your experience, which I haven't had. But you need my direction so we can achieve results together."

We ended up by winning the sales trophy one of the three months I was there. So Valdosta seemed to work, but there were a lot of things the person who is now in that position has done, based on his 15 years experience with the company, that make me ask myself why I wasn't smart enough to do them. Okay, partly that's experience, partly that's because I had to face some other problems of higher priority. He and I have kept up a good rapport; I joke "You wouldn't be where you are today if I hadn't been there to fix things first!"

When she declined the Valdosta branch manager position, Janet felt one year's experience with the company was not enough to assume the role of branch manager. She discusses part of her reluctance to pursue the job when the opportunity was there.

I don't think I'd be too happy in a small community. My aunt, who has lived there for almost 25 years, advised me very bluntly that my opportunity for any kind of social life in Valdosta's conservative, family-oriented community would be minimal. As a single parent, she has survived the social vacuum caused by her divorce by relying on her son and his friends. She certainly felt strongly that I should consider the social implications of living in Valdosta as a single, professional woman. That was the major factor that convinced me not to pursue Valdosta. At times, however, I wonder if I gave too much weight to her attitudes and advice; the branch manager responsibility is necessary for substantial career advancement.

Janet feels that becoming a corporate orphan so early in her career is one of the main reasons for her current dissatisfaction. In her line responsibilities, she enjoyed having people report directly to her, as well as being able to see the effects of her organizational and managerial skills. In the company's main office, however, she feels she has "too many people in my way, rather than having somebody pushing me to do the best I can."

I don't have a mentor, I'm not under anyone's wing, and I don't have anyone coaching me, providing some of the contacts I think I need. It's just a result of circumstance. And while I get along well with my current boss, I just don't interact with him as often as I'd like. In a sense, I suppose that's a compliment, because I don't think he feels he has to supervise me very carefully. He can give me a project and say what he wants done, and I'll go back to him if I have questions. If not, I complete the project, and we go from there.

Again, that may be the difference between a man, who would expect such a working relationship, and someone like myself who's not quite comfortable. . . . I think I need more periodic feedback than I'm getting.

Meanwhile, Janet derives a great deal of personal satisfaction from her heavy involvement with the M.B.A. alumni association. With that commitment, her living arrangement obligations, and her work, she has little time for other things.

Margaret Woods

During her fifth quarter of study for an M.B.A., Margaret assumed management of a small personnel agency owned by her father. At 31, Margaret had previously worked for seven years in medical research for the state, a job she considered "as far away from self-motivated as you can get." The opportunity of getting into a business of her own intrigued her, and she hoped to use her new managerial position to accumulate capital and develop a network of contacts within the industry, with the eventual intent of establishing a word processing training school. She took over the agency in April, spending three weeks of intensive research prior to reopening the agency, which had been idle for three months. By the end of July, she had returned the enterprise to her father, who then sold the business. Margaret spent the summer looking for career employment, and in the fall she accepted a position with a large banking corporation.

Corporate Services, Inc., specialized in the recruitment and placement of staff for law offices in a large metropolitan area. The main business was in permanent job placements, although it included some part-time, free-lance referrals. CSI also placed bookkeepers and office managers. The agency had an excellent reputation among law offices. Placement fees, the main revenue of the business, were all employer-paid and were based on a percentage of the employee's monthly salary. This fee schedule was similar to those of most local agencies dealing with legal firms; however, more generally at this level, fees were paid by the employee. All placements carried a guarantee: if the employee placed by the service left for any reason during the first 30 days, a total refund was given to the employer.

CSI had been developed and run profitably by a local recruiter for three years before it first changed management. It was then sold to a corporate executive who employed a general manager. When the executive was transferred overseas a year later, he felt it would be neither feasible nor profitable to continue running the agency. Margaret's father, a self-employed accountant, bought the business as a side interest; he also continued the operation under a general manager. This arrangement lasted for five years, until the departure of the general manager, combined with a severe decline in the health of Margaret's father, left the business idle. Margaret assumed management three months later. She made no capital investment and was subject to little, if any, supervision. Upon occasion, she did ask for her father's opinion and advice. In evaluating the experience, Margaret claims, "It gave me a finer appreciation of why I seldom saw my father during my childhood, and how fast you really have to pedal to stay ahead. But such an experience really does have a lot of things to say for it."

Margaret had no background in personnel work or in the area of legal secretarial skills. The previous manager had been a legal secretary and had done well matching a secretary's skills with the requirements of a job order. Thus, before attempting to reopen the agency, Margaret met with the original owner, both to investigate procedures that had worked successfully in the past and to gain personal insight about the people she would be dealing with. She spent time with the former office manager, discussing similar topics. She also gathered information concerning competing agencies, visited equipment vendors to become familiar with the computerized equipment used by most large law offices, and contacted local training schools and community colleges for potential recruitment sources. She felt confident that a definite need existed in the city for a quality word processing training school. At the same time, she determined she would have to reestablish the placement business in order to have enough income to live on before diversifying into the word processing business.

Margaret's research dealt not only with the technical aspects of the business but also with the nature of her personal commitment:

I really think you should always take advantage of these sorts of opportunities; I don't think you should not do them because it has always been my feeling that if it is a mistake you can move on. I had absolutely no investment there, I just had to give myself "x" amount of time; trying to figure out how long to give it was also interesting.

To help with this decision, she spoke with an executive recruiter:

I was already committed to this project, and he was most discouraging and very negative. Now, however, I think he was really quite shrewd. He told me to give it six months and then to get out. If I didn't get it up and running in six months, he

said, *"Don't waste your time." It was nice to have that as a goalpost because I always would have wondered, "am I being a quitter?" if I hadn't had some objective person saying, "Hey, at six months, bail out!" And it made it much easier when I really didn't think the business was going anywhere after three months.*

On the other hand, immediacy was an important factor in her decision.

I think the reason I did this was because I didn't want to go out and look for a job. It's a godawful reason, but sometimes I'm like that. At the time, I wasn't sure I'd find a job. Basically, I lacked the confidence and thought I'd better try this. Also, I felt that if it worked out I would be making a comparable amount to what I would in an entry level position, and I knew I would probably feel a little happier. But actually, I think I was delaying the corporate job search. I hated, I absolutely hated that cattle car over at the placement center. It just bugged me. It's the way you get exposure, but ugh!—the thought of going out there with everyone looking for a job—and I'm not the kind of person who could really do academics and job search at the same time (at least, I convinced myself that was the case). So, I was putting it off, and putting it off, and this came along, and I thought "Heck! Let's do it!"

At the time of this decision, however, Margaret, as a single woman, was faced with the sole responsibility for student loan payments, car payments, and house payments. She had purchased her home several years before going back to school. Although she prefers living alone, she began renting a room in her house during her M.B.A. study. Margaret noted that interviewing potential roommates, recruited through local newspaper ads, increased her awareness of the importance of interviewing skills. Her first selection, she recalls, was less than acceptable. During her employment, however, sharing her house became an enjoyable arrangement. "It's real hard when you need to share something—

either something good or something bad—and no one's there. You're isolated physically, emotionally, mentally; there's not much stimulation. When it's going great guns, you appreciate the peace and quiet, but. . . ."

Finances continued to be a major problem in her decision.

> I did not like being only on the fringes of financial security. I told myself I would not go through one more winter without an income; I just couldn't face those oil bills.
>
> After two years at school without income, it was probably not the best time for me to be going into an uncertain financial stream. I learned a lot about myself. After being here at the bank for two and a half months and seeing the corporate structure, my desire to get out and do something on my own is starting to reappear. I have to keep reminding myself—you know, it's real intriguing, it's real challenging, and not always fun, but if I ever do it again, I'm going to have to figure out this financial thing. I think it will always eat at me. But I'd almost always rather be the general than the soldier.

CSI was not a profitable venture for Margaret. Office overhead was minimal, as the business was strategically located downtown, near the courthouse where rents were low. However, the personnel industry turned out to be highly cyclic and, unfortunately, CSI's three-month idleness had not gone unnoticed by many clients.

In addition, the low-rent location brought with it personal safety concerns. Transients frequented the area, and Margaret was concerned about the deterioration of local social service programs. Her office was on the third floor, but exit was possible by only one door. The previous manager had been a victim of an attack by someone she had known by sight. Although no significant personal injury resulted, there was an increased awareness of the vulnerability of the location. As a consequence, that manager began to share the reception area with a man who was both a part-time police officer and a part-time attorney. While sharing the office space did reduce the already low overhead, the attorney was rarely there.

Margaret continued to feel nervous, especially with male applicants. During interviews with them she would frequently use the excuse of the building's overheating to prop open the door. Further, she usually left the office by 3:00 P.M. (an aspect of her job she later labeled as "the most fun").

She describes her typical day as "hideous." Several days of silence were not unusual. She arrived at the office at 9:00 A.M.; to arrive any earlier was unproductive, as legal firms were fairly unreceptive to phone calls during their opening hours. She would pick up her phone calls from the answering service, return them, then make some of her own. She ran ads in the local papers on Wednesdays and Sundays, so she was certain to be in the office on at least Thursdays and Mondays.

> If I ever—if I ever!—when I got a job order, I'd go and call on the office manager. That way, I could at least meet them and they could see that I wasn't a cretin, and I could get a better feeling for what kind of operation it was. And hopefully project a solid image. That part was fun; I liked that a lot.

CSI's image did remain a significant problem, said Margaret: "I would never associate myself with the personnel agency business again." As a representative of an agency, Margaret was generally poorly received when making "cold calls" on customers. From her inquiries, she realized this was a result of a history of misrepresentation and aggressive sales techniques used by most agencies. Although she spoke of the necessity of building a good lunch network, she added:

> A lot of the people I was dealing with I wouldn't care to socialize with, nor they with me. There's

a lot of bad feeling toward agencies here in the city. It starts working on your own self-image. And because I have enough confidence and self-respect to know I am somebody, it bugged me. It bugged the hell out of me, to be treated so badly by total strangers.

She found the lawyers she dealt with generally arrogant and covetous of their time. She gave them a "C minus" on personality but admitted that having dated an attorney for eight years, she should have known "what I was getting into." Indeed, the worst part of the job was "probably dealing with some jerk lawyer—or some jerk secretary who thought she was better than you, and you knew she didn't have half the brains, or half the potential, and didn't have the courtesy. . . ." Again, "the worst part was fighting the stigma of being associated with an agency, and probably just the loneliness. . . . There were a couple of times I just wanted to scream obscenities over the phone. It was discouraging, but I guess that's just the way it goes."

Thus, rather than promoting the business by telephone or by in-person "cold calls," Margaret sent a promotional mailing to two hundred attorneys in the downtown area. The difficulty of financing this effort underscored her already precarious financial situation. In addition, this general canvass turned out to be an error, as it elicited little response. Next, Margaret selected about 35 firms, mostly previous clients. To those she added another group, which she identified as rapidly growing but without the staff and finances to recruit internally. Margaret then called each firm to get the name of the office manager in charge of hiring. This approach worked well, and she considers the creative process of developing the promotional materials and the subsequent positive responses the most rewarding experiences of her job. Margaret followed this second mailing with a phone call; she felt it would be to her advantage to build on the good repu-

tation the agency had already established, and aimed to distinguish the business in that manner. With ensuing job orders, she made personal calls on the firms in order to promote her agency's image and assess the office's needs.

Securing secretaries for the positions was more difficult, however. Help-wanted advertising in the local papers had limited results and was costly; respondents were largely underqualified or without experience. Margaret kept a log to determine which type of ad brought the best results but could not find any correlation. Community college and training programs were also of little use as sources.

For the most part, lawyers wanted "local people," but only those who were currently employed with top skills and references. Further, experienced people were so readily placed that Margaret found it difficult to understand why they didn't find their own jobs. Top secretaries earned over $20,000 annually, and many of the larger legal firms did their own recruiting. On the other hand, entry level positions paid extremely low salaries: "That's the only way to get into the legal secretary game; there are a lot of sharp people looking for jobs who wouldn't take those entry jobs, and I don't blame them. I wasn't going to tell them it was the best thing."

Plus, the frequently arrogant attitudes of the would-be employers were often matched by the problem of misrepresentation by those seeking employment.

I've always prided myself on being a fairly good judge of people, but you have to watch out for the ringers; you know, someone who comes in and claims she's been working in the city for twelve years, yet can't give you a reference (now come on!). "Who did you work for last?" "Well, they're all dead."

Trust was also a major stumbling block. Neither employer nor potential employee was always honest with the agency.

I found that you couldn't ever really be sure. You couldn't speak of your product with confidence because it was so variable, and you couldn't really sell an agency because you never really knew—you know, they were desperate, they were sounding good, they wanted someone bad—and then they get someone and treat them like dirt. So it was a real hard thing; there was absolutely no confidence on either side of the game. Now, if you had your own school, you could really assess someone's skills and you could at least sell them with confidence. That would improve the situation, I think.

However, Margaret thinks learning how to handle herself under a variety of adverse circumstances, and learning what she could expect of herself, proved "an invaluable experience. It didn't hurt me any. It certainly gave me a better understanding of what it takes to survive."

While perhaps I'm not the most confident person—I'd probably weigh 20 pounds less and have fingernails if I were—I do have a lot to offer. That's another thing about being in the personnel business: when someone sharp walks into your office, you immediately know you're dealing with a sharpie; when a dud walks in, you immediately know you're dealing with a dud—and there are a lot of duds out there! In turn, you know that whoever has the pleasure of talking to you realizes (or they're stupid) that they are speaking with someone who is fairly astute. And that's not a brag, it's just a fact of life.

Of her personal life during that time, Margaret hesitates:

Let me try to remember; it was either extremely bad or extremely good. Well, the whole thing, being in transition like that, I was not the best of company for anyone. On the other hand, I really made an effort to get out and be with people. It's hard. I don't like being that lonely, that poor. . . . Still, I probably would do it again.

Now, however, Margaret has traded poverty for medical-dental benefits, a paycheck every two weeks—the fruits of employment within a large corporate structure. During the time she managed CSI she also finished her M.B.A.; currently she is employed as a commercial lending trainee with a large bank. After having been involved with the bank's classroom training program for three months, she now begins another five months in case studies, to be followed by a succession of departmental rotations that will acquaint her with various bank procedures. Her ultimate assignment is unknown.

Has she set herself another time limit for success?

Yeah, next Thursday! No. I think if I stay, and I may be totally wrong, you probably need three years to fully evaluate this position, and by then I'll be pushing 34. But I'm thinking career paths—and that's another thing I'm wondering, did I dawdle around too long? But then, you know, you never move, you never move. So, on some days I say three years before I know where this is going, and some days I say three weeks or I'm out. I don't know where it's going to go. But I'll tell you one thing, I'm not going to sit around and take any garbage from anyone. And if that ends my career, so be it.

Electronic Systems Company

The Electronic Systems Company was a growing concern in 1966, having experienced continuous, comfortable growth in its first ten years of operation. Its founder and owner, Francis Walker, was a classic success-story entrepreneur. He conceived an idea for a new electronic component, invented and initially developed it in the basement of his home, and sold it on the basis of quality, price, and quick delivery service. It was an exciting company, created from scratch in Walker's image. It employed around 250 people and its sales approached $4 million. Although the company was molded by him in every significant detail, he had gathered around him associates who shared his passions and his enthusiasms and who expressed outstanding commitments to the goals of the organization.

One such enthusiastic employee was Barry Welch, who came to work at Electronic Systems after having completed his tour of duty with the Air Force in the latter part of the 1950s. Later, around 1962 or 1963, Barry expressed a desire for a college education. The company offered to finance part of the expense, so Barry enrolled in the evening division of a local college, majoring in physics and minoring in math. (When I arrived at the company in 1968, Welch was in the second semester of his junior year.)

It was not uncommon in this young organization to find that several employees wore various departmental "hats." For example, after several years as a process engineer in the research and development laboratory, Barry was the prime organizer and supervisor of the raw-material and finished-goods stockrooms and the production control department. These three areas were managed by Welch until 1967, when Mr. Walker, seeing a need for a new and improved information system and professing great faith in Welch's ability as an organizer and manager, decided to send Welch to one of IBM's data processing schools. Before leaving for school, Welch agreed that when he returned he would devote his full time to the management of the data processing department, relinquishing his responsibilities in the other three areas. (It should be noted here that, in each of the three areas, Welch had developed capable managerial personnel prior to his departure.)

It was at this time that Mr. Walker sensed his business was growing too big for a one-man operation. Numerous new contracts from both government and commercial sources made the future look optimistic, but the workload for one man was difficult. Mr. Walker decided to seek outside help. Therefore, in response to various offers, he sold his company to a Wall Street investment firm that was very much impressed with Electronic Systems' great potential for sales growth. Mr. Walker was retained as a member of the board of di-

This case was written by Craig T. Galipeau under the supervision of Alvar O. Elbing. Used by permission of Alvar O. Elbing. Names of people and places have been disguised.

rectors, and also served in a consultative capacity as vice president for planning and development.

The investment firm hired Mr. Daniel Wilson as the new president of Electronic Systems. He, too, quickly saw the need for an improved information system as a tool for decision making. Therefore, Welch's initial project for the new president was to expedite plans for the proposed IBM equipment by training key punchers and machine operators and designing the initial systems. Organizationally, the new data processing department was to be managed by Welch, who would report directly to the controller, Thomas Haley. Haley had worked for a leading optical company before Wilson asked him to join Electronic Systems in the latter half of 1967.

Although Haley had little knowledge of data processing operations, the organization established by Electronic Systems reflected the organization used by the majority of new companies in the data processing field. Mr. Haley, however, was quite familiar with the application of a total accounting system, which could be generated by the hardware in Barry's department. Even so, the main objective and top priority of the new equipment was to be its use for logistic purposes—production control, production, and inventory control—with the marketing system given second priority and the accounting system given least priority.

In June of 1968 I was hired for the summer to assist Barry in the design and implementation of the management information system. During my second week of work with Barry, I discovered what I thought to be a redundant system in one of the early systems applications. Barry confirmed my finding and showed no particular surprise. He then related how he had argued this particular point with Mr. Haley early in its application.

BARRY: I explained to Haley earlier that this type of thing would happen. And now this proves me correct.

AUTHOR: Well, couldn't he see that eventually we would run into this problem?

BARRY: No. He didn't buy my argument that this would happen in the first place. Besides, it appears to me that as long as we get a system going as fast as possible, he doesn't care if it is right or wrong.

The president, Mr. Wilson, would usually pay a visit to Barry's office several times a week, complimenting Barry on what a fine job he was doing. Since very little application was made of the machines at this time, Mr. Wilson always expressed interest in the proposed overall system that Barry and I were working on. He was very pleased to see some of the ideas we had arrived at already, commenting that we seemed to be in good shape to meet the target date for our oral presentation in August. (Mr. Wilson gave us the go-ahead for implementing logistics subsystems before our August target date, however.)

At the same time, Mr. Haley did not find Barry's work satisfactory. As mentioned previously, the top priority for machine and design time was given to the logistics systems. However, Mr. Haley was continually putting pressure on Barry to get the complete accounting system established on the machines. This irritated Barry, and our conversations at coffee breaks and lunch continually centered around Haley and his accounting system.

Pressured by Haley, Barry devoted many hours in the evenings and on Saturdays and even Sundays in attempting to please him. These overtime hours were always devoted to such things as the budgets, payroll, accounts receivables, etc. Yet no appreciable recognition came from Haley—just complaints about the "bugs" that are found in any new system.

The rest of the workers in the firm, of course, had knowledge of Barry's overtime duties and would good-naturedly kid him about his department. Coffee and lunch breaks were always filled with laughter, with Barry bearing the brunt of all the jokes and harassment. All the men at the table (production men, industrial engineers, accountants, salesmen) were well liked by each other, and the majority would spend much of their social time together outside the plant. Since they all knew the trouble Barry was having with Haley, they, too, began to criticize Barry's work.

PRODUCTION MAN: Hey, "punch-card," those reports your girls passed out this morning were useless garbage.

BARRY: Look, you give me garbage, my machines will give you garbage back. [Laughter.]

SALESMAN: Who are you kidding? I give you good, accurate data, and the reports I get, too, are completely useless. Are you sure you know what you are doing over there, Barry? Maybe Tom will help you get straightened out. [Laughter.]

BARRY: Yeah, by the way, "Little Haley" [referring to Jim, the head of the accounting department], did Tom see that memo I left on his desk this morning?

JIM: Oh yeah, he told me to take care of it as usual, and then went back to reading his *Wall Street Journal* so he could have some free time later on this afternoon to play golf with his kid.

BARRY: Beautiful! That's par for the course.

PRODUCTION MAN: Well Barry, you better get back over there and get those budgets out so Tom won't have so much work during the day. When are you guys going to relieve me of some paperwork?

All this kidding, however, developed into a hassle between the vice president for manufacturing and Mr. Haley. At one of our meetings, the vice president said he felt the data processing department was not living up to its expectations of relieving some of the paperwork from the foremen while at the same time yielding reliable information. He asserted that too much time was being spent on the accounting system and not enough time in the production area. Mr. Haley disagreed vehemently. The vice president then re-

quested that a report be submitted showing the actual time Barry spent in each area. (Although the report showed less actual running time for accounting reports, the production people were not getting the various reports which were promised them in the beginning, nor was their system as completely "debugged" as Haley's system.)

One morning in late July, Mr. Haley called Barry into his office. It was the time of the annual review at Electronic Systems, and I knew of Barry's expectations for a raise in salary. After two hours or so, Barry was back in the data processing department, looking very unhappy.

AUTHOR: Well, how'd it go?

BARRY: I'm sending out résumés starting tonight. I can't hack that bald jerk much longer.

AUTHOR: You mean he didn't give you a raise?

BARRY: Oh sure. I got a raise all right. But even with the raise I'll be making less than I did this year. You see, the raise puts me into another salary bracket where you don't collect any overtime pay on anything less than sixteen hours in a month. Right now, he's got me working about fifteen hours or so, but I get compensated for it. I'm getting the hell out of this joint as soon as I can. By the way, he wants me to get that lousy payroll on the machines soon, and you know what a tough job that will be.

AUTHOR: Yeah, the men from IBM told me it would be a long time getting that baby to work.

Barry just sat in his office the rest of the day, staring at the walls. The next morning he came in with his résumé to get my opinion of it. It looked impressive; and I realized how serious he was about leaving Electronic Systems.

During the first week in August, Barry worked almost exclusively with card design and programming for the new payroll system. Mr. Haley asked Barry to work Saturday to try to iron out some of the problems with the payroll system. Since our presentation of the proposed system was due in a few weeks, I also received the go-ahead to work Saturdays. That Saturday Barry was preparing the cards for all salaried personnel at Electronic Systems from a classified file, and my work was interrupted several times that morning with either Barry's laughter or his cries of disbelief.

BARRY: Boy! You wouldn't believe what this guy is making. You should see the raise he got—and for what? He sure has got the wool pulled over someone's eyes.

Back to work for a few minutes. Then laughter from Barry's corner.

BARRY: Hey, Craig. Here's another guy with a lousy deal. Gee, the job he has done here has been fantastic. Do you know when he's on vacation, he still spends his time in here? Boy, this place doesn't appreciate him. And what a lousy salary.

It was from this time on that Barry felt he was not the only employee of Electronic Systems who was being shortchanged. Of course, this made him sulk even more, and he sat staring at the walls and pondering his future. During the following week and up until the time I left, a steady stream of people came to Barry's office to discuss their common predicament—their dislike of Haley, who handled the majority of reviews and salary allotments. The air was filled with talk of résumés and new employer contacts.

In the weeks before our proposed presentation was to be made, two men from IBM were brought in to consult with Barry and me on the system. They presented some helpful suggestions for our system and were of useful support in many of our departmental meetings. However, they showed great concern that Barry had not yet written any standard operating procedures which would be of use to the company in times of Barry's absence. Barry always countered by saying he would begin writing them and developing a manual

that week. However, Barry and I knew better. Barry had always told me that this knowledge would be kept in his head until he thought it was appropriate to record it. It was, as Barry said, his "job security," for as long as he held that knowledge in his head, they needed him. Besides, he also felt it would be a good way to get back at Mr. Haley if and when Barry left.

It was at this time that Mr. Haley again came under attack from the vice president of manufacturing and the plant manager over the monthly work-in-process inventory. Earlier in 1968, Haley had promised that this would be taken out of the hands of the foremen and handled by the data processing machines. This, of course, would save many man-hours by the production-line workers, and the foremen were pleased to hear they would be spared the task. However, by August (although this system was running in June when I arrived), Electronic Systems was still running parallel systems. One was done monthly by the machines, the other was done monthly by the workers on the line. To top it all off, neither system ever came close to the other in reporting the work-in-process inventory.

This was a great thorn in Haley's side, as he was constantly kept aware of the speech he made promising elimination of the monthly physical inventory by production workers. Again, he was under attack for devoting too much time to the accounting system. Finally, Haley cornered Barry in his office and told him to solve the problem. Barry told Haley what the problem was from the data processing angle. However, this problem could easily have been solved by correcting just one of the daily reporting procedures incurred on the production line. Barry knew how to solve this problem quite simply. Haley did not, and neither would the foremen whom Haley went to question. It was Barry's secret, and he gave me a little smile as Haley left his office.

During the end of the week prior to our week-long proposal presentation, Mr. Haley called Barry into his office and told him he was not to attend the first few meetings but was to continue working on the payroll system. Electronic Systems was experiencing great difficulty with this system—so much that a team from IBM, which specialized in payroll installations, agreed to assist Barry later in the month of August.

Barry missed the first day of meetings, but pressure was put on Haley by the various people attending the meeting to allow Barry to be present at the rest of them. Since Barry was to run the operation, many were very much inter- ested in his views. At the end of the week, we had won over the majority, and Mr. Wilson gave his O.K. to that part of the system that had not already been implemented.

When I was making my rounds of goodbyes to the various personnel, the most common piece of advice given to me was not to come back to work at Electronic Systems full time. Most of the workers told me that if I came back next summer, there was a good chance they would be gone. They were starting to get responses from the résumés they, too, had sent out during the summer.

The Barrel of Lug Nuts

Joe Milano worked on the assembly line in one of the major automobile manufacturing plants. He had been with the company for about three years. Joe's job was placing the tires on the cars as they came down the assembly line. The tires, previously programmed as far as size and styles were concerned, were already mounted on color-keyed rims. Joe worked with an electrically operated torque wrench that automatically tightened the lug nuts to a predetermined torque. At his work station, Joe had a waist-high barrel containing the lug nuts used to attach the tires to the cars. Every morning when he arrived at work he found that his barrel had been filled during the night, giving him a fresh supply for the day's production.

Jim Miller, an experienced worker, was Joe's foreman. During the past year or so, he noticed that Joe's attitude toward his job seemed to be deteriorating. He didn't seem to care much about his job, his absenteeism had been steadily increasing, and Miller noticed an occasional car missing a lug nut or two. In speaking to Joe about this, he got the distinct impression that Joe really didn't care about his job or the company.

Since the company had a staff of highly educated industrial psychologists readily available, Miller decided one day to ask for a psy-

Reprinted from *Organizational Behavior: Concepts and Applications* (3d ed.), by Jerry L. Gray and Frederick A. Starke (Columbus, OH: Charles E. Merrill, 1984): 58-59. Used by permission of the publisher and author.

chologist's help in improving Joe's attitude toward his job and, hopefully, his productivity. The psychologist agreed to help and went about gathering data to bear upon the problem. He interviewed Joe, Miller, and other employees. He watched Joe work for a while and examined many documents pertaining to Joe's work. After gathering a lot of data and retiring to his office, the psychologist returned in about a week to Miller with the following analysis:

Joe, I believe, is performing poorly and exhibiting poor job attitudes because he does not feel important in his job. He is merely putting wheels on cars. Therefore, the solution to the problem is for you to make him feel more important.

After considering the psychologist's advice, the next day Miller decided to embark upon a concerted campaign to make Joe feel more important. During the first coffee break of the day, he found Joe in a corner and said to him, "Joe, have I ever told you how important you are around here? Why, just think, if you weren't on the job, every car coming off this assembly line wouldn't have any wheels on it!"

Joe, of course, did think about it and it didn't take him too long to remember that last week he'd taken one day to go deer hunting and when he came back, he didn't see any cars in the storage lot without wheels on them. The more he thought about it, the more angry he became until late in the afternoon he found himself purposely leaving off a lug nut here and there, under the pretense that the line was moving too fast to get them all on. Almost unconsciously, the next day he arrived at work fifteen minutes late and got a brief feeling of satisfaction as he watched Miller putting wheels on the cars while frantically looking for a "floater" to take over.

Miller, being a man of wide experience, realized that Joe's attitude had not improved and, if anything, had gotten worse. During the day, he also noticed the increased number of wheels with lug nuts missing and became even more concerned—enough so that he called the psychologist again to ask for help. The psychologist returned, listened to Miller's story, and asked for more time to gather more data and study the situation some more.

After more data-gathering and rethinking the problem, the psychologist returned to the foreman with the following analysis:

The first time I was right, but I wasn't precise enough. Joe's real problem is that he doesn't feel as though he is accomplishing anything. All he does is put on lug nut after lug nut and he never sees that he is making any progress or getting anywhere. He needs some kind of challenge in his daily work life. Note, for example, that each day he comes to work facing a barrel of lug nuts that he cannot possibly finish off. By

the end of a hard-working day, he has got the barrel down only halfway; the next day it is filled up again. The poor guy never gets any sense of accomplishment! I think a solution might be to get him a smaller barrel—about half the size he has now—so that by the end of the day he will see the bottom of the barrel and feel as though he has accomplished something.

The analysis made sense to Miller so the next day he ordered a smaller barrel, about half the size of the previous one, filled it with lug nuts and placed it at Joe's regular work station. When Joe arrived at work he immediately noticed the smaller barrel, but before he could question the foreman about it, the line started and he had to jump right into his job. Nothing unusual happened during the day up until the afternoon break. During the break, Joe felt a little "different" but couldn't seem to analyze why he had the feeling. Before he knew it, the break was over and he was back putting wheels on the cars. Along about four o'clock—about a half hour before quitting time—something remarkable happened. While almost unconsciously probing the barrel for another handful of lug nuts, Joe saw the bottom of the barrel, and for the first time in his automotive career (as the psychologist had predicted), Joe's interest and motivation to produce increased sharply.

Pointe-SA Holland

"If I am going to stay with the company, there are four conditions that they will have to meet," said Alain Dubois early in 1970. "First, I will insist that I be appointed a member of the new executive committee. Second, the president will have to agree to leave the sales force alone; he cannot continue to work with them as he has in the past. Third, we will have to discharge some people, regardless of who their friends are in the company. We simply cannot afford to have anything but the most competent people with us now. And finally, I must have the authority to hire the kind of people that I need, both in terms of quality and numbers."

Alain Dubois, 33 years old, was the marketing director of the Pointe-Holland Company, a wholly owned subsidiary in Holland of a large company with headquarters in France. The Pointe-Holland Company manufactured and distributed a line of household and food products throughout Europe and was widely known and recognized because of its extensive advertising campaigns. While company headquarters were in France, the parent company had wholly owned subsidiaries in other European countries, each of which was organized as a separate company with separate presidents and administrative staff.

This case was prepared by Professor Harry R. Knudson as a basis for class discussion rather than to illustrate either effective or ineffective handling of an administrative situation. Copyright by IMEDE (International Management Development Institute), Lausanne, Switzerland. Reproduced by permission.

Each president was responsible for the operation of his organization, and each subsidiary was run as a separate profit center. While there was some centralized direction from Pointe headquarters in France, each subsidiary had wide latitude in determining the nature and extent of its activity, especially insofar as promotion and advertising of individual products or product lines were concerned. It was important for each subsidiary to have this freedom and flexibility to accommodate to national characteristics and demands.

Alain Dubois had been director of marketing of Pointe-Holland for two years. He was responsible for all sales promotion, product development, advertising, and sales management activities. He reported directly to the president of Pointe-Holland and had reporting to him all people in the organization involved with marketing activities.

Prior to joining Pointe-Holland, Alain Dubois had been an executive with an advertising agency in France, primarily responsible for preparation of advertising campaigns for organizations active in marketing consumer products. He was widely recognized in Holland for his knowledge of marketing and was considered to be one of the "bright young men." Just prior to joining Pointe-Holland he had attended two executive management programs in the U.S. and, as a result of these programs and his own study and experience, was a leader in Europe in utilizing some of the newer concepts of marketing and management. In fact, his expertise in applying new concepts was one of the primary reasons why he was highly sought after by the Pointe headquarters in France for his current job.

Background of the Current Situation

In describing the background of this current situation Alain Dubois stated:

> I was really put into Pointe-Holland by headquarters in France to see if something could not be done with our operations here. Up until the time I came we had been losing a great deal of money each year. We are still losing money but the amount of loss has decreased substantially; and according to my plan we should break even next year, and each year after that make a small profit.
>
> My relationship with the president of Pointe-Holland is unique. He is a very fine individual and he and I get along very well on a social level. However, he is not up to date in his methods of management or in his knowledge and understanding of current marketing techniques. In fact, while I report to him I really make most major decisions in the Branded-Good Division for the company in Holland, and most of what happens is done at my initiative. The president is still a figurehead but I really go ahead and do what is necessary without much regard for his opinions or feelings. I have been able to do that because I have had the support of the main office in France. I continue to have this support but some things have happened recently which make me concerned about being able to continue to make the progress that we have made here in Holland for the last two years.

Issues Bothering Alain Dubois

One of the things of concern to Alain Dubois was the formation of the new executive committee, whose purpose was to make and review major policy decisions. The two members of this committee were the president of Pointe-Holland and the vice-president for administration. Alain Dubois was not a member of this committee and thought that he should be. When asked what changes in his status would result if he were appointed a member, he replied that in effect he would be independent of the president's authority. As a member of the executive committee he would be on equal status with the president and consequently would not be subject to his control in any way.

A second issue troubling Alain Dubois recently had been the president's actions with regard to some of the sales managers. The president of Pointe-Holland had had a long career as a salesman and still had very close personal relationships with many of the sales managers who had been with the company for some time. Often, perhaps every two months, the president and a few of his friends who were sales managers would meet to discuss the sales situation. Alain Dubois did not attend these meetings. According to Alain Dubois the meetings were primarily gossip sessions at which information was exchanged, but information that had little basis in fact. For example, he described these meetings as ones in which the sales managers would report rumors from the trade; would predict how they thought people were going to react, based on information acquired during their sales activities; and so on. Usually the meetings were held at rather elaborate restaurants and hotels. As the sales force reported directly to Alain Dubois, he thought that these meetings were not helpful to the overall selling effort and that they should be discontinued. He stated that he objected to the meetings on two counts: first, they diluted his authority over the sales managers and, second, the kind of information discussed and the results of the meetings were not at all useful to the selling effort.

Alain Dubois reported that the president had a very traditional concept of authority and would occasionally walk through the offices talking to the more junior marketing people (for example, product managers), much in the way that a general might review an army. But Alain Dubois felt the president had no real understanding of what marketing people were now required to do. The efforts of the salesmen of Pointe-Holland could affect perhaps 40 percent of the potential market. Many of the products were sold directly to large chains of retail outlets, and the selling was done at the headquarters level rather than in the traditional fashion of a salesman calling on an individual customer.

Alain Dubois was especially concerned, too, about one sales manager in particular—the general sales manager—who he felt was not competent to handle his job. This manager was a long-standing friend of the president, which made the matter more difficult for Alain Dubois.

> I have no personal reasons for wanting to discharge this man. My reasons are entirely professional. He is just not competent to operate in the way that we have to operate now. For example, I am attempting to promote the product manager concept in which we have a great deal of flexibility in our approach for each product, depending on the situation. Unfortunately, the manager in question is very traditional in his approach and cannot adapt to this new thinking. He knows my feelings about this but the support he enjoys from the president on a friendship basis undercuts my efforts to initiate the new concepts and ideas. If we were a very large organization it might be possible to bypass this man, but we do not have enough personnel to let us do this. Each of our people has to be a good producer, and in my judgment this particular sales manager just is not adequate. Many of the people who report to him are more qualified than he—and this, of course, causes a problem of morale.

Another matter concerning Alain Dubois was that he did not have as complete freedom as he would like in hiring new people. For example, he thought that several additions to the marketing staff were very necessary, but he had not been able to secure the authority to hire additional personnel without discussing his reasons in great detail with the president of Pointe-Holland.

In summing up the current situation Alain Dubois stated:

> My relationship with the president of Pointe-Holland has been fine as long as I have been able to ignore him. But with these new developments, especially the formation of the executive committee, I am going to have to get my status clarified.
>
> I am going to see the people in France again very soon, but rather than discuss this matter only with the top management of the parent corporation, I think that all of us should discuss it at the same time. So I plan to ask the president in France to arrange a meeting between him, the president in Holland, and myself for later this month. I will prepare a written statement of my position and give it to each man before the meeting so that each of them will know exactly how I feel. I hope that this can be resolved, for I'd like to continue the work that I have started. But I feel very strongly that I must have the freedom and the authority to do what I think is right.
>
> Of course, I realize that there are different ways of satisfying the conditions I have established for my own involvement, but I feel very strongly that I must have complete freedom in each of the areas I mentioned. For example, if they would agree to appoint me a member of the executive committee but not give me freedom to hire the people I need, this would not be satisfactory. Or if they would give me the authority to hire but not appoint me to the executive committee, that would not be satisfactory. In effect, I have to have all four of the conditions satisfied before I feel I can continue to make a contribution at Pointe-Holland.

PART THREE
Interpersonal Dynamics

Lamson Company

The Lamson Company was a small independent oil company, producers of a variety of oil products that it distributed throughout a midwestern territory covering parts of three states. The headquarters and refinery of the company were located in Cincinnati, Ohio. Part of the refinery equipment of the Lamson Company consisted of two distillation towers, designated as Towers 1D and 2D. These towers served the function of distilling crude oil under heat and pressure into a variety of petroleum components that were, in turn, further refined and processed with other equipment. The operation of each of the distillation towers was controlled by means of semiautomatic equipment that was housed in a control building adjacent to the towers.

Each tower required for its operation a three-man crew for each eight-hour shift. The units were run not only three shifts a day but seven days a week. The crew spent most of their working time in the control house, making adjustments to the control apparatus, doing minor repair work when trouble arose, and performing routine maintenance work.

Henry McMahon, crew foreman, supervised all the crews working on Tower 1D; Andrew Kirk supervised the crews on Tower 2D.

Both of these supervisors, in turn, reported to the distillation foreman, Samuel Wood.

The Lamson Company decided to make certain changes in the plant that entailed training some of the personnel for different types of jobs. The company decided to construct a new distillation tower, incorporating many new technological improvements that were not present in the older existing towers. Among other innovations, the new installation was to include a radically different type of control equipment, which was both more intricate and more fully automatic than the older equipment. Because of these modifications in the new tower, the management decided to give a training course for the crew members who would be selected to operate and maintain the new equipment. The training course material was prepared and presented by one of the company's young engineers, William Downes, with the constant help and guidance of the engineers designing the new tower.

In the selection of men for this course, Samuel Wood made a careful canvass of the entire operating and maintenance force throughout the refinery. In general, he chose only outstanding men since higher management, based on information from the designers, felt that a new unit of this type, which was of such vital importance in its functioning, should be well handled. Also, since the equipment was the first of its kind in the country, it would no doubt receive considerable attention. He finally selected 12 crewmen to take the course.

During the extended course the entire group, including the instructor and the representatives of the designers, became very close knit. Changes were constantly being made by the designers that added to the problems of the students. At the completion of the course, the students and the instructor held a "graduating" dinner among themselves. This "graduation" was subsequently celebrated every year by a dinner sponsored and attended by the original group in the course.

After several delays due to war conditions, the new equipment was finally placed in service. It was operated as Distillation Unit 3D under the supervision of William Downes, who, in turn, reported to Samuel Wood.

The type of work required on the new equipment was considerably different from that on the older units and was more in the nature of a white-collar job. For example, work on the new equipment was cleaner than on the old equipment, as a considerable amount of dirty routine maintenance work was eliminated. Another new feature was that special ventilating equipment was installed to provide filtered air in the control house in order to keep down dust and dirt. Fans were also installed to give additional circulation of air.

As the work proceeded, Wood noticed that the men seemed highly interested in their jobs. They made many suggestions for improvements in order to eliminate some of the "bugs" that showed up in the equipment in the early stages. The designer accepted many of these suggestions. Some of the men felt that they were "even doing engineering work." Wood was pleased with the operating results obtained from the new unit.

After some months' experience in operating the new unit, the management felt that it would be necessary to train six additional men on this type of equipment to allow for turnover, absences, and vacations of the regular crew. Such a plan, however, meant that since 18 men would not be needed at all times, some of the group would have to spend part of their time working on the older towers.

After plans had been discussed, and the training program for the six new men had started, Wood received a letter (Exhibit 1) ad-

EXHIBIT 1
Letter from 3D crewmen

December 7

To: MESSRS. LYNCH
             YOUNG
             TURNER
             STEPHENS
             WOOD
             DOWNES

GENTLEMEN:

This letter is being addressed to you to direct your attention to a problem confronting the crew members at the 3D Distillation Unit.

Plans are being made to combine the operating work of all three distillation units. We believe a proper understanding on your part of our feeling toward these plans will serve to circumvent what possibly could become an unpleasant situation.

First. We are agreed that had we known three years ago, when we were informed of this job, that such a proposition as the above was contemplated, we surely would have made every effort to stay where we then were. Because of the fact that the type of equipment was new, the methods, the whole job itself modern, we were led to believe a chance to work in such would be an advancement.

Second. On the day of our induction into the training course for the new unit, we were informed that the system was so unlike anything we had ever experienced that a close application to the job, frequent "refresher courses," and much diligent study would be required of us in order to stay on top of the job. In the 33 months since that day, we have experienced nothing to disprove this statement. To the contrary.

Third. Not one of us feels that he has mastered all parts of his job to such a degree that he could retain the knowledge he has acquired, if forced to divide his attention between two other dissimilar units. None of us feels sufficiently experienced in all normal job assignments in the new unit to merit the title of "all around man." Add to this the fact that no training has been given on many miscellaneous and routine problems of the job and it will become evident that further dilution of job contact is inimical to giving the kind of service that all informed persons declare is imperative with this type of equipment.

Fourth. If we consider the money spent on training men for this job as an investment in good results, then any plan that would tend to depreciate that investment prematurely would be, to say the least, unwise and inefficient.

However, we realize that the training of additional men for the new unit is good insurance, and we believe that the six men now in school can receive their "on-the-job" training and at the same time be used to relieve the present force for refresher courses and during vacations. We have been given to understand that it would be dangerous to spread our 12 men as thin as was done last summer. So it would seem that more men could be used to advantage.

Finally, while not wishing to appear critical of a proposal which, no doubt, is well meant, we do not want to minimize the intensity of feeling which this proposal has aroused in our group. We trust that you will take this letter as it is intended, that is, as a sincere expression of a group of working men having the best interest of our job at heart.

Respectfully submitted,

dressed to his home and signed by the 12 original crewmen of the 3D unit. In addition to the letter to Samuel Wood, copies were mailed out simultaneously to William Downes, as well as to Wood's superiors in the next four higher levels of authority. In each case the letter was mailed to the home address, signed personally by all 12 men, and bore the names of all the recipients.

The Foster Creek Post Office

The United States Post Office in Foster Creek, New York, is a small, first-class office serving a suburban community of 11,000. Normally, the post office employs eleven people—a postmaster, an assistant postmaster, six carriers (including one parcel-post truck driver), and three clerks.

Each postal employee's job requirements are minutely subdivided and explicitly prescribed by the *Post Office Manual*—a large, two-volume publication of the U.S. Post Office Department in Washington, D.C. There is a "suggested" rate per minute and/or day for sorting and delivering letters, of which every postal employee is well aware. The work is highly prescribed, routine, and repetitive, with little basis for the development of individual initiative. Although each man contrives a few little tricks (which he may or may not pass along to his fellow workers) for easing his *own* work load, there is little incentive for a postal employee to attempt to improve any part of the mail delivery system *as a whole*. Each man performs pretty much as he is expected to perform (nothing more or less). Roger, the assistant postmaster, clearly verbalized this attitude, "The inspectors can't get us if we go by the book [manual]."

The irregular, unannounced visits by the district postal inspectors aroused a strange fear in *all* the employees at the Foster Creek Post Office. Although each of the eleven employees is fairly well acquainted with the inspectors, there is something disturbing about the presence of a man whose recommendations may mean the loss of your job. The security of their positions in the post office is highly valued by employees of Foster Creek, some of whom are no longer young and must provide for their families. It is customary, therefore, to see an entire post office staff snap to attention and work harder at the arrival, or possibility of arrival, of a postal inspector.

Larry, the Foster Creek postmaster, had a philosophy regarding the affairs of his office which was: "Keep the patrons and the inspectors happy." Outside of this requirement and an additional one which made it imperative that each employee punch in and off the time clock at the exact appointed time (this requirement was primarily for the ease of bookkeeping), each man could do his job pretty much as he wished. The clerks reported at 6 A.M. to sort the day's mail into different stacks for the carriers who arrived at 7 A.M. The carriers then "cased" (further sorted according to street and number) their letters and usually were "on the road" by 9 A.M. They were required to be back in the office at 3:30 P.M., if possible, for further casing, and at 5 P.M. all the carriers went home.

In the summer months when the mail is relatively light and the weather is clear, each carrier easily finishes his route (including time al-

This case was written under the supervision of Alvar O. Elbing. Used by permission of Alvar O. Elbing. Names of people and places have been disguised.

lowed for a half-hour lunch break) by 1:30 P.M. It is standard procedure for the men to relax at home for two hours before reporting back in at 3:30 P.M. In the winter, on the other hand, with snow piled high in the yards, each carrier can no longer take the shorter route across the yards, and the men often finish long after 3:30 P.M. Larry is well aware of this procedure and says: "It all balances out, and in the hot summer they can use the extra hours to take it easy."

At 3:30 P.M. (or so) the day's big social event takes place at the post office. With the cry of "Flip for cokes," all the employees except Jane, the one female clerk, match dimes to see who will be the day's loser and provide cokes for the others. This daily gaming is one of the many examples of the free and frequent sociability which exists among the ten male employees. Although the office's formal organization is detailed by postal regulations (see Exhibit 1), owing to the similar socioeco-nomic status and interests of the employees, the post office atmosphere is very relaxed and informal (see Exhibit 2). Many of the men bowl together; they go to the same church; and they often attend high school graduations and funerals affecting the families of their coworkers.

On payday (every Friday), each of the ten male employees contributes 50 cents of his paycheck to "the fund." This fund is used for coffee and donuts, to provide sick employees with flowers and "get-well" cards, and to purchase a ham to be shared at work during Christmas time.

Other important parts of each day are the regular morning and afternoon conversations. In the morning, the talk invariably turns to news items in the morning's paper. In addition, the men often talk about "those politicians in Washington" and the possibility of a postal pay raise. In the afternoons, the men relate any interesting experiences from the

EXHIBIT 1
Foster Creek Post Office formal organization

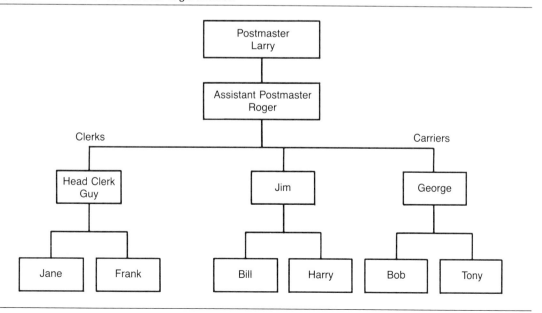

EXHIBIT 2
Foster Creek Post Office informal organization

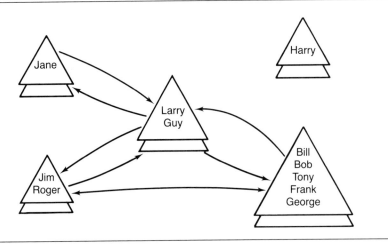

day's rounds. These experiences range from dog bites to coffee with an attractive female patron.

In general the eleven employees of the Foster Creek Post Office enjoyed their work. They constituted a close-knit team doing similar and somewhat distasteful work, but, as George, a senior carrier, put it, "We get good, steady pay; and it's a lot easier than digging ditches."

In mid-June 1968, Larry filed a request for a carrier to replace a regular Foster Creek carrier who had died suddenly. At 7 A.M. on Monday, July 8, Harry reported for work as a permanent replacement.

Harry was a tall, skinny man with thinning hair, long fingers, and wire-rimmed eye glasses. He appeared to be in his fifties. He seemed nervous and shy, and when Larry introduced him to the Foster Creek regulars, Harry stared at the floor and said only "Hi!" Initial opinions of this new carrier were mixed. Jim, another senior carrier, probably best expressed the employees' sentiments when he said: "He's not too friendly—yet; he's probably a little nervous here—but *man* can he case mail!"

Harry was an excellent caser. For 27 years he had been a clerk in the main post office. The attitudes and work environment in big city post offices differ markedly from those in smaller offices (as Larry was quick to point out when any of Foster Creek's employees complained). In the city post offices, where competition for the few available positions is extremely keen, a man must not only be very competent but must follow the postal regulations *to the letter*. As Harry said quietly to Roger upon his arrival at Foster Creek, "Things were just too pushy in the city. And besides, my wife and I wanted to move out here in the country to have a house and garden of our own to take care of."

Harry had a well-kept and attractive house and garden. It was apparent that Harry loved to take care of his lawn and garden, because he spent all day Sunday working on it. As a member of the Foster Creek Building and Loan Association, Larry knew that Harry had purchased the property with cash.

On Wednesday, Harry's third day at work, the opinions regarding Harry had become more concrete. As Jim said: "Harry's strange.

He thinks he's better than all of us, coming from that city office. He never talks to us or says anything about himself. All he does is stand there and case mail, but *man* is he fast at that!''

The first real problem arose on the fourth day. Harry had learned his route well enough so that he, too, was able to finish by 1:30 P.M. His ability to case and ''tie out'' (gather the mail in leather straps) his mail so quickly put him on the road by 8:30 in the morning—ahead of the other four carriers.

On this Thursday afternoon Harry reported back to the post office at 1:15, having finished his entire route. Upon seeing this, Roger's first reaction was to say, ''Go home and have some lunch, Harry. Relax at home for a little while.''

Harry replied, ''I've had my lunch. There are letters on my case. I've got to do them now. I've got to do my job.'' Having said this, he began to case the several hundred letters which had piled up since the morning. He finished these quickly, and then went on and cased all the mail which was lying on the other four carriers' cases. When the four regular carriers returned at 3:30 P.M., they were, to say the least, surprised.

Bill, the youngest and least energetic of the carriers, thanked Harry. However, Jim and George in particular were very angry. They grumbled about having a ''newcomer'' interfere with his ''city tricks'' and ''fancy casing.'' They were especially angry that Harry had violated the 3:30 rule. They were determined that he would not be the one who would make them lose their precious privileges, and they complained to Larry about Harry. The postmaster told Harry to case only his own mail, and to take it easy when walking his route in the future.

The next day, Friday, was payday. Each man contributed his share to ''the fund.'' Harry refused. ''I don't drink colas,'' was his only answer. No one pushed the matter further, although discontent over Harry had developed among all the employees.

EXHIBIT 3
Foster Creek Post Office layout

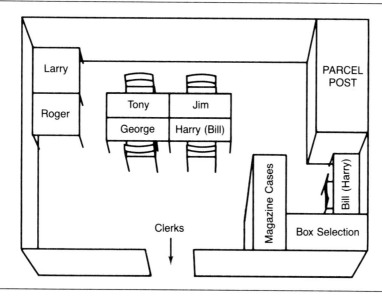

As the next week passed, Harry appeared to sink into an even deeper shell. He punched in at 7 A.M. and punched out at 5 P.M. In between, he neither looked at nor spoke to any of the other employees. He continued to report back into the office before 3:30, case all his own mail, and then sit on the stool in front of his case reading magazines. Larry was worried primarily about Harry's exposure to the public as he sat at his case reading, and so on Friday of Harry's second week, Harry's and Bill's cases were switched (see Exhibit 3).

When each of the carriers reported in on Friday afternoon, Bill was told that his case was moved so as to give him more room to handle his quickly growing route (which, in part, was true). Harry said nothing about the switch, but went straight to work in his new location.

During Harry's third week at the post office, Larry began to worry even more about his behavior. Although the carrier was hidden from the public now, a postal inspector could catch Harry reading at his case very easily.

On Thursday, July 18, Larry's worst fears were realized. An inspector came to the Foster Creek Post Office. As he walked in, Harry was sitting quietly at his case, reading as usual. The inspector looked at Harry, then at Larry.

Larry explained that Harry had an easier route than the other carriers. Because of this and his ability as a caser, Harry was able to finish his route more easily. Larry pointed out that he did not know what to say to the carrier, for he had finished all his *required* work. The inspector suggested that Larry readjust the routes to give Harry more houses to deliver and more mail to case. This was attempted, but Jim, George, and Tony reacted unfavorably.

Northeastern Electric Light and Power Corporation

The material presented in this case study was gathered from the observations made by Bill Peterson during the summer of 1967. Peterson, a newly graduated engineer, had accepted summer employment with the Northeastern Electric Light and Power Corporation in order to earn money to finance a graduate education in personnel management.

Bill, along with another college student, Fred Greene, had been hired as an engineering aide for the company's land surveying department. This was one of the smallest departments in the company, which was one of the largest utilities in the country. There were 14 people in this department: seven aides, three instrument operators, three crew chiefs, and a chief surveyor.

The duties of the crew chief were to plan the work assignments that were given to him by the chief surveyor every week. He was to make sure that the work was finished during the week, take care of the crew's expense account money, make out the daily time sheets, and generally oversee the three or four men on his crew.

The instrument man on each crew had one major function, which was operating and maintaining the surveyor's transit that each crew had. In addition, he was to take charge of the crew in the crew chief's absence and also

This case was written by Andrew P. Krueger under the supervision of Alvar O. Elbing. Used by permission of Alvar O. Elbing. Names of people and places have been disguised.

to assist him in the preparation of charts, maps, and other engineering paperwork.

The aides were responsible for the upkeep of the truck supplies and were required to take turns driving to the sites of various company projects. They were also supposed to help the chief with surface measuring (done with steel and cloth measuring tapes) and to hold range poles and measuring rods for the instrument man. Other duties ranged from washing the trucks each week to sharpening the axes and brush hooks that were needed for cutting foliage in some areas.

The chief surveyor, Don Williams, was the overall boss of the three crews. A large part of his time was spent in the drafting department. Don and the drafting foreman passed information and drawings back and forth between the two departments. Williams was relatively new to the job, having previously been a licensed surveyor in Illinois until Northeastern hired him in May, 1967. At the beginning of the summer, according to the older employees in the department, he did not seem to know his job very well. Up until the end of June, Don Williams spent most of his time working with Mr. James, the company's chief engineer. Mr. James was in charge of the engineering section, of which the drafting and surveying departments were part. The chief engineer had his own office adjacent to the drafting room—located on the third floor of the large building, which also housed administrative offices and a garage for company vehicles—and he was rarely seen by any of the surveying crew. His orders and assignments were usually passed to Don, the drafting foreman, and two other foremen in different departments of the engineering section.

Organization of the Surveying Crews

The thirteen employees—other than Don—were organized into three crews. Each consisted of a crew chief, an instrument man, and two or three aides. One group had three aides and the other two groups had two aides. There was also a panel truck with a complete set of surveying equipment for each crew. The trucks had been specially outfitted with drawers, compartments, and a foldout desk. Thus in most cases, the three groups were completely independent of one another.

In practice, the personnel were switched between crews every week. There were several reasons for this. The aides, some of whom carried quite a bit of seniority, were changed almost every week. Those with seniority were entitled to have the first chance to work on the projects that were more than 40 miles away from the plant. These projects carried more pay than did the "in-town" jobs. The company paid $10.50 per day on "out-of-town work" for board and lodging and only $1.50 per day on in-town work for lunch money. The instrument men were also changed, but with much less regularity than the aides. All three of them had equal seniority, but they possessed slightly different skills with the "gun," which made it desirable to have them working on certain projects. They were usually rotated between in-town and out-of-town very regularly, as were the crew chiefs, because of union rules regarding employees having equal seniority. Most of the time everyone—except Peterson and Greene, who were nonunion and had no seniority—

was satisfied that he was getting his share of out-of-town work. Exhibit 1 gives more explicit data on the personal background, seniority, and work status of the individual members of the surveying department.

Relations Between the Employees

Exhibit 1 shows that there was quite a difference in personal background among several of the men in the surveying department. Bill noticed, however, that these disparities actually made little difference in the status of each group member.

EXHIBIT 1
Background data of the survey crew members

Name and Job	Age	Seniority (in years)	Education	Marital Status
Pat (chief)	50	21	gs	m
Doug (chief)	59	22	hs	m
Jack (chief)	48	20	hs	m
Jim ("gunman")	48	20	2 yrs hs	s
"Stick" ("gunman")	44	21	hs	m
Hank ("gunman")	48	18	hs	m
Fred (aide)	20	0	3 yrs coll	s
Bill (aide)	21	0	coll	s
Ralph (aide)	23	1	hs	m
Dave (aide)	23	1	hs	m
Alan (aide)	19	5 mos	1½ yrs coll	m
Gerry (aide)	24	2	hs	m
Herb (aide)	42	20	gs	m

There was only one striking exception to this. That was Herb, the oldest aide. During the very first week that Bill was with the group, Herb had remarked privately: "This is a pretty good job. The work's not bad—most of the guys have a good time out here. But you got to watch out for guys like Pat. He'll go out of his way to make you look bad if you let him—he's always trying to cut somebody's throat. Some of the others will too, but not as much as Pat."

Pat, a crew chief and union steward for the surveyors, was generally agreed by most to be a tough but fair boss. He had no great liking for Herb, though, as was evidenced by his constant complaining about Herb's "stupidity." At Pat's request, however, Herb was usually put on his crew because he was the most experienced of the aides. This made quite a difference to Pat, who had, on occasion, remeasured some of the younger aides' work because he did not trust them.

Pat was noted for getting work done on schedule. On one occasion, Jim (an instrument man) had said: "If that damn Pat wasn't the steward, he'd probably work everyone to death. No matter what else, he always gets his work done. They see that upstairs and they like it. That's why Pat gets most of the good jobs."

Jim, "Stick" (a contraction of his last name), and Hank were the instrument men. It was generally agreed that they did their jobs well and were good men to work with. Pat was the only one to criticize them, but he was the "complainer" in the group and the instrument men (many of whom had been here as long as Pat) paid little attention to him.

The remaining two crew chiefs were Doug and Jack, both of whom were amiable and easygoing and were highly regarded by the aides and instrument men. Neither of them was noted for being particularly industrious, however, and this was the reason Pat was usually put on the important projects. Don had quickly recognized this and had gone so far as to nickname Doug, the oldest member of the group, "the old speedball."

The remaining four aides were about the same age and had about the same experience. Ralph and Dave had been in military service together before coming to work for the company in 1966. They had gone to high school together, and now lived quite near each other. Alan had started to work for the company in February 1967, after dropping out of an engineering program in college halfway through his sophomore year. Gerry had come to the department from another one of the company's largest generating plants in the middle of May, just before Bill and Fred started their summer work. Thus there were three new men in the department—Bill, Fred, and Gerry.

Company Organization

The Northeastern Electric Light and Power Corporation, which served portions of three large states, was broken into nine divisions. There were three divisions per state: the eastern, western, and central divisions. Each division had its own survey crews that were responsible for, among other things, the layout of new and relocated transmission and distribution lines, the layout of natural-gas pipelines, and the site engineering of new substation facilities.

The area of the crews that Bill Peterson worked with was approximately 6000 square miles. It was frequently a long distance from the main plant to the projects that they were working on. Some jobs were within a mile or two of the plant, while others were as far as 170 miles away. When they employees had to travel more than 40 miles to their jobs, as mentioned above, the company paid extra for board and room if the job lasted more than one day. With this extra pay, the men were expected to stay near the job until it was finished.

Work started at 8 A.M. and was to progress until 5 P.M. with an hour out for lunch between 12 and 1 P.M. In actual practice, however, none of the crews ever operated this way. (The work behavior of the crews is discussed in the next section.)

During the summer months, the crews worked a six-day week. Rarely did anyone complain about this; but if somebody wanted a Saturday off, he only had to tell Don a few days in advance.

Activities of the Group

The work routine of the survey crews started at 8 A.M. on Monday. At this time, everyone checked the crew schedule to find out what crew he was to be with for the coming week. Since Don and Mr. James came in around 8:30, there was a little time for the crew chiefs to make out the time sheets and expense-account reports for the previous week. Usually the instrument men helped the chiefs with this work, while the aides were busy cleaning the trucks and restocking them with supplies. At 8:30 the crew chiefs would go up to Don's office to get the assignment sheets and be briefed on the week's projects. These briefings ran anywhere from one-half hour to sometimes as long as two hours.

As soon as the aides and instrument men were finished taking care of the trucks, sharpening tools, and resupplying, they usually went off to other parts of the garage to talk to friends in different departments. Monday morning was the only time that the members of the surveying department had to get together with others in different groups. Bill eventually became good friends with Pete, a young man who worked in the supply cage. Pete always gave Bill a good supply of pens, pencils, and paper, which Bill felt would come in handy during school the following fall. Meanwhile, Fred, Ralph, and Dave could be found talking to Dave's uncle, who was a "hot wire" line foreman. His truck was always parked down at the far end of the garage. During this time, all the men in the department (except the crew chiefs) were spread out all over the plant. Consequently, each crew chief had to walk around and find his crew members when he was ready to leave.

After leaving the plant, the crews usually met at a prearranged place for coffee and to talk over the upcoming work. (Only if a crew had to travel a great distance for a one-day job did they fail to have coffee with the group.)

Then each crew would go its own way to the job. After working until about 11:30, the crew would load the equipment back into the truck and go to lunch. Most of the chiefs knew all of the good places to eat, no matter where the crew was.

The lunch period lasted as long as the crew chief desired. Pat usually took about half an hour; Jack about an hour or an hour and a quarter; Doug sometimes as much as two hours, depending on the job and the weather. After lunch, the crews would drive back to the job and work until between 3:30 and 5:00 or until they finished, depending on the crew chief.

Pat usually worked until at least 4:30; Doug and Jack were known to quit as early as 3:00 on days when they were doing out-of-town work. After work, the crews with Doug and Jack would almost always adjourn to a favorite bar and have a beer or two before starting for home. Occasionally, the two crews would meet, but this was not the usual case.

The trip home was another story. Everyone always went home at night, even if they had been working hundreds of miles away. This was easy enough to do because, on out-of-town jobs, one member of the crew always brought his car. The truck was left in a company-approved service station near the job. The individuals on each crew would take turns during the week driving to the service station in a car pool which met near the members' homes in the morning. The drawback to this was the fact that in order to get anything at all accomplished during the day, it was often necessary to meet as early as 5:30 in the morning. However, the company's $10.50 a day "handout" more than made up for this inconvenience. Except for the aide whose turn it was to drive, everyone usually slept on the way out to the job, so that no sleep was lost.

Because Don never came down to the garage until he left at 5:30 P.M., it was possible for the "in-town" crews to bring their trucks in as early as 4:00 and quietly leave in their own cars, which were parked in the company's parking lot on the side of the plant away from Don's window.

On two successive Wednesdays in the latter part of July, Bill Peterson made the following observations on the operation of two of the crews:

Jack's Crew ("Out")

7:15	Meet at car pool
8:00	Finish having coffee; drive to the job
9:30	Arrive at project site
10:00	Set up equipment and start work
11:30	Stop work, repack equipment, go to lunch
1:15	Leave lunch, return to work
1:45	Set up equipment and start work
3:15	Pack up and leave work
4:45	Arrive at service station

Doug's Crew ("In")

8:00	Report to plant
8:20	Leave plant (just in time to miss Don coming in)
8:50	Arrive at diner, have coffee, talk about day's work
10:00	Leave diner, drive to work
10:15	Arrive at project site
10:30	Unpack equipment, begin work
11:30	Pack up, go to lunch
1:15	Leave lunch, return to work
1:30	Unpack equipment, start work
3:30	Stop work, pack up equipment
3:45	Leave project site
4:10	Arrive at plant, put truck away, leave for home

Foreman's Reactions and Conclusion

It is obvious from the above schedules that the self-imposed work day of the crews was quite different from the standards which the company had set up. According to Doug, however, it had always been that way, from the time that Clyde Daniels (Don's predecessor) was the chief surveyor. Jack's reaction to Bill's questions on the subject was the same.

"What's the difference?" Jack had said. "We always get our weekly assignments done. You've seen that on some Saturdays, when we're getting time and a half, that we don't have a damn thing to do after lunchtime." To be sure, this was true. The crews always had their weekly work completed by quitting time Saturday. Bill had observed, however, that some projects had to be redone by another crew right after the first crew had supposedly finished them. On one occasion a certain substation layout was done three times in three successive weeks by three different crews before the engineering section was satisfied with the work.

Around the middle of August, Don started to get out of the plant more often than he had when he first came to work for the company. On several occasions he personally visited the project sites where the crews were working. Most of the time he either visited Pat's crew, who put in a pretty full day, or else he dropped by after lunch when the other two crews were working as they were supposed to.

After a while Don began to visit every crew at least three times a week and started to find out how the different crew chiefs went about their work. Now he started to realize that perhaps they were not getting as much work to do as they were capable of doing. In the next few weeks, the weekly work assignments became longer. All assignments were completed, but the quality of the work took a drastic dip. The previously mentioned substation project was a prime example of the problem that Don now realized he was facing. Because of company policies and union contract clauses, it was almost impossible to lay off help that was not needed. There were three crews to watch, plus the fact that he had his own office work to do. The company also advised him that he should not consider laying off the two students because they were personnel the company was trying to attract for full-time employment after their studies were completed.

At the end of Bill's summer employment (the middle of September), the situation was still the same. At this time there had developed a considerable amount of animosity on the part of the workers toward Don. Part of this was due to the lectures on efficiency that the crew chiefs were constantly getting from him, and part of it was caused by the fact that the employees regarded Don's visits to the sites as "spy trips." At the end of the summer, Don Williams was faced with a very real problem.

Acme Wholesale Distributing Company

In February of 1973, I was hired by the Acme Wholesale Distributing Company, a local firm in Portland. The work group consisted of ten students from the local university. We found the job through the university's placement center.

The group members were approximately the same age, ranging from 18 to 23. The reason for the majority of the workers to seek employment was to earn money for school. The social backgrounds of the group were hard to estimate; however, I believe a middle-class background prevailed. Of the ten, I only knew two, my roommate and a friend of my brother.

The job consisted of about a week's work in the evening from 8:00 P.M. to 2:00 A.M. It involved opening old boxes of a nationally distributed brand of imported, and now moldy, salami; separating the salvageable from the unsalvageable salami; cleaning the salvageable salamis with vinegar and a scrub brush; drying, rewrapping, and reboxing them.

The building was an old, cold, gloomy structure, which was primarily used as a warehouse, with a small office in the front. We worked on the second floor, which was accessible by means of an old open-style elevator used to haul the products. Stairs near the front office also gave access to this floor. The floor was filled with boxes of various products, with all but one dirty brick wall covered. The few windows were too high to be of any use.

We had one supervisor who was a day employee at the firm. He also had attended the university. His age was around 30. It was his duty to instruct us and see that we did our work. He also made periodic inspections of the finished product to see if it met quality standards. It became apparent at once that he did not like working nights but enjoyed the overtime pay.

On the first night we were divided into two groups, based on where we were standing at the moment. Instructions were given to each person for his specific job, and we started. A diagram of the work area is shown in Exhibit 1.

Bill, the supervisor, stayed with us the whole first night helping at each position. It was also his responsibility to see that a new pallet of 40 boxes was supplied at the same time the old one was finished. This kept an even flow through the line. We had one major break in the evening, which was at 10:30 for half an hour. This time we spent in a nearby tavern, eating and drinking. Bill and one other member who brought a sack lunch did not attend this gathering. Very little conversation took place that night. What did occur was primarily questions directed at Bill. By 2:00 A.M. we had achieved 170 boxes and 10 sore backs. A thorough cleaning of the area at night's end was mandatory. So ended the first night.

EXHIBIT 1
Diagram of work area

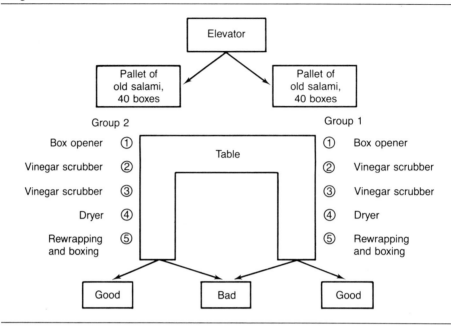

On the second night Bill had been instructed to achieve a production quota of 240 boxes a night, and that we were to produce a higher percentage of good salamis. This meant that we would have to scrub more salamis and scrub them harder to get more mold off.

This, however, produced a conflict of goals between the group and management. We were to work at a rate that seemed impossible and to produce more for the same pay. The incentive was that if we reached this goal early, we were finished for the night and would be paid for the full night. So the work began again, this time with Bill not present but staying in the office, returning only to supply us with more pallets, check our work, and leave again.

Things began slowly, with members changing positions periodically to relieve boredom. Specialization in each job developed, and new methods evolved to increase speed. Rotation slowed when each member found a job he liked best and could do the fastest. If anyone was slow at one position, thus slowing the line and the production, he would give it up for another position. Thus, we all found our optimum spot in the line. On the second night I left group two for group one, in which my roommate and my brother's friend were working. This was the only transfer between the two groups to take place.

We developed a sense of unity which helped our group. Our group talked more, produced faster, and, in general, joked around more. The overall atmosphere changed, with laughter often heard. Someone brought a radio. Individuals were given nicknames, such as "fat man," and so on. Conversations were more within each group, with occasional satirical remarks exchanged between the two groups. It seemed to be our way of communicating to those we didn't know without feeling awkward or leaving anyone open for personal attack. No one spoke of his past. The talk was focused on the strange situation in which we were working. We all decided it was against the law and the health codes. No one seemed to care beyond that point. After all, it was money, which we all needed. Group two spoke little; our group dominated most of what was said. I felt they had less in common with each other. This hampered their overall production, as was demonstrated when short contests between tables took place. One of their members was the individual who didn't go to the tavern with the rest of us. On the fourth day, one of their members left for Washington, D.C., to protest against Nixon.

Members helped out at other positions on their table and at times crossed over to help the other table; this was done to finish faster, both before our break and at the end of the evening. Slacking off was not permitted, and when discovered, immediate verbal attack

occurred. By the third night, production reached a surprising 240 boxes in four and a half hours.

The next night, Bill tightened up on his inspections of the finished product and demanded better quality. This, of course, increased the time required to complete 240 boxes per night. Also, he stressed that his boss still wanted more good salamis from the 240 boxes done each night. A good box had a resale value of up to $25, and the rejects about $5.

To make everyone happy, we cheated. Of course the consumer was the ultimate loser, but that was not our concern. We hid the not-so-good salami at the bottom of each box and placed the boxes of ill repute in the center of the pallet, a hard place for Bill to inspect. So more salamis passed as good ones, thus pleasing Bill; more boxes of good salamis were packed, thus pleasing Bill's boss; all done in less time, pleasing us.

Ex-Policeman Tells What Makes A "Bad Cop"

DENVER, Nov. 4. (A.P.) — What makes a policeman go sour? I can tell you. I was a Denver policeman until not so long ago. Then I quit so I could hold my head up.

Don't get me wrong. I'm not trying to shift the burden of responsibility for the burglaries, break-ins, safe jobs, and that sort of thing. That is bad, very bad. But I will leave it to the big shots and the newspapers and the courts to say and do what needs to be said and done about that.

My concern is about the individual officer, the ordinary, hard working, basically honest but awfully hard-pressed guy who is really suffering now.

Young fellows don't put on those blue uniforms to be crooks. There are a lot of reasons, but for most of the guys it adds up to the fact they thought it was an honorable, decent way of making a living.

Somewhere along the line a guy's disillusioned. Along the way the pressures mount up. Somewhere along the way he may decide to quit fighting them and make the conscious decisions to try to "beat" society instead.

But long before he gets to that point, almost as soon as he dons the uniform in fact, he is taking the first little steps down the road

that does, for some, eventually lead to the penitentiary.

Let me back up a little. I want to talk about how you get to be a policeman, because this is where the trouble really starts.

Almost any able-bodied man can become a policeman in Denver. If he is within the age brackets, if he is a highschool graduate, if he has no criminal record, he is a cinch.

There isn't much to getting through the screening, and some bad ones do get through. There are the usual examinations and questionnaires. Then there is the interview. A few command officers ask questions. There is a representative of civil service and a psychiatrist present.

They ask the predictable questions and just about everybody gives the predictable answers: "Why do you want to become a policeman?" "I've always wanted to be a policeman. I want to help people." Five or ten minutes and it is over.

Five or ten minutes to spot the sadist, the psychopath—or the guy with an eye for an easy buck. I guess they weed some out. Some others they get at the Police Academy. But some get through.

Along with those few bad ones, there are more good ones, and a lot of average, ordinary human beings who have this in common: They want to be policemen.

The job has (or had) some glamour for the young man who likes authority, who finds appeal in making a career of public service, who is extroverted or aggressive.

Case copyright © 1964 by Professor Harry R. Knudson, Graduate School of Business, University of Washington. Reprinted by permission. By a former Denver policeman as told to Mort Stern, the *Denver Post,* 2 May 1962. Copyright 1962 by the *Denver Post.* Reprinted by permission. "Addendum" from *The Wall Street Journal,* 2 May 1962. Copyright by Dow Jones & Company, Inc. Reprinted by permission.

Before you knock those qualities, remember two things: First, they are the same qualities we admire in a business executive. Second, if it weren't for men with these qualities, you wouldn't have any police protection.

The Police Academy is point No. 2 in my bill of particulars. It is a fine thing, in a way. You meet the cream of the Police Department. Your expectations soar. You know you are going to make the grade and be a good officer. But how well are you really prepared?

There are six weeks at the academy—four weeks in my time. Six hectic weeks in which to learn all about the criminal laws you have sworn to enforce, to assimilate the rules of evidence, methods of arbitration, use of firearms, mob and riot control, first aid (including, if you please, some basic obstetrics), public relations, and so on.

There is an intangible something else that is not on the formal agenda. You begin to learn that this is a fraternity into which you are not automatically accepted by your fellows. You have to earn your way in; you have to establish that you are "all right."

And even this early there is a slight sour note. You knew, of course, that you had to provide your own uniforms, your own hat, shoes, shirts, pistol, and bullets out of your $393 a month.

You knew the city would generously provide you with the cloth for two pair of trousers and a uniform blouse.

What you didn't know was that you don't just choose a tailor shop for price and get the job done.

You are sent to a place by the Police Department to get the tailoring done. You pay the price even though the work may be ill-fitting. It seems a little odd to you that it is always the same establishment. But it is a small point and you have other things on your mind.

So the rookie, full of pride and high spirit, his head full of partly learned information, is turned over to a more experienced man for breaking in. He is on "probation" for six months.

The rookie knows he is being watched by all the older hands around him. He is eager to be accepted. He accepts advice gratefully.

Then he gets little signs that he has been making a good impression. It may happen like this: The older man stops at a bar, comes out with some packages of cigarettes. He does this several times. He explains that this is part of the job, getting cigarettes free from proprietors to resell, and that as a part of the rookie's training it is his turn to "make the butts."

So he goes into a skid-row bar and stands uncomfortably at the end waiting for the bartender to acknowledge his presence and disdainfully toss him two packages of butts.

The feeling of pride slips away and a hint of shame takes hold. But he tells himself this is unusual, that he will say nothing that will upset his probation standing. In six months, after he gets his commission, he will be the upright officer he meant to be.

One thing leads to another for the rookies. After six months they have been conditioned to accept free meals, a few packages of cigarettes, turkeys at Thanksgiving, and liquor at Christmas from the respectable people in their district.

The rule book forbids all this. But it isn't enforced. It is winked at, at all levels.

So the rookies say to themselves that this is O.K., that this is a far cry from stealing and they still can be good policemen. Besides, they are becoming accepted as "good guys" by their fellow officers.

This becomes more and more important as the young policeman begins to sense a hostility toward him in the community. This is fostered to a degree by some of the saltier old hands in the department. But the public plays its part.

Americans are funny. They have a resentment for authority. And the policeman is authority in person. The respectable person may soon forget that a policeman found his lost youngster in the park, but he remembers that a policeman gave him a traffic ticket.

The negative aspect of the job builds up. The majority of the people he comes in contact with during his working hours are thieves, con men, narcotics addicts, and out-and-out nuts.

Off the job his associations narrow. Part of the time when he isn't working, he is sleeping. His waking, off-duty hours are such as to make him not much of a neighbor. And then he wants to spend as much time as he can with his family.

Sometimes, when he tries to mix with his neighbors, he senses a kind of strain. When he is introduced to someone, it is not likely to be, "This is John Jones, my friend," or "my neighbor"; it is more likely to be, "This is John Jones. He's a policeman."

And the other fellow, he takes it up, too. He is likely to tell you that he has always supported pay increases for policemen, that he likes policemen as a whole, but that there are just a few guys in uniform he hates.

No wonder the officer begins to think of himself as a member of the smallest minority group in the community. The idea gradually sinks into him that the only people who understand him, that he can be close to, are his fellow officers.

It is in this kind of atmosphere that you can find the young policeman trying to make the grade in the fraternity. But that is not the whole story.

A policeman lives with tensions, and with fears.

Part of the tensions come from the incredible monotony. He is cooped up with another man, day after day, doing routine things over and over. The excitement that most people think of as the constant occupation of policemen is so infrequent as to come as a relief.

Part of the tensions come from the manifold fears. I don't mean that these men are cowards. This is no place for cowards. But they are human beings. And fears work on all human beings.

Paramount is the physical fear that he will get hurt to the point where he can't go on working, or the fear that he will be killed. The fear for his family.

There is the fear that he will make a wrong decision in a crucial moment, a life-and-death decision. A man has been in a fight. Should he call the paddy wagon or the ambulance? A man aims a pistol at him. Should he try to talk to him or shoot him?

But the biggest fear he has is that he will show fear to some of his fellow officers. This is the reason he will rush heedlessly in on a cornered burglar or armed maniac if a couple of officers are present—something he wouldn't do if he were alone. He is tormented by his fears and he doesn't dare show them. He knows he has to present a cool, calm front to the public.

As a group, policemen have a very high rate of ulcers, heart attacks, suicides and divorces. These things torment him, too. Divorce is a big problem to policemen. A man can't be a policeman for eight hours and then just turn it off and go home and be a loving father or husband—particularly if he has just had somebody die in the back of his police car.

So once again, the pressure is on him to belong, to be accepted and welcomed into the only group that knows what is going on inside him.

If the influences aren't right, he can be hooked.

So he is at the stage where he wants to be one of the guys. And then this kind of thing may happen: One night his car is sent to check in a "Code 26"—a silent burglar alarm.

The officer and his partner go in to investigate. The burglar is gone. They call the proprietor. He comes down to look things over. And maybe he says, "Boys, this is covered by insurance, so why don't you take a jacket for your wife, or a pair of shoes?" And maybe he does, maybe just because his partner does, and he says to himself, "What the hell, who has been hurt?"

Or maybe the proprietor didn't come down. But after they get back in the car his partner pulls out four $10 bills and hands him two. "Burglar got careless," says the partner.

The young officer who isn't involved soon learns that this kind of thing goes on. He even may find himself checking on a burglary call, say to a drugstore, and see some officers there eyeing him peculiarly.

Maybe at this point the young officer feels the pressure to belong so strongly that he reaches over and picks up something, cigars perhaps. Then he is "in," and the others can do what they wish.

Mind you, not all officers will do this. Somewhere along the line all of them have to make a decision, and it is at that point where the stuff they are made of shows through. But the past experience of the handouts, the official indifference to them, and the pressures and tensions of the job don't make the decision any easier.

And neither he nor the department has had any advance warning, such as might come from thorough psychiatric screening, as to what his decision will be.

Some men may go this far and no farther. They might rationalize that they have not done anything that isn't really accepted by smart people in society.

This is no doubt where the hard-core guy, the one who is a thief already, steps in. A policeman is a trained observer and he is smart in back-alley psychology. This is especially true of the hard-core guy, and he has been watching the young fellows come along.

When he and his cronies in a burglary ring spot a guy who may have what it takes to be one of them, they may approach him and try him out as a lookout. From then on it is just short steps to the actual participation in and planning of crimes.

Bear in mind that by this stage we have left all but a few policemen behind. But all of them figure in the story at one stage or another. And what has happened to a few could happen to others. I suppose that is the main point I am trying to make.

Addendum

The following item appeared in the Tax Report column of the May 2, 1962, issue of *The Wall Street Journal:*

Denver police salaries would be raised out of a $2.7 million yearly hike in revenues from a proposed boost in the city's sales tax to 2% from 1%. The proposal comes before Denver voters June 5. Officers' low pay has been blamed in part for a recent scandal involving the arrest of 57 Denver policemen on burglary charges. A 2% retail sales tax is levied by the state.

The United Chemical Company

The United Chemical Company is a large producer and distributor of commodity chemicals with five chemical production plants in the United States. The operations at the main plant in Baytown, Texas, include not only production equipment but also the company's research and engineering center.

The process design group consists of eight male engineers and the supervisor, Max Kane. The group has worked together steadily for a number of years, and good relationships had developed among all members. When the workload began to increase, Max hired a new design engineer, Sue Davis, a recent master's degree graduate from one of the foremost engineering schools in the country. Sue was assigned to a project whose goal was expansion of one of the existing plants' capacity. Three other design engineers were assigned to the project along with Sue: Jack Keller (age 38, fifteen years with the company); Sam Sims (age 40, ten years with the company); and Lance Madison (age 32, eight years with the company).

As a new employee, Sue was very enthusiastic about the opportunity to work at United. She liked her work very much because it was challenging and it offered her a chance to apply much of the knowledge she had gained in her university studies. On the job, Sue kept

This case was prepared by Andrew D. Szilagyi, Jr. Reprinted from *Organizational Behavior and Performance* (3d ed.), by A. D. Szilagyi, Jr. and M .J. Wallace, Jr. (Glenview, IL: Scott, Foresman and Company, 1983): 204-205. Used by permission.

fairly much to herself and her design work. Her relations with her fellow project members were friendly, but she did not go out of her way to have informal conversations during or after working hours.

Sue was a diligent employee who took her work quite seriously. On occasions when a difficult problem arose, she would stay after hours in order to come up with a solution. Because of her persistence, coupled with her more current education, Sue usually completed her portion of the various project stages a number of days before her colleagues. This was somewhat irritating to her because on these occasions she went to Max to ask for additional work to keep her busy until her fellow workers caught up to her. Initially, she had offered to help Jack, Sam, and Lance with their portions of the project, but each time she was turned down very tersely.

About five months after Sue had joined the design group, Jack asked to see Max about a problem the group was having. The conversation between Max and Jack was as follows:

MAX: Jack, I understand you wanted to discuss a problem with me.

JACK: Yes, Max. I didn't want to waste your time, but some of the other design engineers wanted me to discuss Sue with you. She is irritating everyone with her know-it-all, pompous attitude. She just is not the kind of person that we want to work with.

MAX: I can't understand that, Jack. She's an excellent worker whose design work is always well done and usually flawless. She's doing everything the company wants her to do.

JACK: The company never asked her to disturb the morale of the group or to tell us how to do our work. The animosity of the group can eventually result in lower-quality work for the whole unit.

MAX: I'll tell you what I'll do. Sue has a meeting with me next week to discuss her six-month performance. I'll keep your thoughts in mind, but I can't promise an improvement in what you and the others believe is a pompous attitude.

JACK: Immediate improvement in her behavior is not the problem; it's her coaching others when she has no right to engage in publicly showing others what to do. You'd think she was lecturing an advanced class in design with all her high-powered, useless equations and formulas. She'd better back off soon, or some of us will quit or transfer.

During the next week, Max thought carefully about his meeting with Jack. He knew that Jack was the informal leader of the design engineers and generally spoke for the other group members. On Thursday of the following week, Max called Sue into his office for her midyear review. Certain portions of the conversation were as follows:

MAX: There is one other aspect I'd like to discuss with you about your performance. As I just related to you, your technical performance has been excellent; however, there are some questions about your relationships with the other workers.

SUE: I don't understand—what questions are you talking about?

MAX: Well, to be specific, certain members of the design group have complained about your apparent "know-it-all" attitude and the manner in which you try to tell them how to do their jobs. You're going to have to be patient with them and not publicly call them out about their performance. This is a good group of engineers, and their work over the years has been more than acceptable. I don't want any problems that will cause the group to produce less effectively.

SUE: Let me make a few comments. First of all, I have never publicly criticized their performance to them or to you. Initially, when I was finished ahead of them, I offered to help them with their work but was bluntly told to mind my own business. I took the hint and concentrated only on my part of the work.

MAX: Okay, I understand that.

SUE: What you don't understand is that after five months of working in this group I have come to the conclusion that what is going on is a "rip-off" of the company. The other engineers are goldbricking and setting a work pace much less than they're capable of. They're more interested in the music from Sam's radio, the local football team, and the bar they're going to go to for TGIF. I'm sorry, but this is just not the way I was raised or trained. And finally, they've never looked on me as a qualified engineer, but as a woman who has broken their professional barrier.

MAX: The assessment and motivation of the engineers is a managerial job. Your job is to do your work as well as you can without interfering wiith the work of others. As for the male-female comment, this company hired you because of your qualifications, not your sex. Your future at United is quite promising if you do the engineering and leave the management to me.

Sue left the meeting very depressed. She knew that she was performing well and that the other design engineers were not working up to their capacities. This knowledge frustrated her more and more as the weeks passed.

PART FOUR
The Influence Process

Hill Enterprises

When Hill Enterprises was founded ten years ago, its total assets consisted of one automatic lathe, one contract worth $2200, and one employee. The employee was Robert Hill, president and sole owner, then twenty-nine years old. He had one objective in forming Hill Enterprises—that of retiring with a million dollars in his personal bank account at the age of forty.

According to Robert Hill, the reasons Hill Enterprises was able to survive the first difficult years were his considerable abilities as a machinist, which he had developed during the nine years he was employed in the machine shop of a large manufacturing company, his willingness to work long and hard hours, and his knack for raising money for working capital. During the early years, he would customarily spend his evenings working at the plant and his days visiting banks, insurance companies, and personal friends in an attempt to acquire sufficient funds to continue operations. For the most part he was successful, and though he often had the feeling he was a bit overextended financially, his business continued to grow and show profits.

Mr. Hill felt that another reason for his success was his ability to inspire the work force to work toward his personal goal of a million dollars. His typical comment in interviewing a prospective employee was: "If you work for me you will have to work hard, for I intend to retire with a million dollars by the time I am forty. This means overtime, long hard hours, and unswerving loyalty to Hill Enterprises. If you are willing to do this, I'll make sure that you will get your share of the profits."

Potential employees who were willing to accept these conditions found that Mr. Hill meant what he said. Loyalty to the common cause was based on the number of hours of overtime a man put in. This high amount of overtime had two effects. First, Hill Enterprises was able to give its employees approximately double the take-home pay they could receive from other companies, thus reinforcing the promises Mr. Hill had made concerning financial rewards to individual employees. Second, even though the company was constantly growing and the work force was increasing in size, the large amount of overtime kept the number of employees to a minimum so that Mr. Hill had continuing face-to-face contact with them and could maintain a personal relationship with each.

As Hill Enterprises grew and progressed Robert Hill continued his earlier pattern of operations. He set a grueling pace, continuing to work long hours late into the night and spending a large share of his time during the day attempting to raise additional working capital and financial support. He often held important conferences at 5:00 A.M. in order that supervisory personnel would be free to handle their

Personality loyal to Hill, not Really to Co.

regular work during the "normal" working hours. Mr. Hill seemed to enjoy the pace and pressure and seemed especially to like his frequent contact with the employees. His office consisted of a single beat-up desk in one corner of the production area. Thus he was immediately available to all to help with any problem, whether it was a production problem or a personal one. Many employees availed themselves of his accessibility, and while he was in the plant he seemed to be constantly talking with one employee or another, either in his "office" or on the production floor. Often he would report on the progress of his personal bank account to the men, a practice which they enjoyed tremendously, as Mr. Hill would very vividly recount his financial manipulations.

The employees of Hill Enterprises responded to the situation by working long hours in poor environmental surroundings and under the constant pressure of schedules and production deadlines. Hill Enterprises at this stage had set up operations in a deserted store building, and physical working conditions were considerably less attractive than those of competing organizations.

Under the constant pressures to meet schedules, tempers were often short. The accepted way to reduce individual tension was to "fly off the handle." It was the privilege of the president as well as of any employee, and it was a privilege that was often used. Robert Hill had the reputation of being able to deliver the best "dressing-down" of anyone in the organization, and it was not unusual for an employee to comment on the skill with which Mr. Hill had "chewed him out." This give-and-take was not all onesided, and employees regardless of their position felt free to talk back to Mr. Hill or the other supervisors and often did. And because this was the accepted way to decrease tension and to achieve action, the incident over which an outburst occurred was im-

mediately forgotten. The employees seemed to enjoy their existence with Hill Enterprises, and underneath the tension and pressure each employee felt that he was capable and that he was contributing to the goals of the company.

But some nine years after the start of Hill Enterprises, as Robert Hill had often feared, his intricate financial dealings caught up with him. His considerably expanded enterprises were without adequate working capital and he was forced to bring in a new partner, Donald Robbins, who was willing to invest sufficient funds to keep the company going.

One faction of the work force thought that the arrival of Robbins was just another of Mr. Hill's seemingly endless manipulations for capital. The other faction believed that his arrival was the harbinger of the end of Hill Enterprises as they had known it. They sensed that it would be only a matter of time until Mr. Hill would lose control of the internal workings of his organization and that the high wages and overtime pay would be cut.

The immediate influence of the arrival of Robbins upon the operations of Hill Enterprises was negligible. Operations continued at the same hectic pace, and Mr. Hill's personal activities did not appear to be appreciably different. He maintained his old "office" and was still available to help out on any particular problems that arose. However, as time passed, it became more and more obvious to the employees that Robbins demanded a great deal of Mr. Hill's time. Although he retained his desk in the corner of the shop for awhile, Mr. Hill soon set up new headquarters in the more plush surroundings of a new building that had been constructed adjacent to the shop facilities to house the sales and office activities of Hill Enterprises. Because of his new location and the demands made upon him by his new partner, Mr. Hill was unable to spend as much time with the men in the shop as before. In addition, Robbins' apparent aloofness to the workings and problems of the production shop and its employees created resentment.

The employees noticed that shortly after Mr. Hill had moved his office, the time-honored method of "blowing off steam" as a prelude to constructive effort on a problem became more and more ineffectual. Mr. Hill was no longer around to arbitrate really serious disagreements and his customary "O. K., now that we've got that out of our system, let's get to work," was absent. While blowing off steam was still an accepted practice, an element of bitterness seemed to be apparent in such outbursts that occurred. This bitterness and a sense of resentment toward Robbins permeated the atmosphere of the shop, with the result that many employees adopted a fatalistic attitude toward both the future of Hill Enterprises and their own personal futures.

In this atmosphere a second major organizational change occurred. A new man with the title of "Works Manager" arrived to fill the vacuum created by Mr. Hill's forced attention to matters other than production. This man, Rob Bellows, was the son-in-law of Donald Robbins, the new partner. He was thirty-five years old, a graduate of Eastern State College, and had had ten years' experience as an industrial engineer with a large chemical company. He was hired by Hill Enterprises on the insistence of Donald Robbins, who felt that the production activities were inefficient and excessively costly. His appearance on the scene came as a surprise to the shop and production employees.

During his first few days with the company, employees often saw Bellows and Robbins in the production area. The men appeared to be conversing in earnest, and often pointed and gestured toward machines or individuals. Bellows continually took notes on a large clipboard which he carried with him. During this period, none of the employees was spoken to by either of the two men. The men in

the shop had not had official indication of Bellows' duties, responsibilities, or position in the company. They knew only by rumor that he was the new works manager.

Bellows made the following comments about his responsibilities at Hill Enterprises shortly after his arrival:

This Company has a tremendous potential and an unlimited future. Robert Hill is a dynamic individual with great skills. He has certainly been successful to date. Mr. Robbins and I, I think, will complement these skills and make the company even more successful. Mr. Robbins has the ability and experience to do some long-range planning and get our financial affairs in order, and I have the responsibility and ability to make our production activities more effective. A major part of the problem as I see it is that we use our time inefficiently in production. We don't have any effective scheduling procedures of channels or responsibility and authority, with the result that the men spend a lot of time bickering with each other and conversing about things with which they should not really be concerned. Their job is to get out the production. Our job is to organize the production activities in such a way that this can be done at least cost. The whole basis for the situation is that in the past Hill Enterprises has been small enough to be controlled effectively by one man. Now, however, we are no longer really a small firm and we cannot continue to operate like one. I have some ideas and some techniques which I plan to initiate that I think will increase the effectiveness and efficiency of our production operations by 50 percent in very short order.

At the beginning of his third week as works manager, Bellows issued a series of changes in procedures to the production employees. Without exception these changes were made without consulting any of the men in the shop. All of them were issued in typewritten memos, a new practice which many of the employees felt was unnecessary and undesirable because of the effectiveness with which they felt the existing informal channels of communication had been used. The extent of the changes requested by Bellows was significant, ranging from changes in production scheduling techniques to changes in working conditions for individual employees. One employee estimated that to carry out those written orders, hundreds of additional man-hours "which were just not available" would be required.

Bellows' personal contacts with individual employees were limited and consisted mostly of quick and forceful answers to any questions or problems that might be brought to his attention. Many of his decisions seemed to indicate a lack of awareness of the capacity of the tools used in the production processes. For example, because of his insistence on machine speedups for certain operations, several expensive tools were ruined and valuable production time was lost. After having received several memos from Bellows which they considered unreasonable, one small group of employees had christened him with the nickname "The Fool." As the number of written memos coming from Bellows' office increased, the resentment toward these memos became more apparent, and a strong adverse reaction to his presence was evident on the part of the production employees.

Some four months after Bellows' arrival, cooperation between the "old-timers"—both the supervisors and the workers—hit a new high. Unfortunately, this "cooperation" was used to undermine any and all changes that the new works manager attempted to put into effect. As new orders and procedures originated from Bellows' office, the employees carried out the orders to the letter of the law because, in many cases, they afforded a justified means of wasting time and reducing

production. Bellows gave no indication that he was aware of this situation.

Bellows also attempted to establish formal channels of communication within the production operations, for he felt that much needless discussion and confusion was in existence under the present system. He issued several organization charts which described the "approved" way in which communication was to be effected within the organization. These charts were uniformly ignored by the employees, who continued to rely on the previously accepted informal channels of action. It even became an unwritten policy that all information channeled to Bellows under the new system was censored and reviewed by the person or persons to be affected before it was sent to Bellows.

Yet in this new atmosphere the old loyalties to Robert Hill did not fade entirely. The office manager, the plant superintendent, and several foremen attempted to get his ear from time to time to inform him that things were not running smoothly. Mr. Hill was always surprised by such comments, and he attempted to reassure the men by making remarks such as "It will take some time for us to get to know each other well, but I'm sure that everything will be straightened out in a little while." In addition, he made several trips to the production area, talking with the men individually and asking them to give Bellows a chance, as it was important for the success of Hill Enterprises.

Morale seemed to improve for a short while until Bellows issued a statement stating that no one in the plant was to bother the president with plant problems without consulting with him first. Shortly after this statement was issued by Bellows, Robert Hill again made several trips to the production area, talking to individual workers and attempting to explain that other problems prevented his spending as much time in the shop as he previously had. In several instances, he started to report on the status of his personal bank account. Noting that this was not too well received, however, he discontinued this practice.

As time passed, the situation continued to deteriorate. Many of Bellows' acts and orders seemed to be in direct contradiction to Mr. Hill's former policies and procedures. The individuals affected were confused as to which procedure to follow. Attempts to have Bellows clarify his orders either left the questioner more confused than before or were greeted with a curt, "We don't have time to discuss that. It is perfectly clear. Just read the memo."

Within a few months, many of the personnel talked of leaving to look for other employment and a few did. Nine months after Bellows had taken the position of works manager approximately 25 percent of the production force had taken new jobs. The morale among those remaining was poor and a significant increase in product rejects was experienced. But during the same period both Robbins and Bellows felt that important advances had been made in "cleaning up" production activities and that the company was "looking better all the time."

Polar Star Beverages Company (A)

Ken Kirk and three other Polar Star managers had just settled down in Kirk's office. Kirk had returned to the San Francisco plant from San Eduardo, where a regional preview of the company's soft-drink promotion plans had been held. Kirk had made the forty-mile trip back because he wanted to meet with an executive from the Seattle home office who was in town for the meeting. He and Kirk had been joined by two other managers who wanted to talk about some current concerns of the San Francisco plant.

Although it was only 3:30, it had been a long day, and it felt good to sit back and rehash the day's events. Kirk had almost gone directly home from San Eduardo, but changed his mind so that he and the others could meet with the visitor.

The conversation was interrupted by a phone call from a supplier, which Kirk answered at his desk. Suddenly, Kirk heard the sound of bottles falling on the sidewalk below. When he looked out the window, he saw a group of young people gathered on the sidewalk, carrying placards and sacks of bottles and cans. He could also see TV cameras and what seemed to be newsmen on the street.

Reprinted by permission of Anthony G. Athos.

By this time, all four men had joined him at the window. The signs indicated that the kids were from Montview High School in a nearby town that Kirk knew well. Many of the students were the same age as his children, and knowing the high school, he imagined that they were a pretty bright and articulate group. The kids were all wearing worn and faded jeans and all seemed to have long hair.

The plant was on one of the busiest intersections in the Bay Area, and the rush-hour traffic was beginning to swell the normally heavy traffic on both streets. Kirk asked Ed Hall, the plant superintendent and one of the men in the room, to go down and bring them around to the side door. "At least they'll be away from some of the traffic," he thought. "Invite them in for a Polar Star," he added, almost automatically. Kirk tried to finish the phone conversation as quickly as possible; he noticed that the crowd had begun to move around the side of the building at Hall's request.

Before Kirk could finish, Hall returned to say that the students demanded to talk "to the top man in the company." Kirk immediately ended the phone conversation. As general manager of the San Francisco bottling plant and a vice-president of the Bay Area subsidiary, Kirk was the "top man."

Polar Star Beverages Company (B)

The four men started down the corridor, and Kirk tried to imagine what the students had on their minds. They were probably protesting Polar Star's one-way, nonreturnable containers, he guessed, because of the bottles and cans they had brought with them. Although he had become very conscious of the ecology movement and shared its goals, he also knew that it was a practical impossibility for Polar Star to go out of the nonreturnable business and survive in the Bay Area market. The Bay Area's consumers preferred nonreturnable bottles and cans, and all the large-volume chains reflected that preference. None of the chains sold returnables for this reason. In addition, the chains did not like the extra work that returnables entailed for store personnel. But this was not the kind of statement that could be made in front of TV cameras without offending the chains, who were Polar Star's largest customers, and other independent dealers.

Yet at the same time, he thought, Polar Star also relied heavily on the Bay Area youth market. Local universities, colleges, and high schools were an important part of the market. Also, the company's reputation for having an honest, quality product had been basic to its

Reprinted by permission of Anthony G. Athos.

success and expansion. It was crucial not to have the company's image damaged by such a confrontation.

When they reached the bottom of the stairs, Kirk could see the students through the garage doors, chanting, "Recycle now, recycle now." Plant employees had begun to close the garage doors, and Kirk could sense their uneasiness. He knew that most of the inside men as well as the driver-salesmen had little sympathy for protestors, and the possibility of a physical confrontation could not be taken lightly. He also realized that within half an hour, a class for supervisors being held in the plant would be breaking up. They, like the plant employees, were apt to be antagonistic to the protestors. He could also see that Polar Star trucks were beginning to return from their day's deliveries and would continue to do so for the next couple of hours.

Kirk stepped outside and found 75 or 80 kids shouting and chanting. They had begun to empty their sacks of bottles and cans. The TV cameras had come around, and he also noticed several people with still cameras and tape recorders. The students had lined up the bottles and cans against the building; the pile included all brands of soft drinks, including national brands and private labels, as well as Polar Star products. Kirk looked into the crowd and wondered what to do.

Polar Star Beverages Company (C)

The last student protestor had left, and Kirk returned to his office to try and reconstruct what had happened. No outbreak of hostility or violence had occurred, and he felt a sense of relief for that reason alone. He knew that he and the students remained far from agreement on some issues, but it seemed to him that everyone, including himself, had gained a better understanding of the problem. It certainly could have been worse, he thought.

Seattle would want a report on the protest and on the way in which it was handled. The whole episode had come up so suddenly, and everything had happened so rapidly; it could have taken a very different course. So Kirk settled back to retrace the events of the two hours that had just passed.

It was not easy to sort out what had happened and what it meant. In a way, he thought, he had seen it coming. He had tried to keep up on the latest developments in the ecology crisis and had thought a great deal about its implications for companies like Polar Star, but he had never really organized his thoughts into either a defensive or an offensive position. In fact, he found that he agreed with the protestors on most of what they had to say. His responses to them, he thought, were more or less intuitive, but what they had talked about was certainly not new to him.

Reprinted by permission of Anthony G. Athos.

In an effort to reconstruct what had happened, Kirk tried to review the events as they had occurred. He remembered the men closing the garage doors when he had started out to meet the protest group, and he could feel the tension in the building. His first reaction was to instruct Hall not to have anyone talk to the students except himself. He also recalled seeing the television cameras and the large group of kids and placards. It was hard to tell who their spokesman was because of all the activity and shouting. Kirk remembered walking into the crowd and asking if he could meet their spokesman. He sensed that they were somewhat surprised by his presence, possibly because he had come out of the building so quickly.

Kirk also remembered introducing himself to the group's leader and extending his hand to him. The boy pointedly ignored the gesture and immediately launched into reading a statement. He seemed well-spoken and articulate, but with a certain sharpness in his voice. Kirk found it hard to describe the boy's reaction. It was not really belligerent, but definitely hostile and aggressive. The boy read the prepared statement, and when he finished, the crowd cheered. Then he gave Kirk a copy of it and asked him to pass it along to his superiors, which Kirk assured him he would do. Another student gave Kirk a "Fact Sheet" and he paused for a moment to read it. (See Exhibits 1 and 2.) Kirk also remembered being asked who he was and what his title was by a

EXHIBIT 1

DUMP-IN

The use of non-returnable cans and bottles is a blatant example of poor ecological planning. The use of disposable aluminum cans is an unnecessary, if not a serious, waste of our natural resources. Non-returnable bottles add conspicuously to the accumulation of garbage in urban areas. This act of protest is not belligerent in nature. We realize that the Polar Star Company is not solely responsible for adding to the country's refuse problems, but it is a prime offender. If this amount of bottles can be collected in only a week and a half among such a small group, it is obvious that the amount of trash that could build up in a longer period of time is excessive. We hope that today's Dump-In will serve notice to all consumer industries, and to the packaging industries on which they depend, that people in this community want to see the recycling of metal, glass, and paper. We hope that profit-motive will not blind manufacturers to their social responsibilities and that our presence here today will stimulate cooperation between industries themselves and between industries and the people, in an effort to improve our environment.

We strongly suggest that the Polar Star Company be the first to return to the use of returnable bottles and cans in the hope that other manufacturers will also realize their responsibility to our environment.

Montview Students for
Ecology Action

---

woman reporter. Somehow, he felt that his answer was important to the group, because he remembered stressing the fact that he was a vice-president.

He also remembered the barrage of questions that followed. Some of the questions were asked so rapidly that they could not possibly be answered. It almost seemed as if their purpose was more to harass him than to get answers. Several kids in particular seemed to be pushing him, repeating the same question over and over again. It felt as if they were trying to get him to say something he didn't want to say. After several minutes, however, the group seemed to settle down and there was less shouting. As they talked, he began to sense that they were pretty well informed and appeared to know what they were talking about. It almost seemed more important to understand what they were saying than to respond with answers. Maybe it had something to do with having kids of his own who were the same age, he thought. The students seemed to be not only knowledgeable about ecological problems but also sincerely concerned about them. Possibly for this reason, he tried not to dodge their questions, but to be honest and candid, and to let the "chips fall where they may."

Several times he did not know how to answer a question, and he had to stop and collect his thoughts. But he remembered three of the kids as being real needlers. Even when he tried to answer a question as well as he could, and the subject moved to something else, one of them would bring the question back into the discussion and push him further on it. He remembered feeling harassed at these times, as if they were trying to get him to say something out of context. He also sensed that some of them felt frustrated, and he wondered if his basic agreement with them on much of what they were saying didn't underlie this frustration.

Kirk also remembered that after things had settled down, he asked the group to move off the street and into the building where they could see the plant. Part of his reason was to get them out of the way of the rush-hour traffic. Delivery trucks were beginning to return to the plant, making the situation even more hazardous. Moving them into the building required stopping the truck traffic so that they could all file in. He also remembered being

EXHIBIT 2

Recycle   Recycle   ᴿᴱᶜᵞᶜᴸᴱ

Fact Sheet

"Each family in the United States discards, on the average, a ton of empty packages each year." _Environment_ Nov. '69

"Packaging wastes are increasing at the rate of six percent a year, against a one percent increase in population." _Environment_ Nov. '69

"It costs the U.S. taxpayer over one and one half billion dollars a year to dispose of refuse." _Boys' Life_ March '70

"It costs from 20 to 30 cents to dispose of the "disposable" can of 10 cent soda." _Boys' Life_ March '70

"We are rapidly running out of 'sanitary landfill' space." _Boys' Life_ March '70

"Reusable bottles can be reused about 20 times, so they cost the bottler almost nothing." _Forbes_ Aug. 1, '69

"Although there is an abundant supply of aluminum for the foreseeable future, the fact remains that the supply is not unlimited - and aluminum usage has doubled roughly every ten years." _Scientific American_ Sept. '69

"Aluminum scrap offers a worthwhile incentive, a ton of aluminum brings $200 from dealers." _Scientific American_ Sept. '69

"The average American throws away each day about 4½ pounds of trash-cans, bottles, paper, foodstuffs, etc." _Boys' Life_ March '70 aware of the continued presence of the television cameras and lights and wondering why they were still there. He couldn't help speculating that they were expecting something dramatic to happen that he could not foresee. However, he also sensed that the TV reporters didn't like his moving the students inside.

Angrily, one of the reporters asked him why he was bringing them into the building, and Kirk answered by saying that he was going to show them one of Polar Star's recycling machines. "What kind of a recycling machine?" he was asked. Kirk answered, "A paper recycling machine." The machine's purpose was to compress and bale paper products such as cartons and boxes. Kirk brought the group over to the machine and tried to explain that it was, in effect, a recycling machine that Polar Star had developed long before recycling became an important issue.

Inside, the questions still continued to come, and they were hard questions. The group asked about the landfill problem and biodegradable products. Kirk told them about the biodegradable plastic bottle that Polar Star was trying to develop. This seemed to surprise most of them. Other questions were not quite as easy to answer, such as why Polar Star simply did not stop making nonreturnable bottles. He remembered trying to explain that it was impossible for Polar Star to take that step by itself, because all its competitors emphasized one-way bottles, and the consumer preference in the Bay Area was overwhelmingly for nonreturnables. Polar Star could not dictate to a market that wanted nonreturnables without going out of business. The Bay Area, he added, was one of the first markets in the country to demand nonreturnables. He also pointed out that the pile of bottles they had brought showed that the problem was one that Polar Star alone could not solve. The bottles included chain-store private labels, as well

as other brands. He remembered explaining how everyone would be ahead economically if they used returnables and that Polar Star had always supplied dealers with returnable bottles and would continue to do so.

There were several questions Kirk felt he could not answer, because they dealt with confidential information of potential value to competitors, such as the plant's production by bottle type. Kirk explained this and tried to answer giving only percentages. He also felt he could not say anything about whether the company would support proposed state legislation banning nonreturnables, because he had not seen any of the legislation. They asked him this question several times, and he felt that they wanted him to either endorse it or take a stand against it. Although he didn't feel he could comment on the matter, he assured them that the company would comply with any legislation that was passed.

The group moved through the plant as they talked, and Kirk showed them the stacked cases of returnable empties waiting to be reused, as well as the empty fountain and vending-machine syrup containers, which were also continually recycled. Several times during the tour, Kirk had to stop traffic while the group moved within the building. He also remembered pointing out the returnable empties coming back on the trucks. At one point, one of the girls lost her contact lens, and again traffic had to be stopped while they found it. At another point the supervisors' class let out, and Kirk wondered what would happen. Fortunately, the men simply stood around and watched. Similarly, the plant workers and the returning drivers had also kept at a distance, somewhat to Kirk's relief. It had been quite an afternoon, he thought.

During all this, it was apparent that there were several issues on which he and they did not agree. However, he also sensed that he was more aware of some problems that they pointed out, and that they had also begun to see some of the problems facing Polar Star. Much of the hostility he had sensed earlier had gone. If fact, when the students started to leave, he remembered going up and shaking hands with them. Several who had started out the door returned to wish him well.

It had all happened quickly, and he felt a considerable sense of relief that it was over.

Yet some of the questions they had raised, and the episode itself, posed a number of questions. Kirk decided that it might be useful to just sit down and try to write out what had happened and what implications it might have for the San Francisco plant as well as other Polar Star bottlers.

Judy Simpson

Judy Simpson sat at her desk reviewing the department year-end statement that highlighted the Fort Smith Franklin Manufacturing shipping department's performance at $150,000 under the budget allowed for the year. She was especially proud of the $115,000 savings in variable labor since this was a direct reflection of the increase in productivity within the shipping department.

Employee morale was now tops, and everyone seemed to be working together as a team. Nevertheless, this work situation had not always existed. The department had made a complete turn-around in the past year and one-half, and Simpson was indeed pleased to have played a major role in the change.

She had come to the traditionally all-male shipping department in April a year ago as a management associate. She had been working for Franklin Manufacturing as a customer service sales assistant for seven years and had a good knowledge of the business. Realizing that the customer service job was a dead-end position, Simpson began taking courses at Westark Community College and College of the Ozarks in June three years ago. Her enthusiasm and intense drive were demonstrated by her taking double academic loads while continuing to work full-time in the customer service position. At the time she joined the

shipping department, she was preparing to receive a B.S.B.A. degree from College of the Ozarks in August last year. As graduation time had approached, Simpson talked with the Franklin Manfacturing management personnel to determine if advancement within the Fort Smith plant was a possibility. If not, she was prepared to search elsewhere.

Conditions in the Forth Smith Franklin Manufacturing shipping and warehouse operation were at best described as "substandard" in April of last year. Thousands of damaged cases of finished product were strewn in the truck loading doors, rail dock area, conveyor delivery area, and generally throughout the warehouse. Product was protruding in aisles making it virtually impossible to drive a fork lift through the warehouse without hitting merchandise. Poor warehouse layout hampered loading of outbound product and receiving of raw materials.

Due to numerous incidents of telling half-truths or evading issues, employees had little trust or respect for John Dempsey, shipping department head, or other department supervisors. The long-standing position of the hourly workforce was to work against management whenever possible. Two department supervisors, Joe Cox and Howard Corley, were on the verge of retirement and simply biding time. Shift supervisors Tom Wilson and Charles Mitchell could only be considered mediocre at best. The culture of shipping management seemed to be "We know things are not ideal,

This case was prepared by Phyllis Duncan, with the assistance of Professor Robert D. Hay, University of Arkansas, as a basis for class discussion and analysis of an administrative situation. Used by permission of Robert D. Hay.

but they can't be helped. We're doing the best we can." Although only three months into the year, the department, as a result of poor planning and poor warehouse layout, had incurred $50,000 in demurrage from railroads on inbound materials.

The shipping hourly workforce comprised sixty men, 90 percent of whom were considerably older than Simpson, who was 30. None of the employees had been in the department for less than three years. All first shift personnel had been in the department a minimum of fourteen years.

Shipping department employees had been looked down on by plant management for years. For the most part, employees had tough-guy images with attitudes of "do as little as you can get by with—don't care about anything." No one had given them credit for being anything but a liability to the plant.

The only other woman who had attempted to supervise in the department had lasted barely two months before leaving. Shipping employees proudly told Judy Simpson about "running out" Mary Turner.

Jim Basham, plant superintendent of production and planning, who was directly in charge of the shipping operation, had been at the Fort Smith plant for nine months. Keenly aware of the disastrous shipping department situation, Jim began looking for the right people to assist him in turning around the operation. His first move was to ask for Judy Simpson as a management associate. Next, John Dempsey was replaced by Jim Kennedy as department head. Cox and Corley, offered generous severance benefits, opted to retire. Wilson and Mitchell were assigned to other plant positions.

Basham knew what had to be accomplished. He had designed new warehouse layouts for finished product, raw materials, and manufacturing packing materials. Basham recognized Kennedy as being somewhat an au-

thoritarian leader who was consistent with policies. Simpson, through some guidance from Basham in the art of patience, would be the source of getting the work-effort from the employees. This three-member team would be the base for establishing the new shipping operation. The overall objective of the team was to make Fort Smith shipping the most efficient operation of the six plants in Franklin Manufacturing. Honest and fair treatment of employees was decided to be the code for shipping management. Initially the three met daily to discuss department activities and assure consistency in management direction.

Systematic planning of daily work for employees was Simpson's first target. Rather than adopting the previous method of haphazard assignment of work, she attempted to distribute workloads more fairly and consistently among employees and shifts. The new approach was to anticipate "opportunities" and plan accordingly rather than react to the problem after the fact. Shift rivalry had been a major problem in the past, but Judy felt a full team spirit would be required if best department efficiency was to result.

It was soon evident to employees that Simpson was a hard driver. She expected much from herself and also expected a "fair shake" from her subordinates. Nevertheless, she attempted to make the daily drudgery less a drag by expressing genuine interest in the employees—really talking with the people about work and their outside activities—something that would have been unheard of in the past. Realizing she could not force the people to get the job done, she strove to make each employee feel the importance of his efforts in the total department performance. It became commonplace to shake a hand or pat a back to let an employee know good performance was appreciated.

Basham and Kennedy were likewise attempting to raise employee morale by improving working conditions through a more efficient layout of the warehouse, and by adding heating in the warehouse, lighting on the rail dock, new shipping cafeteria facilities, and new dock plates at the truck loading doors.

As productivity increased, little expressions of appreciation were bestowed by management, such as buying cokes for the crew, bringing in rolls for coffee break, or letting employees leave five or ten minutes early after a hard workday. The shipping employees began to take pride in their work, and quantity and quality improved. After three months, the department had increased 20 percent overall in productivity. Even the appearance of the shipping worker changed. The disheveled, unshaven look was gone; employees were neater and better groomed.

By communicating with employees, Judy Simpson found numerous shortcuts that increased output: eliminating loafing of carrier truck drivers around the loading docks by having carriers drop trailers for loading; insisting on carriers being prompt on appointment times; eliminating double handling of product by "pulling and loading" virtually all freight from the warehouse (no pre-staging). To accomplish and maintain warehouse cleanup, four full-time employees were assigned specific areas of responsibility. In the past, common practice had been for employees who had caused product "spills" or left freight in the loading areas to leave the product for the next guy to run over with a fork lift and strew further. A new rule was established and enforced: Anyone responsible for a mess will clean up after himself.

As the Christmas holiday approached, Simpson decorated the office with a tree and tinsel. An informal luncheon was scheduled. She prepared the sandwiches and the employees pitched in with complementing cakes, chips, and salads. The plant manger, Don Sargent, was asked to join the employees for the luncheon. It was apparent the shipping department was becoming a real winning team. As Don spoke to the group, he complimented them on their accomplishments and let them know he was counting on shipping to help make the Fort Smith plant number one.

Simpson continued to groom her relationship with the employees by communicating with them individually and in groups. She arrived at work well before shift change in the morning to see the third shift people and stayed through the first and well into the second shift. It was evident that each shift had its own personality and required "different strokes for different folks." Communications and feedback through personal contact and shift departmental meetings were keys to department morale and productivity.

In an effort to stress the importance of each team member, Simpson took individual pictures of employees and mounted them on a display in the shipping office with the caption "Fort Smith Shipping—No. 1 Next Year." Just to say thanks for their hard work, she prepared and served a spaghetti dinner in the spring for the first and second shift employees and came in at 5 A.M. to prepare and serve breakfast for the third shift.

In May, Jim Kennedy was promoted to a department head position in manufacturing. Judy Simpson was in turn promoted to shipping department head. Richard Long, after having worked in production/planning for the previous five years, had joined the shipping management team five months earlier as second shift supervisor. Tom Craig, long-time shipping clerk, was promoted to receiving/warehouse foreman. Both Long and Craig were competent in their present position, but neither one could handle the first shift supervisor slot due to their lack of skill in interpersonal relations and departmental planning. Mike Jones, a 24-year-old hourly employee, had performed well as a temporary first shift supervisor but did not feel comfortable about the transition from hourly to supervisory and decided to return to his fork lift driver position.

Basham interviewed Ray McGee, a former Mead Container shipping supervisor, and was impressed with his credentials and ambitious outlook. Simpson likewise thought that Ray would be an asset to her department, and he was hired. Basham and Simpson stressed their redefined management philosophy: working through proper channels (lowest level before upward), proper planning, and honest, fair treatment of employees. The department objective was to maintain the credibility of Fort Smith shipping from within and without the Fort Smith Franklin Manufacturing plant.

Believing that her office should always be open to employees, Simpson maintained an open-door policy and continued to make herself accessible in the warehouse. Rather than force unnecessary changes on employees, she stressed the importance of stability in the work environment even if it meant bucking the system with plant management. Although accused by other department heads of "mothering" her employees, Simpson felt the importance of employees being able to depend on their leader.

By providing guidance to the supervisors, McGee, Long, and Craig, Simpson hoped to maintain a high level of performance and competence by the department. Shipping office clerks Evelyn Davis and Paula Griffin were brought into the overall activities of the department and willingly accepted additional responsibilities. McGee was clearly promotable; he demonstrated good leadership skills in working with Long and Craig as well as with the

EXHIBIT 1

Fort Smith Franklin Manufacturing shipping department organizational chart

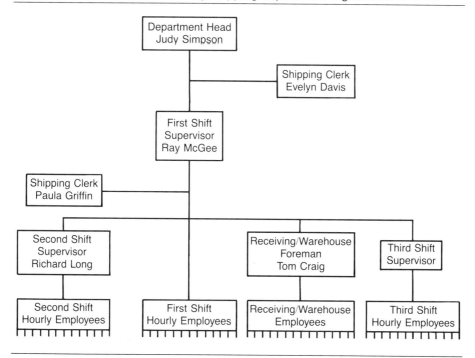

hourly employees. Simpson realized, however, that McGee would need to develop better planning skills in ranking importance of tasks. Long and Craig were stable followers but lacked the initiative for advancement. These two, for the most part, could work effectively through their employees if tasks were assigned by Simpson or McGee, but neither wanted to be the "bad guy" to his workers.

In early August of this year, after an extremely demanding two-month shipping period, Judy Simpson treated the shipping department employees to a chicken dinner, which she again prepared and financed to demonstrate to the employees that their efforts were appreciated. Clearly, the image of the department had changed, which could not have been accomplished with a one-member effort.

Corporate management recognized Fort Smith shipping as the number one Franklin Manufacturing shipping/warehouse operation. The professional shipper image was likewise noticed by plant management and union officials, as was demonstrated by upgrading the labor grade for shipping personnel in the new labor agreement of October this year.

In looking back to her beginning as a "shipping person," Simpson found it difficult to recall exactly how bad things had been. She knew her employees remembered, however, and were rightly proud of the professional but easy-going atmosphere that now prevailed. It had been a give-and-take proposition; as a group spokesman recently told her, "We know some people around here think we should go by the book, but we don't want to go by the book. We like the way you treat us, and we want to do the job for you."

Savemore Food Store 5116

The Savemore Corporation is a chain of 400 retail supermarkets located primarily in the northeastern section of the United States. Store 5116 employs more than 50 persons, all of whom live within suburban Portage, New York, where the store is located.

Wally Shultz served as general manager of store 5116 for six years. Last April he was transferred to another store in the chain. At that time the employees were told by the district manager, Mr. Finnie, that Wally Shultz was being promoted to manage a larger store in another township.

Most of the employees seemed unhappy to lose their old manager. Nearly everyone agreed with the opinion that Shultz was a "good guy to work for." As examples of his desirability as a boss the employees told how Wally had frequently helped the arthritic black porter with his floor mopping, how he had shut the store five minutes early each night so that certain employees might catch their buses, of a Christmas party held each year for employees at his own expense, and his general willingness to pitch in. All employees had been on a first-name basis with the manager. About half of them had begun work with the Savemore Corporation when the Portage store was opened.

Reprinted by permission of John W. Hennessey, Jr., The Amos Tuck School of Business Administration, Dartmouth College. At the time of this case, the author, a college student, was employed for the summer as a checker and stockboy in store 5116.

Wally Shultz was replaced by Clark Raymond. Raymond, about 25 years old, was a graduate of an Ivy League college and had been with Savemore a little over one year. After completion of his six-month training program, he served as manager of one of the chain's smaller stores, before being advanced to store 5116. In introducing Raymond to the employees, Mr. Finnie stressed his rapid advancement and the profit increase that occurred while Raymond had charge of his last store.

I began my employment in store 5116 early in June. Mr. Raymond was the first person I met in the store, and he impressed me as being more intelligent and efficient than the managers I had worked for in previous summers at other stores. After a brief conversation concerning our respective colleges, he assigned me to a cash register, and I began my duties as a checker and bagger.

In the course of the next month I began to sense that relationships between Raymond and his employees were somewhat strained. This attitude was particularly evident among the older employees of the store, who had worked in store 5116 since its opening. As we all ate our sandwiches together in the cage (an area about 20 feet square in the cellar fenced in by chicken wire, to be used during coffee breaks and lunch hours), I began to question some of the older employees as to why they disliked Mr. Raymond. Laura Morgan, a fellow checker about 40 years of age and the mother of two grade-school boys, gave the most specific answers. Her complaints were:

1. Raymond had fired the arthritic black porter on the grounds that a porter who "can't mop is no good to the company."
2. Raymond had not employed new help to make up for normal attrition. Because of this, everybody's work load was much heavier than it ever had been before.
3. The new manager made everyone call him "mister. . . . He's unfriendly."
4. Raymond didn't pitch in. Wally Shultz had, according to Laura, helped people when they were behind in their work. She said that Shultz had helped her bag on rushed Friday nights when a long line waited at her checkout booth, but "Raymond wouldn't lift a finger if you were dying."
5. Employees were no longer let out early to catch buses. Because of the relative infrequency of this means of transportation, some employees now arrived home up to an hour later.
6. "Young Mr. Know-it-all with his fancy degree . . . takes all the fun out of this place."

Other employees had similar complaints. Gloria, another checker, claimed that "he sends the company nurse to your home every time you call in sick." Margo, a meat wrapper, remarked: "Everyone knows how he's having an affair with that new bookkeeper he hired to replace Carol when she quit." Pops Devery, the head checker, who had been with the chain for over ten years, was perhaps the most vehement of the group. He expressed his views in the following manner: "That new guy's a real louse . . . got a mean streak a mile long. Always trying to cut corners. First it's not enough help, then no overtime, and now, come Saturday mornings, we have to use boxes for the orders 'til the truck arrives.[1] If it wasn't just a year 'til retirement, I'd leave. Things just aren't what they used to be when Wally was around." The last statement was repeated in different forms by many of the other employees. Hearing all this praise of Wally, I was rather surprised when Mr. Finnie dropped the comment to me one morning that Wally had been demoted for inefficiency, and that no one at store 5116 had been told this. It was important that Mr. Schultz save face, Mr. Finnie told me.

A few days later, on Saturday of the busy weekend preceding the July 4 holiday, store 5116 again ran out of paper bags. However, the delivery truck did not arrive at ten o'clock, and by 10:30 the supply of cardboard cartons was also low. Mr. Raymond put in a hurried call to the warehouse. The men there did not know the whereabouts of the truck but promised to get an emergency supply of bags to us around noon. By eleven o'clock, there were no more containers of any type available, and Mr. Raymond reluctantly locked the doors to all further customers. The 20 checkers and packers remained in their respective booths, chatting among themselves. After a few minutes, Mr. Raymond requested that they all retire to the cellar cage because he had a few words for them. As soon as the group was seated on the wooden benches in the chicken-wire enclosed area, Mr. Raymond began to speak, his back to the cellar stairs. In what appeared to be an angered tone, he began, "I'm out for myself first, Savemore second, the customer third, and you last. The inefficiency in this store has amazed me from the moment I arrived here. . . ."

---

[1] The truck from the company warehouse bringing merchandise for sale and store supplies normally arrived at ten o'clock on Saturday morning. Frequently, the stock of large paper bags would be temporarily depleted. It was then necessary to pack orders in cardboard cartons until the truck was unloaded.

At about this time I noticed Mr. Finnie, the district manager, standing at the head of the cellar stairs. It was not surprising to see him at this time because he usually made three or four unannounced visits to the store each week as part of his regular supervisory procedure. Mr. Raymond, his back turned, had not observed Finnie's entrance.

Mr. Raymond continued, "Contrary to what seems to be the opinion of many of you, the Savemore Corporation is not running a social club here. We're in business for just one thing . . . to make money. One way that we lose money is by closing the store on Saturday morning at eleven o'clock. Another way that we lose money is by using a 60-pound paper bag to do the job of a 20-pound bag. A 60-pound bag costs us over 2 cents apiece; a 20-pound bag costs less than a penny. So when you sell a couple of quarts of milk or a loaf of bread, don't use the big bags. Why do you think we have four different sizes anyway? There's no great intelligence or effort required to pick the right size. So do it. This store wouldn't be closed right now if you'd used your common sense. We started out this week with enough bags to last 'til Monday . . . and they would have lasted 'til Monday if you'd only used your brains. This kind of thing doesn't look good for the store, and it doesn't look good for me. Some of you have been bagging for over five years . . . you oughta be able to do it right by now. . . ." Mr. Raymond paused and then said, "I trust I've made myself clear on this point."

The cage was silent for a moment, and then Pops Devery, the head checker, spoke up: "Just one thing, Mis-tuh Raymond. Things were running pretty well before you came

around. When Wally was here we never ran outa bags. The customers never complained about overloaded bags or the bottoms falling out before you got here. What're you gonna tell somebody when they ask for a couple extra bags to use in garbage cans? What're you gonna tell somebody when they want their groceries in a bag, an' not a box? You gonna tell them the manager's too damn cheap to give 'em bags? Is that what you're gonna tell 'em? No sir, things were never like this when Wally Shultz was around. We never had to apologize for a cheap manager who didn't order enough then. Whatta you got to say to that, Mis-tuh Raymond?"

Mr. Raymond, his tone more emphatic, began again. "I've got just one thing to say to that, Mr. Devery, and that's this: store 5116 never did much better than break even when Shultz was in charge here. I've shown a profit better than the best he ever hit in six years every week since I've been here. You can check that fact in the book upstairs any time you want. If you don't like the way I'm running things around here, there's nobody begging you to stay. . . ."

At this point, Pops Devery interrupted and, looking up the stairs at the district manager, asked, "What about that, Mr. Finnie? You've been around here as long as I have. You told us how Wally got promoted 'cause he was such a good boss. Supposin' you tell this young feller here what a good manager is really like? How about that, Mr. Finnie?"

A rather surprised Mr. Raymond turned around to look up the stairs at Mr. Finnie. The manager of store 5116 and his checkers and packers waited for Mr. Finnie's answer.

Out of the Frying Pan

How in the world am I going to untangle the situation that has developed in the purchasing department? wondered John Sterling, the president of a small paper products distribution firm. Did I read something more than I should have when Pete Brown said he could handle it? Was I too quick to agree with him because the problem needed so badly to be solved? But, really, what choice did I have? Clearly, there was a need for action, prompt action. My God, the department was disintegrating! So. . . .

No one in the company doubted that there were significant problems in the purchasing department, for there were few secrets in this small organization. At the same time there was little sympathy among other employees, many of whom thought that the three buyers in purchasing considered themselves a cut above the rest. Company salesmen grumbled frequently about out-of-stock situations and seemingly "lost" deliveries from distant suppliers to the company's own warehouse. The order-takers, who worked downstairs from purchasing and were in another department, had believed for some time that the buyers had certain working privileges not available to

others. Not only did this belief rankle them, but also the fact that they, as order-takers, had to take flack from customers who were not always gracious when told the items they wanted were not available. As the buyers dealt primarily with suppliers, they were buffered from any direct heat emanating from disgruntled customers. Not surprisingly, the order-takers did not relish such a role and tended to compensate for this harassment with frequent criticism of any real or imagined shortcomings on the part of the buyers.

Background

Over 30 years ago, John Sterling and Tom Fenton bought the fledgling company organized a year before as a branch office of a much larger firm. As a consequence of astute and aggressive operations, the company grew and prospered in the very competitive paper products distribution industry. This was largely due to the drive and stimulating example of the president. From the outset Sterling concerned himself with overall company operations while Fenton narrowed his attention to sales. Over the years, this arrangement prevailed without major alteration. Although a principal stockholder and member of the board, Fenton never questioned who was the boss, seemingly content with his subordinate and much-circumscribed role in the company. Within broad policies and goals set by Sterling, Fenton was expected to proceed on his own initiative.

Operating in a city of over 200,000, the firm not only expanded within the municipality but also was able to extend its business to roughly a one-hundred-mile radius. In seeking national accounts, the company commenced a concentrated effort to develop institutional accounts as opposed to the smaller retail customers previously solicited. With some 60 employees, the firm had annual sales of about $25 million, offering such products as matches, toilet and facial tissues, paper towels, packing materials, business forms, paper cups, plates and napkins, and so on. Having acquired some 20 acres of highly suitable commercial property serviced by rail, the company had built its own warehouses adjoining the office facilities. Deliveries to customers were accomplished by its own fleet of trucks. Company salesmen were divided into local and regional components. The organization chart is shown in Exhibit 1.

As the company's business had risen sharply and rather abruptly, Sterling had become increasingly concerned about the performance of the buyers. Their decisions and actions determined whether the company obtained the right products in the right quantities at the most favorable cost. With profit margins at two percent or less, there was little room for inventory mistakes. Sterling thought that he had made a needed change when he decided to turn the purchasing department over to the sales manager, who said he was willing to take on this added responsibility. A member of the firm for more than 15 years, Pete Brown had always been in sales in one capacity or another. He had confidence in himself, and now that he had acquired two principal assistants and a most competent secretary, Brown told Sterling that he was sure he could improve the unstable situation in purchasing.

One of the difficulties in making this new assignment was the need to tell Tom Fenton. As the senior vice-president of the company, Fenton now would have to relinquish his au-

thority over purchasing after considerable time as the chief of that function. Another complication was the fact that previously Fenton had been Brown's supervisor for several years. Some time ago Sterling had placed Fenton in charge because of his extensive knowledge in this area and his passion for detail. Fenton also was well known to all the company's major suppliers and respected by the top managers as well. He liked working with figures and was especially intrigued by the challenge of developing new procedures, especially if they could be put on the company computer. He was not, however, a programmer or an analyst, depending on others for these skills, but he believed that he appreciated reasonably well what a computer was suited to do. The computer impressed Fenton as a superior management tool; as he observed, "In today's environment, we can't function without it."

Fenton's Management Style

A working supervisor, Fenton applied himself strenuously, never complaining about the time he spent beyond normal working hours. He liked to write numerous short memos to his subordinates whenever he wanted to bring something to their attention:

Harry, I've been checking on your purchases for the last month and they are way off base. I want you to tell me why you haven't been following the recommended buys programmed into our computer, and what you are going to do about it. We've spent a lot of money on this program and it *works*. Let me have this tomorrow.

Peggy, you are making far too many errors in computing these supplier invoices. Here's a sample of what I've found in just the last week. You've got to be more careful, for these mistakes are costing the company money. I've been over this with you three times in the past month.... Come and talk to me about this.

If he decided to talk with a buyer directly, Fenton typically would approach the buyer in this fashion, "Charley, I just don't know what's

EXHIBIT 1
Organization chart

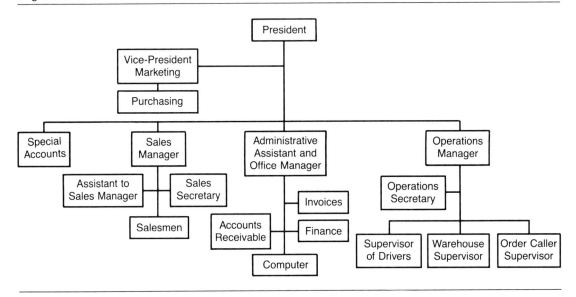

the matter with you! Just look at this! I've forgotten now how many times I've been through this with you, and you keep screwing up. . . . Are you ever going to get it straight? What does it take to penetrate your brain?"

"Gee, I'm sorry, . . . I thought I had it right. I . . ."

"Well, it isn't, damn it! I figured you could understand something as simple as this purchase. Maybe you'll never get it. . . . I don't know. . . ." At that point Fenton would turn away and go back into his office. Picking up a stack of computer printouts, he would resume an item-by-item review.

A newly hired secretary, having overheard this exchange, went over to another buyer nearby and asked, "Is Mr. Fenton like this always?"

"Oh no, he's pretty calm today. . . . Let me say this: Mr. Fenton is an expert, and he expects us to follow his instructions—"

"Exactly?"

"You get the idea."

"But, isn't there a lot to remember? I was told that each of you buyers handles nearly 400 items; is that right?"

"Yes, to both questions. Weren't you told about the book of instructions, where all the individual tasks are listed? Mr. Fenton wrote it himself."

"Book? No, I don't remember that. Do you have one?"

"No, there's only one and Mr. Fenton keeps that in his office. Now don't get the wrong idea. When I came here for this job, Mr. Fenton called me in to his office and went over all of it with me. If I have a question, I can always go in and ask him."

The Purchasing Department

The purchasing department consisted essentially of three areas: The industrial accounts (IA), the commercial accounts—industrial (CAI), and the commercial accounts—non-industrial (CANI). Each area was under one buyer (see Exhibit 2). Generally, the three buyers shared the same workload, although the 1200 line items the company carried were not neatly divided into three equal parts. Computer programs provided the basis for decisions on what and when to purchase, through a variety of printouts. Among these were the Recommended Buy Report, the Expedite Report, the On-hand Report, the Daily Receiving, the Stock Adjustment, and other reports on special items prepared on different time periods, such as weekly, biweekly, or monthly. The Recommended Buy Report contained specific quantities to be purchased on a standard pack basis; it also reflected recent customer usage rates by company identification number, word description, and the like. The quantities to be purchased were computed automatically in accordance with a special economic order quantity (EOQ) formula, which was updated periodically.

Pointing to the EOQ column on this report, Fenton declared to the buyers, "This is what you will order."

Orders were placed by telephone and confirmed by an appropriate purchase order (PO). Subsequently produced by the computer, these POs were based on punched card input from a form completed by the buyer. Occa-

sionally the buyers were expected to adjust item quantities to be ordered to constitute a full railcar load to minimize freight charges. A special computer program was called upon to assist the buyers in making such a determination, yet buyers did alter some computer recommendations on their own initiative. Another important duty for each buyer was to record and keep track of the increasingly frequent price changes that suppliers submitted.

Fenton also expected each buyer to seek special promotions from as many suppliers as possible and as often as feasible. A promotion involved a limited period when price reductions provided an incentive to increase sales.

Concerning a typical day for these varied tasks, one buyer commented, "I estimate that I spend about 50 percent of my time placing orders, with follow-up delivery status accounting for 10 percent of my total effort. The balance of my time is consumed by trouble-shooting for 20 percent and about the same for administrative demands."

When asked how much time was devoted to studying the market for his commodity area, he replied: "I don't have time for that."

On the subject of personnel turnover, this same buyer remarked, "Well, there's been a lot. For example, shortly before I came here,

EXHIBIT 2
Purchasing department organization

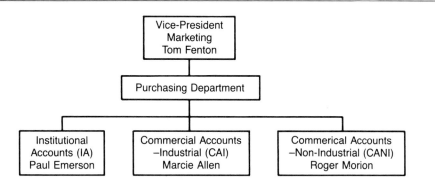

and I guess that was about nine months ago, there was Peggy on CANI, Charley on CAI (he pronounced it "Kay") and Mary on IA. Mary quit and was replaced by Stella. That didn't seem to work out, so Rozella switched from being a secretary to IA buyer when Stella quit. A few weeks later, Rozella was fired and I found myself as the new IA buyer. I tried to pick up the pieces as best I could, and. . . . Well, I'm still here."

"Did the department settle down after that?"

"No, it didn't. Three months after I came, why, Charley—he was the CAI buyer—was fired. About the same time, Peggy quit and Marcie became the CAI buyer. Oh, yes, Roger was hired for Peggy's job. We had to juggle things around to cover all the accounts, and finally I ended up as the IA buyer. Thinking about all the time involved when this was happening, I'd say that it was from May to October in 1978."

The New Chief

This was the period when Fenton was in charge of the purchasing department. These circumstances led Sterling to seek a change by asking Pete Brown if he would assume the responsibility for purchasing in addition to his position as the sales manager.

I need someone who gets along with people, Sterling mused, and certainly Pete fills that bill.

So he called Tom Fenton to his office and told him that he needed him to work on some high priority matters that only Fenton could handle, and further, that Sterling believed Brown could step in and assume Fenton's purchasing role. While Fenton may not have entirely agreed that Brown could handle the complexities of that department, he acquiesced to Sterling's urging.

Accordingly, Brown moved into the front office in purchasing and assumed the full responsibility for it. As he viewed what he thought was a chaotic situation in the department, he decided to bring in Ron from his sales department to take over the IA desk. Since this position already was occupied by a buyer named Paul Emerson who had been in that function for approximately five months—the fourth in somewhat less than one year—Brown realized that initially this move would not ease the unrest that had prevailed for so long. Nevertheless, he considered that this action should be taken.

After he summoned Paul to his office, Brown said, "Paul, I need to talk to you about the IA desk which you've been breaking in on for the past several months. I've been observing your work, and it seems to me that you are having more trouble with it than you should. There still are instances where you order too much of an item on the one hand, and too little of something else on the other. Perhaps it's because you've never been a buyer before. . . . I don't know. . . ."

"Could you give me some specific example?"

"Of course I can, but I don't think it's necessary to repeat what I've discussed with you before on the cups and plates. . . . Let's just say that the job is too much for you at this time," Brown hastened to add as he noticed a puzzled look spreading across Paul's face. "So, I've decided to make a change and move you over to CANI, which is not so complicated. I'm going to bring Ron in from sales to work the IA desk."

"Ron Fisher? Has he ever been a buyer?"

"What? . . . Now, Paul, I want you to spend some time with Ron helping him get adjusted as fast as possible . . . and, of course, you'll also be handling the CANI desk at the same time. I don't think you'll have any real trouble. Okay, Paul?"

"If that's what you want."

The New Look

For a few months matters in general appeared to improve in the department, and the buyers apparently were more content than under Fenton's control. The working atmosphere gradually became quite relaxed, almost gay at times. At least this was the impression gained by some employees in other, nearby offices. One, perhaps envious, worker was overheard exclaiming, "Why, that place has turned into a —— country club."

Unfortunately, performance in the department did not match Sterling's expectations. His concern deepening as reports continued to reach him that the buyers were more interested in their own well-being than in doing a better job, Sterling began to press Brown for details. At this juncture, Sterling's suspicions grew that discipline was overly lax and that Brown tended to let too many details get by him. The deeper Sterling probed into the circumstances developing in the purchasing department, the more acute was his feeling that Brown really was not cut out for that job.

What appeared at the outset to be a welcome change when Brown moved to purchasing, now was turning sour. Initially successful in curbing the anxieties of the buyers under Fenton, which had adversely affected their performance, Brown apparently was more pleasant than demanding. Sterling was convinced that it was imperative that the buyers recognize immediately that they had to knuckle down—or else. The inventory situation remained in an unsatisfactory state: too many dollars tied up with dormant stock concurrently with too many out-of-stock items. After discussing this state of affairs further with Brown, Sterling's anxiety deepened that the purchasing task needed more attention.

The Asgard Petition

When the petition first came around, I'd worked at Asgard Advertising for three months. A large, national retail firm, Asgard has stores across the country and is renowned for its high-quality, fashion-forward merchandise. Before this, I was employed in the Asgard credit department for three years—a part-time position I held as I worked on my B.A.

I came out of the university with a B.A. in English/Creative Writing and a lot of disillusionment—with Asgard, with the idea of graduate school. I wasn't sure what I wanted to do, and I was even less sure I'd find a job, at least not one I'd enjoy—nowadays, an English degree doesn't mean much to a lot of employers. With this in mind, I'd planned to continue working part-time at Asgard after graduation; the pay was comparable to anything I expected to find, and I would have enough free time to work on my own writing. I wasn't really interested in taking on a lot of responsibility in the credit department or in getting involved with the company, although I'm certain if I'd shown any interest, my manager would have promoted me. But after three years, I'd seen how management worked there, and it just seemed too constricting; the last thing I wanted was to have to conform to someone else's rules, be under anyone's thumb—especially when I knew I didn't care much

about credit or retail or climbing the corporate ladder.

However, things happen. About a week after graduation, I heard about a position in advertising. On a whim, I decided to interview. And I got the job.

I didn't have any specific advertising experience and not much of a portfolio. In fact, I'm still not sure how I got them to hire me. But as it turned out (and to my great surprise!), I was a "natural." I caught on very quickly. I worked at a faster rate than most of the other writers, and I asked for extra work when I had completed my own. During the first few months, I was assigned several special projects usually reserved for people who'd been there a considerable time. My boss told me the executives really liked what I'd done. I became recognized as the top writer in the department. And I got my six month raise at three months—a 12 percent jump in salary!

In addition, the people were nice, creative—a fun, close-knit group. And the hours were terrific: we only worked 9:00 to 5:00, with an hour and a half as our *standard* lunch break. Plus, we had a great deal of flexibility in terms of vacation time, days off, sick leave, and so forth, and depending on the project, many people were able to work at home for two to three weeks at a time. There was no punch clock, no time card, no Big Brother watching. Somehow, I had landed a fun, "plush" job, and I was doing extraordinarily well at it. All things considered, the world looked very rosy indeed, and I made great plans for my future advancement in the company.

Of course, no person, or department, can stay on the upswing all the time. Soon after this period of Shangri-la, my boss called us together for our weekly meeting and announced that effective the following week, our hours would be changed to 8:30 to 5:30. The decision had been handed down by Marcia, one of the top executives, who felt this additional hour would allow us to be more efficient and less rushed during our busy seasons. Our salaries were not to be adjusted upwards for the extra hour.

Immediately, the department was in an uproar. Before we'd even gotten out the conference room door, I'd learned that "no one really liked Marcia anyway," and that she had a reputation for being a "puppet" for the other higher (and all male) executives. To say that people were upset would be an understatement—all afternoon, our bosses bore the brunt of it, meeting with angry employees behind closed doors, soothing, discussing, explaining. However, most of them didn't seem to know much more than the rest of staff, and many didn't seem to be too happy with the decision either.

For the most part, people felt taken advantage of. Because the pay scale at Asgard Advertising was one of the lowest for advertising in the city, the shorter work day was seen by employees as both a justifiable and even expected perquisite. However, it soon became obvious that management didn't see it this way. Later that afternoon, when the situation had become its most unbearable, Marcia called us together for a meeting. We quickly gathered in the hall, whereupon Marcia, dressed to kill in her fanciest Asgard suit, stepped out of her office, stalked over to the reception area table, and *climbed up on top of it*. From this unique vantage point, she lec-

tured us for half an hour on the merits of the proposed hours increase. In conclusion, she stated that in order to allow people to make arrangements for transportation, after work activities, and so on, the new hours would not be put into effect for another month. Her mind was made up on the issue, she added, although she would be willing to listen to any response we might have. And she avoided the salary issue completely.

At this point, I wasn't sure what to think. Marcia's table scene had disgusted me. And although I'm not usually one to follow the crowd, I wasn't sure I liked Marcia very much either, especially after such a display. Most of all, because I knew how management sometimes went at Asgard, I wasn't at all sure that Marcia *wasn't* a "puppet." The whole thing left a bad taste in my mouth, and I was determined not to get involved.

Two weeks later, a petition started around. Apparently, people had met after hours, feeling angry and misused. Many were "old-timers" in advertising and felt doubly put upon—the "I've been here 'x' years, how can they do this to *me*?" thing.

In essence, the petition stated that it wasn't necessary to add an extra hour; we already produced good work, and we produced it on time. More importantly, the petition stated that any increase in hours should be accompanied by a relative increase in pay. Anything less was essentially the same as either a reduction of salary, a devaluation of an annual raise, or both.

The petition was passed around "secretly," although most of the managers knew about it and half even signed it. A spokesperson accompanied the petition at every stop; most were old-timers, and all were extremely persuasive and not beyond putting a lot of pressure on whomever they were trying to convince. The person who spoke with me was a man I respected a lot. Determined to stay out of it, however, I told him I didn't want to get involved, that I hadn't been there long enough to make such a decision. He disagreed quite vehemently, said I'd been there long enough to know what was what; certainly, I didn't think the hours increase was *right,* did I? I told him I'd think about it overnight (the petition was to be turned in the following evening) and let him know. But I knew I wasn't going to sign, no matter what I thought; I was just too new, and it would be just too foolish. I talked it over with a friend who'd been hired about the same time I had. We both agreed with what the petition said, but still felt we shouldn't sign it.

The next day, my spokesperson came by for my answer. I told him that while I agreed in principle, I'd still decided not to sign. He looked pretty disgusted at that, and I guess I didn't blame him. I've always hated the wishy-washy, the brown-noser. Besides, he was right—I *did* know what was what, and yet I wasn't strong enough to commit to it. I began feeling guilty for not supporting the people I worked with, many of whom by this time had become my friends, and for not having the guts to follow through with my own beliefs. In fact, I felt very hypocritical. I looked at the petition, brimming with signatures, and saw the names of all the people I liked and respected. What the hell, I thought, and signed it. And I felt a lot better. A little bit later, I spoke with my friend and found she'd done exactly the same thing.

These things always come back like a slap in the face. The next day, top management sent us each a copy of the petition, with our own signature circled in bright red ink. (If that isn't enough to put the fear of God in you, I don't know what is.) I stared at my copy, knowing the punishment was on its way; now, too late, I kicked myself for having gotten involved.

Rumors flew. One man told me he'd heard we were all going to be fired. Another disagreed—said we would be fired later, during the slow season. Yet another said only those managers who had signed would be fired. After lunch, we were individually summoned to our manager's office. Two women later told me they were so upset they cried. I didn't. Manager or no, I like to think I have some self-respect. I'd made a corporate mistake, perhaps, but in the big scheme of things, I'd really just stood up for my own beliefs. Of course, as one of the newer members on staff, and especially after getting such a good raise, I was worried about getting fired. But at this point, there was nothing I could do to change the situation. And while I was feeling far from cocky, my three months at Asgard Advertising had shown me that I had considerable talent, enough so I didn't have to worry *too much* about getting another job.

I think I handled myself fairly well in my boss's office. He asked why I'd signed the petition, and I told him. I didn't get defensive, and I didn't blubber. In return, he didn't threaten to fire me or tell me how stupid I'd been. He did say he felt the petition was unprofessional. I agreed, but added that Marcia *had* asked for a response, and this was one of the few ways we had of making our feelings known without being singled out. Looking back, I realize how lucky I am to have such a wonderful boss: instead of getting on a high horse or spouting off the company line, he listened. And we talked it out as two adults rather than boss and employee. By the end of the meeting, neither of us had changed our view much. But I think he got a clearer picture of me, and of how much I value my independence. And I left our meeting with a great deal of respect for him.

Things simmered down. Marcia went on vacation, and we waited. Marcia came back, had a long talk with the spokespersons who had initiated the petition, and the event slowly faded. The new hours began, and we went willingly, like cattle. Any resentment was repressed; people felt lucky to have their jobs.

Now, months later, I realize Marcia probably couldn't have given in to our demands; to do so would have been the same as admitting mutiny. But I still don't think she handled the situation very well. In fact, I don't think she handled it. She just waited it out, first putting it off for a month, then (with the exception of her talk with the spokespersons), she ignored it. I think her mind was indeed made up from the beginning. It's possible she was just following orders from higher up, and she was as stuck as the rest of us. But her table dramatics and general lack of concern didn't show this. I think by handling the situation the way she did, Marcia built up a lot of resentment that hadn't been there before (or at least hadn't been given a target for expression). Mostly, I think Marcia set a precedent that management didn't listen—not even if 90 percent of the staff held the same view.

Soon after the new hours were put into effect, several top people left, most of them old-timers. I guess they'd just had it. They were replaced, as they always are. But no matter how smooth the surface looks, those who stay remember. And I know from my own experience at Asgard, both in my part-time position and in my job at advertising, I don't want to be in management there. It's just too much headache, too much dealing with people with an inflated sense of self. And while I'm glad to say I still get along with my own boss, I can't pass Marcia in the hall without feeling frustrated, knowing that she, and people like her, have the power to either raise me up or fire me, subjectively, without a moment's notice. Maybe it's like this everywhere. Maybe it's just me. But I don't think so. And while I'm glad I didn't get fired, I'm not at all sorry I signed the petition. Because somewhere along the line a certain integrity needs to be maintained. And somewhere along the line, Marcia needs to get down from her table.

PART FIVE
Change and Conflict

Village Inn

T he Village Inn, located on Bermuda Boulevard in San Diego, was only a few blocks away from San Diego State University and was within several miles of some of California's largest tourist attractions. Visiting lecturers, speakers, professors interviewing for jobs, and people attending conferences at the university resulted in a considerable amount of business for Village Inn.

The Inn was also near a concentrated area of light and heavy industry. The largest shopping mall in San Diego was under construction across the street from the Inn. A relatively new VA hospital and the University Community Hospital were both located within one mile. The Inn's very favorable locational features, together with the fact that it was a franchise of a major national chain, had made it a profitable investment. During the past 12 months, the Inn had an average occupancy rate of between 65 and 70 percent, some 15 or more percentage points above the break-even occupancy rate of 50 percent.

Although the Village Inn had only modest competition from other hotel or motel facilities in the immediate vicinity, a new Travelodge Inn was under construction next door. The other closest competitors were nearly three miles away at the intersection of Bermuda Blvd. and Interstate 8. Village Inn offered a full range of

This case was prepared by Diana Johnston, Russ King, and Professor Jay T. Knippen, the University of South Florida. Reprinted by permission of Jay T. Knippen.

services to its guests, including a restaurant and bar. The new Travelodge next door was going to have just a coffee shop. Insofar as its restaurant/bar business was concerned, the Village Inn's strongest competitor was the popular-priced University Restaurant, two blocks away. Village Inn did not consider its own food service operations to be in close competition with the area's fast-food franchises or with higher-priced restaurants.

Ownership of Village Inn

Mr. Johnson, a native of Oregon, opened the first Village Inn in San Diego in 1958. Since that time, he had shared ownership in 15 other Village Inns, several which were in the San Diego area. He opened the Bermuda Blvd. Inn in October 1966. Prior to his focusing on the motel and restaurant business, Mr. Johnson had owned and operated a furniture store and a casket manufacturing plant. A suggestion from a business associate in Oregon influenced his decision to seek out Village Inn franchises and get into the motel business. In some of his Village Inn locations, Mr. Johnson leased out the restaurant operations; however, the restaurant and bar at the Bermuda Blvd. Village Inn was not leased out. Mr. Johnson felt that because the occupancy rate at this location was so favorable it was more profitable to own and operate these facilities himself.

Management of the Inn

Mr. Johnson had employed Ms. Deeks as the innkeeper and manager of the entire operation. She had worked in Village Inns for the past seven and one-half years. Previously, Ms. Deeks had done administrative work for Davis General Hospital and before that had been employed as a photo lab technician for two years. Her experience in the motel/restaurant business included working for several restaurants and lounges for five years as a cocktail waitress just prior to joining Village Inns.

Ms. Deeks stated that her main reason for going to work for Village Inns was because she felt there was more money to be made as a waitress than anything else she had tried. Her formal education for her present position of innkeeper consisted of a three-week training course at the Home Office Training Center, in Louisville, Kentucky, and one-week refresher courses each year at the Training Center.

Recently, the assistant innkeeper had been promoted and transferred to another location. Both Mr. Johnson and Ms. Deeks agreed that there was a pressing need to fill the vacancy quickly. It was the assistant innkeeper's function to supervise the restaurant/bar area, and this was the area which always presented the toughest problems to management. Unless the food was well prepared and the service was prompt, guests were quick to complain. Poor food service caused many of the frequent visitors to the area to prefer to stay at other motels. Moreover, it was hard to attract and maintain a sizable lunchtime clientele without having well-run restaurant facilities. With so many restaurant employees to supervise, menus to prepare, and food supplies to order, it was a constant day-to-day struggle to keep the restaurant operating smoothly and, equally important, to see that it made a profit. Ms. Deeks, with all of her other duties and re-

sponsibilities, simply did not have adequate time to give the restaurant/bar enough close supervision by herself.

While searching for a replacement, Mr. Johnson by chance happened to see a feature article in the *Village Inn Magazine,* a monthly publication of the Village Inns of America chain—copies of which were placed in all of the guest rooms of the Inns, describing the operation of a successful Village Inn in nearby San Bernardino. The article caught Mr. Johnson's attention because it described how the Inn at San Bernardino had gained popularity and acclaim from guests because of the good food and fast service provided by the head chef of the restaurant operations. After showing the article to Ms. Deeks, Mr. Johnson wasted no time in getting in touch with the head chef of that Inn, Mr. Bernie, and persuading him to assume the new role of restaurant/bar manager for the Bermuda Blvd. Village Inn in San Diego.

Food Service Facilities and Layout

Exhibit I depicts the arrangement of the lobby area and food service facilities at the Inn. A brief description of the restaurant/bar area follows.

Restaurant   The restaurant itself consists of a dining room which seated 74 people, a coffee shop which seated 62 persons, and a bar which seated 35 people. The Inn's banquet facilities were just behind the main dining room and could seat 125 people.

The essential role of the restaurant and bar area was to provide pleasant and convenient facilities for the Inn's guests. The contractual franchise agreements with the national chain required all owners to provide these services in conjunction with the overnight accommodations. There were periodic inspections of the

EXHIBIT 1

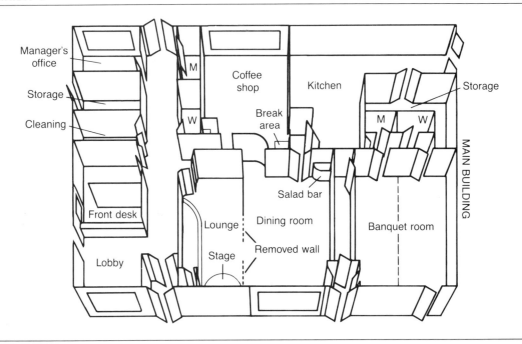

facilities by a representative from Village Inn's corporate office. Village Inn required each franchisee to comply with minimum standards for its food service facilities in an effort to promote comparability and ensure attractiveness. Restaurant services were to be available to guests from 6:30 A.M. until 11:00 P.M.

Coffee Shop   The coffee shop was open from 6:30 A.M. to 11:00 A.M. to serve breakfast to motel guests. At 11:00 A.M. these facilities were closed and the main dining area was opened. The coffee shop was occasionally used beyond scheduled hours to serve customers for lunch and dinner when there was an overflow from the dining area. Tables in both the coffee shop and the dining room were decorated and set uniformly.

Dining Room   The dining area was open from 11:00 A.M. until 11:00 P.M. It was located next to the lounge and was physically sepa-

rated from the coffee shop by a wall. The lunch and dinner offerings featured a salad bar along with menu items which were somewhat uniform with other Village Inns and which were prescribed by the franchise agreement. However, menu deviations were allowed if approved by corporate representatives from Village Inn's central office.

Bar   The bar, separated from the dining room by a partition, was open for business from 10:00 A.M. until 1:00 A.M. It had tables and booths, and customers who preferred to do so could have their food served to them in the bar area. A small dance floor was located in front of the entertainer stage near the front window; a juke box furnished music when there was no live entertainment. A small bar stockroom was located at one end of the bar counter. The cash register area was centrally located to receive payments from customers in all three areas—dining room, coffee shop, and bar.

Kitchen The kitchen facilities, located beside the coffee shop and dining room, had a stainless steel counter at the entrance door from the restaurant area. It was here that waitresses turned orders in to the cooks and that the cooks served the orders up to the waitresses. The cooking area was located in the center of the room and sinks were located along the sides of the kitchen.

Restaurant Operations

As was to be expected, customers' activity in the restaurant area fluctuated widely. Busy periods were generally at the traditional meal hours, but the peak load at any given mealtime period often varied by as much as an hour from one day to the next. At lunchtime, for example, customers sometimes seemed to come all at once, while on other days the arrival times were more evenly distributed throughout the 11:30 A.M. to 1:30 P.M. interval. Experience had shown that these peaks were hard to anticipate and that the staff had to be prepared for whatever occurred. Moreover, on Monday, Tuesday, Wednesday, and Thursday evenings, the customers were mostly business people, sales representatives, and university visitors, whereas on weekends there were more family travelers. Because of the Inn's location, its clientele consisted somewhat more of the former than the latter.

The Inn's restaurant business was also subject to some seasonal fluctuations. There were always a certain number of people who spent the winter in Southern California to escape the harsh northern and Canadian winters: these included not only winter tourists but also the "Canadian Snow Birds" who came to Southern California to work in the late fall and returned to Canada in March or April. In addition, the Inn's business picked up noticeably during the June graduation exercises at San Diego State University and during the week when the fall term opened. By and large, the daily fluctuations were harder to predict than the seasonal fluctuations.

Restaurant Staffing

Because of the alternating between peak periods and slack periods, the employees in the food service area tended to work together, take breaks together, and eat their meals together. In commenting on the kind of people who tended to work in hotel-motel operations, Ms. Deeks indicated that employees were typically gregarious and were there because they wanted to be. They had to contend with an uneven work pace, a low wage scale (often no more than the minimum wage), and irregular working hours. Since waitresses often earned only a token wage ($0.75 to $1 per hour) and relied mainly on tips for their income, they could not afford many "slow days" or "bad days" at work. Their livelihood and degree of service were dependent upon how well they greeted customers, a friendly smile, prompt service, and, in general, an ability to make customers feel satisfied with the attention they received. When the food was cold or ill-prepared or the service less than expected, customers left smaller tips and the waitresses' disgruntlement carried over to the kitchen staff, the hostess, and the busboys. But even more disruptive than the loss of tips were the customers who complained directly to the Inn's management; if this occurred frequently, then the pressure and anxiety felt by the restaurant staff increased noticeably. Ms. Deeks noted that people who could not adjust to the tempo and temperament of the restaurant business usually did not stay in it long. She noted further that it was extremely difficult to "standardize" the human service aspects of the restaurant business and that trying to attract and keep a good, experienced food service staff was a challenging task.

Ms. Deeks supplied the following job descriptions of the restaurant staff; these descriptions, however, came from her thoughts and perceptions and had never been formally set forth in writing to the Inn's employees:

Bartender   Cut up fruit for drinks, wash glasses, serve counter drinks, clean behind bar, stock liquor and mixes, stock bar, fill room service orders, ring up checks, balance register, and help with inventory.

Hostess/Cashier   Take room service orders, seat guests, deliver menus, direct seating, supervise waitresses and busboys, perform any functions within their prescribed area to speed service, check out customers from dining area, check out register, file cash register receipts, and assign stations.

Waitress   Take food orders, deliver order to kitchen, pick up and serve orders, serve food and beverages, and perform any function that speeds service as directed by the hostess.

Busboy   Bus tables, put clean place settings on tables, clean dining rooms, stock supplies, take ice to all areas, get supplies for cooks, help set up banquets, deliver room service orders, help with maintenance, and perform any function that will speed service as directed by the hostess and manager.

Dishwasher   Wash dishes, pots, and pans, and sweep and mop floors.

Cook   Prepare meals, schedule meals for prep cook, assist management in stock orders, receive food supplies, supervise and direct kitchen help, and assist management in menu changes. Report to management any changes or problems that occur.

Prep cook   Prepare all food that the cook needs for the dinner and evening meals. Assist cook in any meal preparation that is necessary to expedite service to guests. Inform cook of any problems that need attention and help cook see that facilities are clean at all times.

Breakfast cook   Open the kitchen in the morning. Prepare breakfast food for motel guests. Provide information necessary to maintain in-stock supplies.

Mr. Bernie

When Mr. Bernie arrived to assume his new duties as restaurant/bar manager, he wasted no time in demanding and receiving total obedience from the personnel under his direction. He made it clear that he would not tolerate insubordination and that the consequence would be immediate discharge. Although Mr. Bernie stayed in his new job less than three months (from January to March), he nonetheless created an almost instantaneous climate of ill will and hatred with his subordinates. The intense dislike for Mr. Bernie was voiced by nearly every employee. One example of this was a statement by Elaine, the day hostess/cashier who had been employed in this capacity for the past two and one-half years: "I enjoy my job because I like people. But Mr. Bernie was something else! I generally do not use this term in my vocabulary, but Mr. Bernie was a bastard from the day he arrived until the day he left."

Mr. Bernie's unpopularity was further brought out by a busboy's impromptu comment. Elaine was trying to possibly justify Mr. Bernie's temperament by pointing out that he was not of American nationality. Unable to recall his nationality she inquired of a nearby busboy if he could remember. The busboy immediately and sincerely replied, "He crawled out from under a rock."

Mr. Bernie spent considerable time trying to impress upon his staff the "right way" (his way) of accomplishing tasks (see Exhibits 2 and 3). Most of the employees resented Mr. Bernie's close supervision. And one veteran

EXHIBIT 2
Memo 1 from Mr. Bernie to food service staff

People,

Please help keep the floor clean.

If you drop something, pick it up.

Wipe table off in a trash can.

If you spill something the mops and brooms are outside.

It's no fun scrubbing the floor Saturday, and if you don't believe it, be here Saturday night at 11:00 P.M.

Mr. "B"

---

employee and waitress, describing her resentment, said, "No one really needs to supervise us, especially the way Mr. Bernie stood over us. Usually the hostess is the supervisor, but all the old girls know what they are doing and everyone does their job."

Although an intense dislike for Mr. Bernie was foremost in the minds of the employees, he did manage to make a number of improvements and innovations. Physical changes became obvious within all departments under his authority. In the kitchen a general cleanup campaign was instituted, an order spindle was added, and new oven equipment installed. In the coffee shop and restaurant, new silverware, china, and glasses were purchased, and the menu was improved and complemented by the use of a salad bar. *Explicit* work duties were written and verbally defined to all employees under Mr. Bernie.

Mr. Bernie separated the cashier/hostess function into two distinct jobs. The cashier was confined to the cash register station and given instructions as to the duties she was to perform in that area. The hostess was given instructions to greet people, seat them, and

supply menus. When Mr. Bernie was absent, he instructed the hostess to see that the waitresses and busboys carried out their jobs efficiently and effectively. According to Gay, one of the two day hostesses:

> When Mr. Bernie was here I never had any employee problems. Waitresses and busboys did what I asked. But now if we have a busboy absent or we are crowded, some of the waitresses inform me they will not bus tables. Today there's no one in charge of anything. We need more employees here. It is always better to have more help than not enough. That's one thing Mr. Bernie did, he doubled the help the day he came.

The changes which Mr. Bernie instituted regarding the waitresses were significant in several aspects. All waitresses were required to wear fitted uniforms. This necessitated their driving across town for a uniform fitting. Mr. Bernie's detailed scrutinizing consisted of specific instructions on how to serve customers and which station locations each waitress would serve. He even went so far as to show them how to wrap the silverware and the napkins, and gave explicit instructions to veteran

EXHIBIT 3
Memo 2 from Mr. Bernie to food service staff

March 11

TO ALL FOOD AND BEVERAGE EMPLOYEES:

I wish to thank each and every one of you for the very good job you have done in the past two weeks. The service has greatly improved on both shifts. There has been a better customer/employee relationship, but there is a long way to go yet. We are nearing the end of our winter season so it is most important to all of us that we concentrate on more service in order to obtain a local year-round business. Appearance, neatness, and good conduct on the floor will obtain this, along with good food.

A waitress and busboy are like salesmen. The hostess/cashier can determine the quality of service in this organization.

I expect my waitresses and busboys at the cashier stand only when getting a ticket or paying a check.

I smoke myself—probably more than the rest of you put together. Your service area is beginning to look like a cigarette factory. I do not expect people to give up their smoking habit, but I do expect them to adhere to the rules and regulations of Village Inn, Inc., and those of the health department, "No Smoking on Premises." I would not like to enforce this law.

In the last two weeks I have walked into the operation after a busy breakfast or dinner and found everyone sitting around the first three booths of the cafe. I do not say it cannot be used, but when I find no waitresses on either floor day or night and customers have to call for service because waitresses are off the floor, I believe each waitress and busboy on all shifts should ask themselves one thing: what kind of service would I like if I were a guest? There is only one thing I know, in this part of California when the tourist is gone, half of the employees are worked on a part-time basis, which is not good on anyone's pocketbook. Therefore, I say let's not be second best but let's be first.

With regard to employees taking their meal breaks, I do not wish to schedule them but I cannot have everyone eating at once. Busboys will eat one at a time.

Thank you once again for your good performance.

Mr. "B"

waitresses on how to fill out the order tickets.

Mr. Bernie had the wall between the dining room and the bar taken down. He then brought in an entertainer who supplied dinner music for both the restaurant and bar guests. Today, the waitresses are getting some dysfunctional effects from this innovation; according to one:

> Mr. Bernie brought in an organ player. While this was conducive to a more pleasant dining atmosphere, the organist was not good enough to keep the people beyond their meal. But now that Mr. Bernie is gone, our new entertainer is causing some serious problems. For example, last night I had a family of five sit at a table in my station for two and a half hours after their dinner. If people won't leave and they won't buy drinks, I can't make tips.

Mr. Bernie instilled an atmosphere of insecurity and day-to-day doubt in the minds of the employees as to how long they could weather the barrage of innovation and directives. To some, just remaining on the job became a challenge in itself. Elaine (the day hostess) phrased it in this manner:

> I have been employed with the Village Inn for almost two and one-half years. I have worked most of my life and have never felt insecure in any of my jobs. The last job I held was a swimming instructor for ten years with the Academy of Holy Names in San Diego. The reason I had to leave there was because of the change in the educational background requirement which called for a college degree.
>
> My children are all college graduates with highly responsible positions. They achieved this by hard work. I instilled this in their minds because I am a hard worker. But when Mr. Bernie was here, I experienced for the first time in my life the feeling of not knowing from one day to the next if my job would be there when I came to work. What few personnel he failed to drive away, he fired.

Linda, who was a bartender in the lounge area, commented further on Mr. Bernie's supervisory tactics:

> Bernie was a rover. When he walked into an area, including my area, the bar, he could not stand to see someone not involved with busy work. He even made me clean under the bar on the customer's side. I'm not a maid and I often wanted to tell him so. But the way he was hiring and firing employees, I just kept my mouth closed and did as he told me. My experiences with Mr. Bernie were nothing compared to the relationship he had with the busboys. From the bar he would sneak around and watch them in the dining area. If they did anything the least bit out of line, he would call them aside and give them lectures that could last for half an hour. He really treated the busboys like the scum of the earth. When the boys did get a break, they would come over to the bar and get a coke and ice. You know, he even started charging them 25 cents for that!

Sam, a cook hired by Mr. Bernie, offered a slightly different view of Mr. Bernie:

> My wife was working here as a hostess, and I used to bring her to work every day. One day I came in with her and for some reason they were short of help in the kitchen. They needed a dishwasher. I was sitting in the coffee shop and Mr. Bernie walked over and asked me if I could use a job. I had been interested in cooking ever since I was in the Navy. There are two things you can do in your spare time in the Navy . . . drink and chase women, or find a hobby. I found a hobby, which was cooking. On my two days off I used to go down to the galley and help the cooks. There I learned everything I know today. When I got out of the service I worked as a prep cook in a restaurant in Pennsylvania for a year or so. My real specialty is soups, though. Anyway, I had been a dishwasher here for about two days when the cook walked off the job after three years of service here. Mr. Bernie came in and asked how I'd like to be the new cook and here I

am today. Mr. Bernie really taught me a lot. He taught me that a restaurant has three things it must give a customer: service, good food, and a pleasing environment to dine. If you have these three, customers will return.

I've spent most of my working career in the automotive business doing such things as driving trucks. But I'm really into this cooking thing. Mr. Bernie taught me that about 50 percent of the customers who come in and order from the menu have no idea what they are ordering. The menu is too complicated. The customer doesn't know what he thinks he ordered and what you think he ordered. Another thing that fascinates me is trying to think like the customer. His definition of rare, medium, and well done is altogether different from my idea of how it should be. One addition by Mr. Bernie was the salad bar. This is a tremendous help to my job. If the waitress can get to the customer before they go to the salad bar and take their order, this gives me plenty of lead time to be sure the meal will be cooked right and served in the attractive manner that Mr. Bernie was so particular about. This lead time is especially important on those days that we are unusually busy. For example, I have prepared as many as 250 meals on some days and as few as 40 on others.

The employees who left or were dismissed by Mr. Bernie included two hostesses, two waitresses (one had an employment record at the Inn that dated back five years), and two busboys. Two of the personnel that Mr. Bernie fired have since returned to their old jobs. One of the waitresses who subsequently was rehired described her reason for leaving as follows:

I really enjoy being a waitress and have been here for about five years. The work isn't really too hard and the pay is good. I took all the "directives" I could take from Mr. Bernie! A week before he left, I gave my resignation and took a vacation. When I returned, I learned of his departure and here I am again. I'm really glad things have worked out as they did.

Ms. Deeks' opinion of Mr. Bernie's performance was one of general dissatisfaction with the way he handled his dealings with employees:

Mr. Bernie was highly trained, but he was an introvert who stood over his subordinates and supervised everything they did. Cooks are a rare breed of people all to themselves. The help situation has changed greatly in the past few years. It used to be that you could give orders and tell people what they were supposed to do. Now, you have to treat them with "kid gloves" or they'll just quit and get a job down the street. This problem is particularly true with cooks. They are very temperamental and introverted and they expect to be treated like prima donnas.

Mr. Johnson and I really tried to work with Mr. Bernie during his 90-day trial period. We knew that terminating him without a replacement would be hard on us, but we had no choice. We are now without a restaurant/bar manager or assistant innkeeper. We have been looking for a replacement, but finding a person that is knowledgeable in both the hotel and restaurant management is something of a chore.

Conditions after Mr. Bernie's Departure

Since Mr. Bernie had departed, the restaurant personnel were in general agreement that their operation was understaffed. Often guests were seated in both the dining area and coffee shop waiting to be served; even though the waitresses were apparently busy, many customers experienced waits of 20 to 30 minutes. Elaine, one of the two hostesses, explained the lack of prompt service as follows:

The coffee shop is supposed to take care of the guests until 11 A.M. and then the restaurant part is to be opened. Mr. Bernie handled the situation differently than we do now. When he was here he would not open the dining hall in the morning no matter how crowded the coffee shop was. I *can remember mornings when people were lined into the hallway and all the way outside the front door. I guess he knew two girls and two busboys could not handle two rooms.*

But today we handle the situations differently. If the coffee shop gets crowded or we have many dirty tables we open up both rooms. This really makes it hard on the girls trying to serve both rooms. What we generally have when this happens is poor service to all concerned and consequently some guests leave unhappy and without tipping the waitresses.

Ralph, a busboy, indicated the problem was not exclusively felt in the restaurant only. He seemed to feel the lack or absence of a manager was the primary problem:

Ms. Deeks just can't run this operation by herself. It is physically impossible for her to be here seven days a week from 6:30 A.M. until 11:00 P.M. and manage the kitchen, restaurant, bar, coffee shop, front desk, maid service, and maintenance crew all at the same time.

Some of the employees perceived their duties and functions differently. For instance, the restaurant's two day hostesses alternated work shifts. Elaine would seat customers, give them their menu, take beverages to customers to help out the waitresses, help out busing tables when it was very busy, and have very little to say in supervising the waitresses and busboys. On the other hand, the other day hostess, Gay, would seat customers and give them menus but would not do what she perceived to be the duties of waitresses and busboys. Instead, she exercised supervisory authority over these personnel, and when they were not able to get everything done, she would try to find out why not, rather than doing the job herself.

There were similar discrepancies in the ways the waitresses and busboys performed their duties. In some cases, waitresses would help busboys clear tables during overcrowded periods and busboys would also help out the waitresses by bringing water and coffee to the people who were waiting to be served. On the other hand, some of the waitresses, particularly those who had been employed for some time, felt that it was the busboys' responsibility to clear tables and would not lift a finger to help them. In these instances the busboys did not go out of their way to help the waitresses.

Gene, the other bartender, offered yet another view of the Inn's problems:

You know, I could tell management a few things about the restaurant business if they asked me. I knew from the first day Mr. Bernie arrived that he wouldn't work out. But Mr. Bernie is not the only problem they had. One of the biggest problems they have with this restaurant is in the banquets they have. We have a luncheon here every week with such clubs as the Sertoma, Kiwanis, and the like. Their luncheons start at noon and last until 1:30 or so. Have you ever noticed how they park outside? Well, I'll tell you they park all over the front parking lot and when local people drive by they assume our restaurant is full and go on down the street. These businessmen tie up most of our help and yet the dining room may be empty. These banquet people don't buy drinks with lunch like the local businessmen do who take clients out to lunch and often have a bar bill bigger than their restaurant checks. There's only one successful way to have a banquet business and that's not next to your dining room. If the banquet room was on the opposite side of the restaurant, then it would be okay.

Employee Training

The Village Inn provided a minimal amount of job training for employees with the exception of the management staff. The contractual agreement between franchise owners and Village Inns of America required all innkeepers, assistant innkeepers, and restaurant managers to attend the Home Office Training Center within a year of being hired. They also had to attend refresher courses on a yearly basis.

The restaurant personnel, in contrast, were given little job training. Instead, efforts were made to hire cooks, waitresses, and bartenders who had previous experience in the field. But in practice this policy was not always adhered to—as was exemplified by the way Linda became a bartender:

My training on the job was really short and sweet. Mr. Bernie came in one day and inquired, "How would you like to be a bartender?" At the same time he handed me a book on mixing drinks. I went home and studied it and "poof" I was a bartender.

Within a short time on the job I began getting a lot of help and advice from the waitresses who came over to the bar for drink orders. Sometimes when we do get a drink mixup they are very nice about it. I've even had people from other departments in the Inn to help me when the situation called for it. One night I had two ladies in here, one from the "crazy house" and the other her bodyguard. After a few "shooters" as they referred to the drinks, they asked for their check. They wanted to use a credit card instead of paying cash. This was not a problem but so I would get my tip I offered to carry the check and credit card to the front desk. Then they said I would cheat them on their bill once I was out of their sight. The front desk man heard the hassle and came in and escorted the ladies to the desk. This type of working together happens here all the time. Ms. Deeks, my boss, is really a nice person to work for. She doesn't come around very much, except if she needs information or to advise me about something.

Pay Scales

Management indicated that there was a shortage of good employees and that a low pay scale was characteristic of the restaurant business. Some of the employees expressed their awareness of this also.

LINDA (bartender): The pay scale is really low compared to other areas. My first job as a cocktail waitress in San Diego was in a dive downtown. They paid us 50 cents an hour plus tips, but the tips were lousy. Here they're paying 80 cents an hour plus tips which is somewhat better, but it's still way below the wages elsewhere. I really don't feel like I'm suited for this work, but I make more money at the bar than I did as a cocktail waitress.

GAY (hostess): I make $2 an hour here. With all the responsibility and experience I've had, the pay scale here compared to other parts of the country is deplorable. The busboys make almost as much as I do. They make $1.45 an hour plus 15 percent of the waitress's tips. Even though the pay scale is low, there is always overtime available to most of the employees who want it. My husband, who is a cook here, has worked 145 hours so far in this two-week pay period and he still has five more days to go.

Barb, one of the waitresses, further substantiated the availability of overtime by saying she got at least one hour overtime each day. She attributed the extra hours of overtime to the fact that the Inn's restaurant staff always seemed to have at least one person unexpectedly absent each day.

The problem in the restaurant was apparently compounded by the fact that it was operating with a minimum number of employees. Timmy, a busboy, indicated the wide range of activities expected of him and the other busboys:

We do everything; I clean and bus tables, sweep floors, and do janitorial work. I don't mean in just my area either. If the front desk needs a porter or runner, or if some type of room service is needed, I do that too. Mr. Bernie was really hard to work under, but he always confined us to restaurant duties. When he was here we didn't do all those jobs outside our area. Those duties were handled by a front desk porter. But I'd still rather have to do things all over the place than have to put up with Mr. Bernie.

Searching for Mr. Bernie's Replacement

In outlining her thoughts on trying to replace Mr. Bernie, Ms. Deeks stated:

I really had a good track record with personnel before Mr. Bernie came along. I strongly objected to his dictatorial supervision. In my experience I have learned employees perform their jobs better when left alone most of the time. I once tried to set up off-job activities for my employees. I reserved a room at the hotel for employees to meet together after working hours to play cards and drink coffee. Unfortunately the room was not used enough to merit keeping it on reserve. However, I still support functions that the employees suggest. We are presently sponsoring a bowling team that two of my waitresses belong to.

Most of the waitresses would rather work night shifts if they have their choice. Some of the girls have children and husbands who require them to be home at night. This balances the shifts real well. One reason I prefer to schedule the waitresses is because of peculiar problems which occur. For example: I have two extremely good waitresses that will not work on Saturdays and Sundays. The other waitresses do not know this and I feel if I were to allow the hostess to do the scheduling I would have some immediate personnel problems. To further complicate any benefits that might be derived by allowing the hostess to make out schedules, it would be necessary to reveal my awareness of the slower waitresses we have that I schedule on Saturday and Sunday—our slower business days.

I am really more active in management and day-to-day problems than most of the employees realize. Any significant changes in rules or policies are usually passed in the form of a written memo. I prefer to handle communication in this way for two reasons: first, there is no room for distortion, and second, it does not give the employees a feeling that they are being closely supervised. However, I do need an assistant to help me manage this place. I have verbally put the word out to other inns and motels. I'm really not concerned whether I get a restaurant manager or an assistant innkeeper so long as he has a knowledge of the food and beverage service. I'm really going to be cautious in the selection of this person as I don't want to jump out of the frying pan into the fire.

The absence of Mr. Bernie is now a well-known fact to all of the Inn's personnel. However, it was not known to everyone. One day, Mr. Trainor, a well-liked sales representative, walked into the restaurant and inquired, "Where is Mr. Bernie today?" There was a hush of silence and then, in answer to his own question, he replied, "Why is everyone smiling?"

Watson Siding

Bob Jackson picked up the phone.
"Yes?"
"Mr. Jackson, there's been a derailment at Watson Siding. The ten o'clock freight hit a split switch and jumped the track. It skidded over to the second main line, and the whole railroad's blocked!"

"Who is this?"

"I'm Baxter, the Yardmaster at Daggett."

"Baxter, you know that Watson Siding is in the Westport subdivision. The responsibility for the wreck belongs to Atkins at Westport. I handle only the road up to Juniper—and that's four miles this side of Watson Siding."

"Yes sir, but the wrecking crane for the Westport subdivision is tied up in the shops. Yours is out at Juniper, and it would only take a few minutes to run it down and clear the main line."

"Baxter, have you ever read the delegations of authorities to subdivision superintendents? It says very clearly that they will not, under any circumstances, move their assigned equipment to another subdivision without written authorization from the division superintendent."

"But, sir, Mr. Bagley is out of town!"

Reprinted by permission of Professor Richard N. Farmer, Graduate School of Business, Indiana University.

"Well, wait till he gets back in town! If you think I'm going to lose my job just because someone made a mistake in the Watson subdivision, you're crazy."

Baxter drew a deep breath. "Mr. Jackson, we have the whole railroad tied up. You have at least two trains waiting now for clearance because of the wreck. We have our crack passenger train tied up at Watson Siding now, and all the passengers are having a good look at a bunch of boxcars scattered all over the right of way. I'm sure that many of them ship by our railroad. Can you please send over your wrecking crane for a few minutes, so we can clear one track at least?"

"Confound it, Baxter, no!" Bob slammed down the phone. He remembered once in 1937, when he tried to help those people over in the Westport subdivision. He had sent them a wheel car, and as a result he had been suspended for a month. This time, he was not about to get in trouble. He sighed. The trouble with these young kids trying to run the show these days was that they just didn't realize how important it was to maintain proper channels.

He picked up the phone. "Jim, check on how many trains we'll delay if the line stays closed for a couple of days. It looks like we'll be sitting here for some time. Those Westport subdivision people are not very efficient."

Metrocenter Police Department

This case concerns the mission and operations of the police department in Metrocenter, Ohio, a city with population in excess of 400,000 people. To protect individual privacy, the names of the city and the people involved are disguised.

The Department and Its Mission

Two years ago, the elected city council of Metrocenter, reacting to strong public sentiment, redefined the mission and organization of the department. The mayor's office and the police commissioner's office had jointly assigned three people to gather facts on (1) crime and public safety in the city, and (2) the public's view of what city government should do in police operations. Statistics were gathered which showed, for example, a significant increase in both the number of deaths and of serious injuries in auto accidents. Mayor Boyle states,

In addition to facts of life about public safety in Metrocenter, our office did a complete public opinion survey. Particularly in elected office, one should not only find out what is factually happening, but also what the public thinks about it. We found that 72 percent of the people of Metrocenter believe that the rate of injury and death inflicted on innocent parties by careless use of automobiles is far too high. When we asked for examples of what the public means by

"injury to innocent parties," 68 percent of our people cited instances such as elderly or young pedestrians killed by drivers not obeying established rules (running red lights, using alcohol, speeding) or families hit in head-on collisions by careless drivers.

Organization of the Department

Metrocenter Police Department (see Exhibit 1) is organized into four main divisions, each headed by a Captain. The Traffic Division operates patrols for vehicle operation; the Detective Division investigates various crimes by use of non-uniformed officers; the Patrol Division uses uniformed officers to watch for and aid in preventing general infractions of the law; and the Police Administration Division provides administrative services such as telephone and radio communications, data processing and fingerprinting, booking policies and procedures, and budget.

Captain Terenzio, 38, head of the Traffic Division, has been with the Department 16 years. With a degree from Ohio State, he is highly respected by the Mayor, Commissioner, and fellow division heads for his technical knowledge of traffic patrol work. It is also common knowledge in the Department that the officers within the Traffic Division respect him. Lt. Baker says:

He knows a lot about traffic enforcement from practical experience and constant attendance at national training institutes, and he carries the banner for traffic when it comes to dealing with

EXHIBIT 1
Metrocenter Police Department

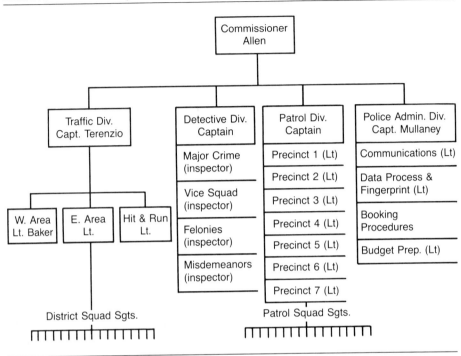

other divisions. For example, he succeeded in getting $200,000 for improving ready rooms where traffic patrolmen meet for their work in our three area headquarters. Other divisions also wanted money and there wasn't enough to go around. The old facilities were really bad on the men.

Captain Mullaney, 39, head of the Police Administration Division, has been with the Department eight years, having come to Commissioner Boyle's attention during nine years' service in the Kansas City Department. In the eyes of a large number of officers throughout all divisions, he has made significant contributions to the whole Department. Lt. Jackson, head of the Felony Section of the Detective Division, puts it this way:

He came here from Kansas City, which we all know is an excellent department. And we know via the grapevine that he is largely responsible for K. C.'s excellence in some vital services with the department. In his eight years in Metrocenter, he has vastly improved the 24-hour, seven-day communication system which receives calls and radios out information. He and Lt. Rankin (a lawyer who heads Booking Procedures) have helped the department devise procedures that protect civil rights of the innocent public and minorities, yet legally implicate real criminals. He has been a factor in the good public image of Metrocenter police. Unlike a lot of large cities, we have very few public charges that the police run roughshod over civil rights. Mullaney and Rankin (Mullaney also got a law degree at night in Kansas City) deserve much credit.

Problems in Planning Public Safety

According to Captain Mullaney,

Three years ago I hired a research team from Northwestern University to help us look at why traffic deaths and serious injuries were noticeably higher in Metrocenter than in most other U. S. cities of comparable size. We concluded that one factor was a lack of serious and scientifically modern planning of accident prevention—not a lack of good competent traffic patrolmen who by their presence tend to prevent reckless driving and who watch for violations. Both the number of total patrolmen and the competence level of individual patrolmen are comparable here to other cities. By planning, I mean research on where accidents occur, at what hours, and under what conditions.

If we know this, we can do two things that use men and dollar resources most efficiently to reduce accidents. First, we can invest in safety equipment at the right spot at the right time. For example, under our new system I can tell you that in the 28th census tract, at the corner of Lansing Street and Lake Drive, there are slightly more accidents than at any other corner in the city; that there is an 80 percent probability these occur between 10 p.m. and midnight; and that accidents have occurred there in approximately stable frequency for 4 months. The intersection at Huron and Chicago Avenues ranks 31st in accidents with 75 percent probability of occurrence between 4 p.m. and 6 p.m. Given the amount of money we can put into traffic lights, do you see how constant research can yield much more public safety for a given amount of citizens' money if we allocate this properly? Second, do you see that with a given investment of resources in competent patrolmen, we can assign these to areas, and at times of day, that will save more lives of citizens?

To put this into practice, we have purchased an electronic data processing system. The Northwestern experts provided experience of the public safety planning systems in Chicago. Portland, and other cities. They designed computer programs—software—and computer

specifications—hardware—that will analyze the information.

The second thing necessary to do this planning has developed a hitch. Computer systems are one thing. But maybe you've heard the quip "garbage in, garbage out." It means that the best computer system won't work without the cooperation of thinking human beings to put facts into the computer memory. We designed a new citation form. The old one had only two parts to it. Very brief, and on a 3-inch-by-6-inch card which the public calls a "ticket." The new one is in five parts. It requires the patrolman to give more specific clear information on the type of violation, and the exact location. For example, for accidents at the Lansing-Lake Drive location, the patrolman is provided with a very small code book. He enters the name of the streets with the code (1236 for Lansing and 1892 for Lake Drive), the exact time-of-day code (we use the 24-hour system so that 10:45 p.m. is 2245), and other information. He also provides a code indicating which of the 81 census tracts (geographic areas) of the city the incident occurred in.

Commissioner Allen, along with myself and Rankin, covered the purposes and mechanics of the new system in a special meeting called by Division Captains. The patrolmen seemed impressed, but not really enthusiastic. The commissioner told them that last year an angry group of citizens called him, demanding a traffic light. He called the Administration Division and said, "I want an analysis of the accident rates at that corner compared to others."

He said he couldn't get accurate information quickly because the Administration Division didn't have quick methods. Worse, he wasn't getting accurate information. It was grossly inaccurate because patrolmen write illegibly or incorrectly on their citation forms. The new system, he said, would correct many problems, including this one.

I also explained that we could develop better training and concentrate on the right hazards. We could ask the computer to give us, for four census tracts, statistics on types of violations: careless driving, reckless driving, speeding, running red lights, improper equipment (lights, etc.), and double parking. With this information, we can train patrolmen on what to look for, and this may differ for different parts of the city. Suppose we have a bad double-parking problem in one section, causing head-on collisions or ramming of parked cars from the back at night.

Finally, I said that the commissioner needs good data in his monthly problem diagnosis report, and that the mayor needs hard facts when he allocates city money in the budget.

Captain Terenzio reviewed the matter with the three lieutenants and various district sergeants at his monthly staff meetings. He showed them the new citation form and passed out new citation forms and code books. He explained that the coding by patrolmen was decided on because of the necessity of precise information, and that illegible writing in a city the size of Metrocenter meant an impossible job if the codes were entered by a clerk in the Booking Section of headquarters.

Actually one reason for asking patrolmen to code was the very bad writing and illegibility problem. Patrolmen didn't take time to think about the important administrative use made of citation forms and weren't too concerned about legibility. We thought that coding would not only eliminate this but would cause patrolmen to stop and think about accuracy.

Three months after Terenzio's staff meeting, the system still wasn't working. About 30 percent of all citations that came in had either the census tract code or one of the street location codes missing. On more than a quarter of these, the original data was written so illegibly that we could not determine accurately the street names and census areas to do the coding in the office here. The whole planning system, and even our investment in that expensive computer, will be down the drain if we cannot correct it.

Initially, I asked the booking clerks to put on my desk all citations that were either incomplete or illegible. Then I went directly to the patrol officer's immediate boss, his district sergeant. I did not want to go raise hell with bigger bosses right away. This took enormous amounts of time over the next two months. With about half the sergeants I could handle it quickly. They would

cooperate, though I noted most of them cooperated for a few weeks and then the accuracy and incompleteness problem reappeared.

With the other half, I got immediate and firm opposition. They told me that patrolmen in their districts had a lot on their mind besides paperwork, that there was enough paperwork in the department before these new citation procedures came out, and that they just could not face their men if they were constantly giving out orders for petty paperwork details.

One day I had a number of unreadable or incomplete violations from the Western Area Traffic Headquarters. It had been five months since Terenzio's first announcement in his staff meeting. I went to Lt. Baker and pleaded with him. I gave him all the arguments I've mentioned so far, and added the fact that we're so far behind in processing accurate citations for court dockets that the whole process of justice in Metrocenter is in jeopardy.

In the conversation it became apparent that Baker just didn't see the importance of the whole thing. He said he would mention it to his sergeants at the afternoon muster. But most of the conversation time was taken by his constant repetition of the same theme: "Our patrolmen are out there with a lot on their minds when they cruise and stop violators. They do the best they can in administrative work. We'll cooperate when we can, but don't expect them ever to become clerical experts."

Over the next three months this occurred two more times. Each time, I was pleasant and logical in my conversation with Baker and each time he was pleasant and logical in his conversation with me. I could see that I was getting nowhere with this lieutenant. I didn't want to tread on anybody's toes. At this point I could go to the Commissioner, but I thought I'd be a nice guy and go to the the Traffic Division head, Captain Terenzio. It had now been 8 months since he had announced the program to his men.

Terenzio listened to the whole story, almost all of which was repetition of the original explanation given at the Commissioner's meeting. He said, "I agree that the forms should be filled out properly. But I have been a patrolman for many years and it is just impossible to do everything according to standard procedures. I will be glad to remind all lieutenants and sergeants that these forms are very important to the Police Administration Division and do it at my next monthly staff meeting!''

I decided to give it one staff meeting more to see if there were positive results. As a matter of fact, results weren't positive. If anything, the citations got a bit sloppier.

After 9 months of trying other methods, I decided it was either my hide or one of the Division heads. I had been hired and promoted to do a good job in Police Administration, just as Terenzio had been hired and promoted to do a good job in Traffic Patrol. All my training had been along this line, and I was convinced that the people of Metrocenter had a right to good safety planning as well as good patrolling.

So I went to the Commissioner. I told him the whole situation, from beginning to end, just as I'm telling it now. I told him that I thought we had to correct the situation regardless of whose toes got stepped on.

He asked my opinion as to how to correct it. There were two alternatives, I said. One would be a general briefing by the Commissioner in the muster rooms at the Eastern and Western Traffic Patrol Headquarters. We would ask Capt. Terenzio to sit on the platform and introduce both the subject and the Commissioner. The same logic we've used before would be used, but the entire Traffic force, from top to bottom, would be there face-to-face with the Commissioner.

A second alternative would be for the Commissioner to request all traffic personnel, from top to bottom, to spend a bit of their time off, rotating them over the next two months, coming to headquarters and following one of their citations through key operations. They could watch key-punching of codes onto cards with the clerk trying to read it, watch the booking section entering their citation on a court docket, watch other operations taking place.

Then we would ask them to punch a computer terminal on either a census tract or street corner in their area, asking the computer a question of their own interest, such as, How many careless drivers per capita does the Eastern Headquarters have compared to the Western Headquarters? or, Is our problem worse in speeding or in general reckless driving?

Commissioner Allen was much more attentive and concerned than either Terenzio or Baker. He had come up himself through traffic control work. Did I make a mistake in coming out into the open and telling him the whole story, including the implied charge that Terenzio and Baker were dragging their feet? Does he think I am a trouble-maker? Does he think I don't know how to get along with a management team (this term was always a favorite of ours in Kansas City)?

He said he would think about it and let me know by next Monday. Today is Wednesday. I never knew I could get as anxious wondering what he will do. He gave no real indication.

Aspen County High School

The following is part of a conversation between the Superintendent of Schools and Mr. Don Mason, Aspen County High School Principal, that took place at the regular Wednesday meeting of the Aspen County School District Board of Trustees during the last week of March.

SUPERINTENDENT: Don, it seems like every time you come to our meeting you've got your hand out for more money. Last month it was money for new band uniforms. Before that you were trying to tell us the athletic teams needed $2,000 worth of equipment. Now you hit us with this across-the-board raise for your faculty. You know we're working on a very limited budget and we have other demands that must be met, too.

DON MASON: Of course, it costs money to run a school district. I can understand your problems. But remember, the only way we're going to be able to offer good instruction to this community is by having well-qualified teachers on the staff. And good teachers cost money! Besides, remember you promised us last year when we asked for a raise that we'd get it this year, and. . . .

SUPERINTENDENT: Now, just a minute, Don. We never promised you that you'd get a raise this year. We simply said that it was impossible to give you a raise *last* year because Western Steel had closed down as a result of the

strike and the district's income was decreased substantially.

At that time we thought that Western Steel would soon be operating at full steam and that we would have the funds available for a raise *this year.* As everyone knows only too well, Western still is only operating at about one-third capacity. This means that their payroll is only about one third. Quite a few people have moved from the area to get jobs. Business income is low and some of the shops have closed their doors permanently. We just don't have the money in the General Fund and we probably couldn't pass a special bond issue at this late date anyway.

Aspen County School District was a unified district comprising four elementary schools, two junior high schools, and one high school. The district served the entire population of the county. The major source of income for this small western community was Western Steel. Strikes and slowdowns at Western Steel often had resulted in extreme fluctuations in the population and the financial well-being of the community. As a result of these problems and others, the superintendent and the board experienced frequent discord with the teachers and administrators on financial matters.

At 8:30 A.M. the following Monday, the thirty-seven faculty members and administrators of Aspen High School held their weekly faculty meeting. The meeting was called to order by the vice-principal of the high school, Bob Lane.

This case was developed and prepared by Professor Sherman Tingey, School of Business, Arizona State University. Reprinted by permission.

BOB LANE (Vice-Principal): We have a lot of business to cover in our meeting this morning, but first I think it is appropriate that we hear from Don. As most of you know by now, Don went to bat for the faculty against the board for a salary increase, and he wants to bring this item up first so that everyone will understand exactly how things are progressing.

DON MASON (Principal): I met with the board last Thursday and asked about that raise they had promised us. They gave the same old excuse of no funds. It looks like we're going to have a tough battle on our hands if we expect to get an across-the-board raise this year. Since their major objection appears to be lack of funds, the Teachers' Welfare Committee has been working over the weekend on possible ways that the funds can be obtained. They have worked up a couple of alternatives that can be presented. The most attractive one involves not receiving your three summer months' checks in one lump sum in June as some of you have been doing. Phil, why don't you explain just how that is going to work?

Phil, the chairman of the Teachers' Welfare Committee, then explained to the group that approximately one half of the teachers had been exercising the option to receive their three summer checks in a lump sum at the beginning of the summer. If receipt of these checks could be postponed until after June 30, the expense would appear in the next fiscal year. This could be a permanent postponement. If only 75 percent of those now exercising this option were willing to forego this advantage, enough funds would be created to finance the desired salary increases. A hand vote of those who were willing to give up this option indicated that 16 of the 18 teachers involved would probably be able to rearrange their financial affairs to support the proposal.

DON MASON: Thanks very much for your support. I'll present this proposal to the board this Thursday and see if we can't work something out. Bob and I were talking just yesterday and we both expressed the opinion that we have an excellent staff here at the high school and we think that you deserve a raise in the salary schedule. Besides, Bob and I are on a schedule, too, and we'd benefit from a raise the same as you would. Both "X" County and "Y" County received schedule increases this year and our county is falling behind.

The meeting was turned over to Bob, who conducted the remaining business. That same afternoon a group of teachers were discussing the situation in the teachers' lounge after school.

TEACHER A: I heard Bill [an English teacher] say that he was going to investigate the possibility of a position at Sacramento if it looked like we weren't going to get a raise this year. Do you think we'll get the raise?

TEACHER B: Naw, we probably won't. But I wouldn't leave because of that alone. Money isn't everything. I think the kind of work environment we have here is worth something. Not very often will you find a school where both the principal and vice-principal will stand behind their teachers and support them 100 percent. I think that's one of the reasons Don and Bob are so well liked by the teachers.

TEACHER C: I'll agree with that! I'll never forget that incident with Bob Lane when I first came here. You remember that he asked me to be the Lettermen's Club advisor? None of the coaches wanted the job because it takes a lot of time and the kids are pretty rough to handle. Well, anyway, when he introduced me to the club members, he said that the administration would stand behind me in whatever I wanted to do as long as I thought it was for the best benefit of the club.

Later, when I told the club members that the initiation had to be toned down considerably because of the danger of seriously hurting someone, they stormed right into Bob Lane's office complaining. They figured that since they had to go through all that rough stuff to be initiated, it was only fair for them to "get revenge" against the new members. Boy, it really made me feel good when I found out Bob had told them, "If that's the way your advisor wants it, then that's the way it's going to be." It surely made my job a lot easier from then on.

TEACHER A: Do you remember that problem I had in the boys' cooking class right at the first of the year?

TEACHER B: No, what was that?

TEACHER A: Well, it really wasn't a problem. I was nervous since this was my first teaching job. We were supposed to be making cookies. Two boys were laughing and goofing around and somehow they broke a bottle of milk. I was so upset that I sent them to the office. Really it was just an accident, but Don gave the boys a talking to anyway and told them not to goof off in class. I realized afterward that sending them to the office was too strong a discipline measure, but I was surely glad that Don stuck up for me anyway.

TEACHER D: I really think a lot of Don and Bob. Remember last fall when I was teaching that adult evening class in bookkeeping? Dayle [another teacher] and I had gone out for a little deer hunting after school one afternoon. We shot a three-point near the top of Hogback Mountain and it took us a lot longer than we expected to get that deer out. The class I was teaching was supposed to meet at 7:00 and we didn't get back to town until about 7:30. When Don phoned my home about 7:20 and found out that I was still out deer hunting, he said, "I'll tell the students to go ahead and work on their own. He's probably shot a big one and is having difficulty getting it out."

When I got to class 40 minutes late all my students were still there waiting for a deer-hunting story. After class I met Don in the hall and he asked just one question: "Did you get your deer?"

The following Thursday at the Board of Trustees' meeting, Principal Don Mason presented the proposal of the Teachers' Welfare Committee in an effort to show the board members where they could get the funds for a salary increase. After considerable discussion of the proposal, the board said they would take it into consideration but still didn't feel a salary increase would be forthcoming.

At this point in the meeting, the board revealed to Don Mason that during the week they had decided to set his salary for the next year at $12,000. They emphasized that he would be receiving $900 increase in addition to the regular yearly increment of $400. They also emphasized that they expected a lot more cooperation from him in the future.

Mason expressed his thanks for the raise but also expressed his opinion that the teachers should also receive a salary schedule increase. He then rose to leave. As he was leaving he heard one member of the board whisper, "Boy, talk about ungrateful!"

At the next board meeting, Mason had arranged for members of the Teachers' Welfare Committee to meet before the board in an effort to convince the board members of the necessity of a salary schedule raise and that the means for the raise were accessible. After the presentation by the committee, the board said they would consider this information and requested time to verify the data the committee were using. They also expressed their opinion that there was little hope of obtaining raises this year.

Three days later, all the teachers at the high school received notification of a special faculty meeting to be held immediately after school for the purpose of discussing recent events in the negotiations of salary increases.

As some of the teachers met in the hall on the way to the meeting, Teacher G was asked if he knew what was going on. He replied, "I don't know for sure, but Bob Lane said it was 'something big' and for everyone to be sure to attend.''

TEACHER H: Maybe we're going to get our raise after all!

TEACHER G: Not a chance! You know as well as I do the board isn't going to let Don tell them what they should do. Something else must be in the air.

As Bob Lane, the vice-principal, called the meeting to order, some of the teachers were commenting on the absence of Principal Don Mason.

BOB LANE: I think everyone is here now. We've called this special meeting because we think that you should know exactly what has been going on during the past few days. Apparently Don has pushed the board a little too hard for salary increases for the teachers. The night before last one of the board members called me at my home around 9:00 and asked me if I could come over to his house. When I arrived, three of the board members were there to greet me. They asked how I liked my job as an administrator in the high school and I told them I really enjoyed my work here. Then they asked me if I would like to be principal of the high school next year with a nice increase in salary. [Several oh's and ah's were heard in the group.] All I could think of was: What about Don? I asked them if Don had quit and they said, ''No, but we aren't going to offer him a contract for next year.'' [Looks of astonishment and surprise appeared on many faces as a few teachers leaned over and whispered to each other.]

When I asked them why they weren't offering Don a contract, they said it was personal and they didn't want to discuss it with anyone. Well, I didn't hesitate to tell them if they didn't offer Don a contract for next year, they needn't offer me one either because I wouldn't sign it. Now I think this is information that you should know. I think Don finds himself in this position because of his efforts to help you teachers. If

there is any way that you can support Don in his fight, I certainly think you should, and I know that he would welcome your help.

At this point Bob Lane left the room and Teacher P, the president of the High School Teachers' Association, took over the meeting. The room was filled with loud talk and excitement.

TEACHER P: May I have your attention, please! I know that this is quite an unexpected turn of events. It surprised me as much as it did you when Bob explained the situation to me about an hour ago. But you haven't heard the whole story yet. Don met with the board in a special meeting that was called at Don's request last evening. He specifically requested reasons for his dismissal, but the board said they did not have to give any reasons for their actions.

Contracts will be offered on the first of May—that's about ten days away. What can we do to help Don?

TEACHER D: (jumping up excitedly): Well, I'll tell you one thing! If they fire Don they can find a replacement for me too. I don't want to work for a board that can fire someone without any reason other than disagreeing with them.

TEACHER E: I have no ties here. The main reason I stay is because I like to teach under Don and Bob. If they go I'll go too, and I'd like to see the rest of you do the same.

The faculty meeting continued for another hour. It was determined by secret ballot that approximately 90 percent of the faculty would be able and willing to support Principal Mason in the following manner: If Don Mason was not offered a contract, the teachers would not sign their contracts. It was also decided that this information should be conveyed to the board immediately.

On May 1, the teachers received their contracts in sealed envelopes. Also in each mailbox was a mimeographed note saying Don Mason had not received a contract. All contracts were to be returned to the Board of Trustees by May 15.

During the next two weeks the following appeared in the local newspaper:

Dear Editor:

I read in *The Daily Times* this evening that Mr. Don Mason has requested four times a statement from the school board as to why his contract was not renewed as principal of the Aspen High School.

I do not know much about civil law, but I do know of a moral law that reads: "Do unto others as you wish them to do unto you." Any person who has been employed in a school system whether principal or teacher for a period of years is definitely entitled, as a matter of courtesy, to be given an explanation as to why his contract is not renewed.

I feel this very unjust to the man and the teachers as a whole. No teacher can feel secure under an administration of this caliber. I think the public should demand an explanation. Any innocent member of the school board who sits back and lets this go on is as guilty as the rest.

Sincerely,

A parent

The following letter was signed by approximately one fourth of the 650 students at Aspen High School.

Dear Editor:

What is the school board trying to do by dismissing Mr. Mason without giving any reasons? We feel that Mr. Mason has done an excellent job of building up our high school.

We have been told that better than 90 percent of our teachers have refused to sign their contracts for the coming year. This would result in drastic conditions for our school system. If this happens our school could possibly become a nonaccredited school. This could pose many problems for the seniors planning to attend college.

Parents! Are we the only ones concerned about these problems?

A citizens committee had been formed to investigate the current school "crisis." This committee had requested the investigating services of Dr. Williams, an executive from the State Education Association. A special meeting was held at which Dr. Williams reported his initial findings to the Citizens Committee. The newspaper printed the following as part of the report of that meeting:

It was stated during the meeting that there has been a complete breakdown of the communications between teachers, administrators, and school board members, thus creating a crisis in the education system. There has been unwillingness on the part of the school board, it was said, to discuss the situations as they arise with the persons involved. In addition. . . .

Dr. Williams stated that he had checked with attorneys on such a problem and he was now certain that a school board has the right to refuse to give new contracts to teachers without having to give an explanation of the refusal. However, to prevent the type of breakdown that now exists here, that person should be called in and an explanation given as to the cause for action.

Five days prior to May 15, the date the contracts had to be returned to the board, the local paper printed the following in its editoral column:

This week appears to be the week of decision, for the contracts are supposed to be returned to the school board within five days. The board is apparently counting upon most of the good teachers signing up by the deadline.

Thinking on the basis of the present situation and eliminating what is already "water under the bridge," there seem to be three things that could happen: (1) the school board could reverse its decision regarding the principal, or (2) the teachers could decide they want their jobs even more than they want victory in this strange fight, or (3) the board and the teachers could remain adamant and the board could attempt to recruit as many new teachers as needed.

A Matter of Priorities

Ted Michod graduated from the Newark College of Engineering as an electrical engineer and went to work for a small but growing computer manufacturing firm in Philadelphia which employed about 10,000 people. His first position with the company was that of a junior engineer in the data processing systems division. He worked with twenty other junior engineers designing primary computer circuits and electromechanical linkages. Basically, Michod's job consisted of fitting various electrical and mechanical components into a package which would perform logical and arithmetic operations with the greatest reliability for the least cost. Most of the time he worked out designs on paper, although, on occasion, Ted actually tried his ideas out in the lab.

After two years, Ted received a promotion which, along with an increase in pay and status, provided him with an opportunity to expand greatly his knowledge of the industry. As an associate engineer in the programming systems division, he served as a liaison between his old design group and a systems engineering team which was responsible for the creation of new programming languages. Ted's duties were to make sure that the programming languages being developed were consistent with design capabilities which were being incorporated into new computer systems by his old work group. Thus, he was able to relate his previous experience with hardware (circuits) to the creation and design of software (program languages) and round out his technical education.

After a year in his new position, Ted began to realize that while he was mastering the technical end of the computer business, he was unprepared for the managerial responsibilities it entailed. Furthermore, it seemed to him that a graduate degree in business administration would improve greatly his chance for promotion in the future. After giving the problem considerable thought, Ted decided to take a two-year educational leave of absence to work on an M.B.A. degree. His decision was based on the fact that in addition to his need for managerial development, his interests had gradually shifted from the technical to the administrative aspects of the industry.

Ted Michod graduated from the local university finishing in the top twenty percent of his M.B.A. class. Within two weeks of graduation, he was married and he decided to return to work with his old company. This time, at his request, he was assigned to the midwestern marketing regional office in Chicago as a customer engineer. Ted felt that experience in the field of customer relations together with his previous technical work would increase greatly his worth to the firm and thus his chances for success. For this reason both Ted and his bride viewed their move to the Chicago office as a "step in the right direction."

This case was prepared by Professor Robert A. Ullrich of the Graduate School of Management, Vanderbilt University. Used by permission. All names and places are disguised.

Once settled in Chicago, Tod reported to the customer engineering manager, John Lucas. Mr. Lucas assigned Michod to the customer education section as an instructor. The section's purpose was to train customer employees in the installation and use of computer systems. Since this was not considered to be a full-time assignment, Ted was given additional duties as the supervisor of a program modification team. This second job consisted of giving technical assistance and direction to a group, consisting of four programmer trainees, which was modifying existing computer programs written by the manufacturers for the customers to keep them consistent with improved methodology and technology. Both positions required that he report directly to Mr. Lucas. On the average Ted taught about thirty hours a week and devoted fifteen hours to his second job.

As a result of the group's work modifying a set of market forecasting programs, Ted hit upon the idea of using a form of the Markov Process to predict growth in sales of new industrial products. [The Markov Process is a statistical approach which basically views life as a series of probabilities that an event will (or will not) occur given that it has (or has not) taken place in the past.] Ted had learned about this technique in his M.B.A. program. He studied the problem evenings at home and in mid-October submitted his idea to Lucas in the form of a well researched and documented proposal. Lucas seemed interested in the project but told Ted it would have to be shelved until the necessary manpower and finances became available.

About two months later, however, Ted's program modification team completed its assigned projects and the group was disbanded. When he reported to Lucas to be re-assigned, Michod was instructed to see Wayne Smith, the head of the computer installation department. Smith, like Lucas, was the head of a staff department. Smith and Lucas enjoyed equal rank within the firm and reported to the same district manager.

Smith outlined Ted's next assignment as follows. Ted would supervise two junior systems engineers in the installation of small computers and would have complete responsibility for each installation project. The job, at first, would require about twenty hours a week of his time. In addition Ted would continue to serve in his present capacity of instructor until the middle of the year. At this time, an additional instructor would be transferred to the midwestern region and Ted would be relieved of his teaching responsibilities to devote his entire efforts to the installation department. Until then, however, he would report to Smith concerning installation problems and to Lucas for matters involving the education program.

The following day Ted received a note from Lucas to see him as soon as possible. Upon entering Lucas's office, Ted found himself engaged in the following conversation.

TED: You wanted to see me, Mr. Lucas?

LUCAS: Yes, Ted. Sit down. You know, I liked the proposal you submitted for forecasting with Markov processes. I'd like you to work up some programs and make it operational. Do you think you could wrap up the job in two months?

TED: Well, I could if I had the time, but as you know I'm still working as an instructor and I've just taken over an installation team for Wayne Smith.

LUCAS: Yes, I know about that. You'll have some free time on Wayne's project though. I don't see why you won't be able to fit my project around your other work. It won't take long, will it?

TED: I just don't know. I can make a wild guess at a hundred and twenty man hours. I don't think I'll have the time to tackle it.

LUCAS: Sure you will, Ted. Smith's project won't take all your time. Besides, a hundred

EXHIBIT 1
Midwestern marketing region partial organization chart

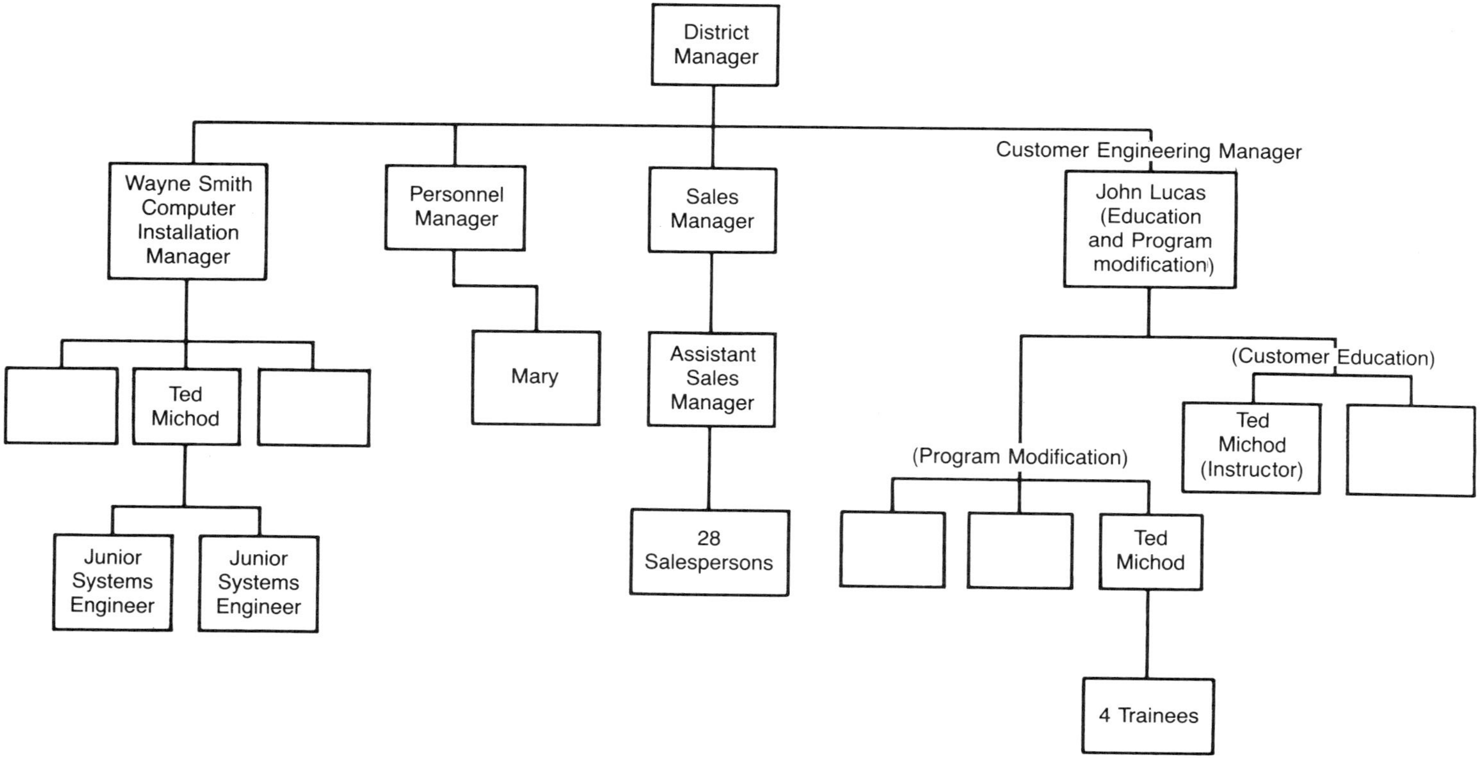

and twenty hours isn't very much. Why, it's not even two weeks' work.

After leaving Mr. Lucas's office, Ted stopped in to see Wayne Smith.

TED: Hi. I was just wondering when I should start working for you.

SMITH: (Jokingly) Today! Now!

TED: Well, what I mean is will it be full time at first or will I have some time on my hands?

SMITH: No. It should be a full twenty hours a week right from the start. Why did you ask? Any special reason?

Michod told Smith about his conversation with Lucas and explained that he didn't think he would be able to handle all three projects. Wayne Smith agreed but felt that there had been some misunderstanding. He told Ted that he would talk to Lucas that afternoon and that Ted should let the matter ride until it had been looked into further.

TED: Good. I hope this gets cleared up soon.

SMITH: Don't worry, Ted, we just have our wires crossed. Stop in and see me first thing in the morning.

The next day the following conversation took place between Ted and Mr. Smith.

SMITH: Ted, I saw John Lucas yesterday and I'm not sure I've solved your problem. He said that the project he had in mind wasn't very big and that you should have plenty of time to get it done.

TED: But I told him it would take a hundred and twenty hours. Since then I've been worried that my estimate was way too low.

SMITH: Well, you'd better talk with him again. I understood that I was to have you for twenty hours a week, and believe me, I need every bit of that time!

Ted saw Lucas a few hours later and explained again his commitments and lack of available time. He went on to suggest that he could instruct a new man to carry out the project if that was acceptable to Lucas.

LUCAS: I don't know who else would be available to do this type of work. . . . Look, Ted, just fit it in around your other work. You'll have time to do it. . . . Oh, before I forget, see Mary in Personnel on your way out. They need some information for your records. And tell my secretary to come in, will you? I have a stack of letters to get out.

Ted walked down to Personnel wondering how he wound up in the middle of all this. Furthermore, he wondered what he should do next.

PART SIX
Human Resource Systems

"Perfectly Pure Peabody's"

The Peabody Soap Company was founded by Joshua Peabody, a small-town pharmacist who patented his formula for "Perfectly Pure Peabody's" soap in 1909. By 1973, Peabody Soap had grown from a one-product mail-order house to a $100 million publicly held beauty business with 2,500 employees. The founder's grandson, George Hinton, now chairman and chief executive officer, had masterminded the recent growth, divisionalization, and international expansion of the company.

During the last ten years, Peabody Soap had received national recognition for its achievements in pollution control, community relations, and minority employment. George Hinton was personally responsible for spearheading activities in these areas, and he was proud of the company's fine record.

Hinton was known throughout the industry as a business leader with outstanding instincts for developing both quality products and a sound management team. He began his career at Peabody Soap in 1945, having spent a year at a well-known consulting firm after graduation from Stanford Business School. He assumed the presidency in 1956 and became chairman in 1965.

However, in January 1973, the resignation of Chemical Research Manager Sarah

Barrington (the company's top-ranking woman) made Hinton aware that he had not adequately addressed himself to a key corporate problem: women in management.

Peabody's Marketing: 1965-1973

Prior to 1965 the company had limited production to a highly successful and profitable line of soap, shampoo, and related skin-care products. "Perfectly Pure Peabody's" consistently maintained better than a 20 percent share of the face soap market. In the mid-1960s George Hinton decided to expand product lines domestically and open up new foreign markets.

To meet the domestic objective, he promoted Herbert Richardson, a forty-six-old production manager, to vice-president of marketing. Richardson, who had come up through the ranks, was considered a rugged individualist. His energy, directness, and work record made him a prime candidate to succeed George Hinton, who had already announced that the next chief executive officer wouldn't be a "member of the family."

Richardson's first move was to create a market research department. After a year of thorough market analysis by the new department, Richardson recommended that Peabody expand into the hypoallergenic skin-care products field. Because the company had experienced little need for research before the decision to broaden the line, its chemical laboratory was inadequately staffed for experimen-

Reprinted from *Stanford Business Cases 1974* with the permission of the publishers, Stanford University/Graduate School of Business. Copyright © 1974 by the Board of Trustees of the Leland Stanford Junior University.

tation. As a result of his industry review, Richardson knew that several companies were experimenting with hypoallergenics. He was convinced that the growth objective of the company depended on the caliber of the chemical research section and the speed with which it could develop new products. A "blind" ad for a product research manager, placed in several trade publications, *The Wall Street Journal,* and *The New York Times,* brought in nearly eighty applications.

Richardson, who prided himself on his young and eager management team, was particularly impressed with one applicant—thirty-two-year-old Sarah Barrington, an unmarried research chemist. Barrington had spent the last three years as assistant laboratory director for Peabody's nearest competitor. Born and educated in England, she held a graduate de-gree in business economics and a doctorate in organic chemistry. Her total work experience was only four years, but she had an outstanding record with both of her previous employers. Furthermore, her salary requirements were low ($15,000 per year) compared with those of other applicants.

After her initial interview with Richardson, Barrington was sent to the company's industrial psychologist, who summarized his findings: "Sarah has good management potential, she is highly results-oriented with the proper balance of deference to authority. If, however, she cannot see the logic of a superior's request, she will seek an honest explanation. She is respectful, but also inquisitive and direct. She is ambitious as well, and will benefit from working toward long-term career goals." (See Exhibit 1.)

EXHIBIT 1
Industrial psychologist's report on Sarah Barrington: 1/5/67

Miss Barrington is a conscientious, industrious, dependable woman who takes herself and her responsibilities seriously. She enjoys her work, is ambitious for career progress, and is willing to work as hard as necessary to achieve her goals.

She is alert, intelligent, and perceptive of what goes on around her, and is eager to learn all she can about the processes with which she works. Her strong points are troubleshooting and problem solving; she is analytical, critical, and objective in her approach to situations of a technical nature. She works at a brisk pace, with strong focus on tasks, and takes pressure well. She plans effectively, is well organized and methodical, and can be counted on to meet requirements. She sets high standards for herself and others and faces up to issues squarely.

She likes activities that are challenging, stimulating, and rewarding, in which her capabilities will be utilized fully and which will provide opportunities for further growth. Initiative is readily available; she welcomes responsibilities and is eager to show what she can do on her own. She likes to explore wherever clues lead, will innovate and improvise as warranted, and is not reluctant to take calculated risks to test the validity of her ideas.

Verbal and social skills are very good. She is articulate, precise, and fluent or terse as necessary, and typically puts people at ease. While initially reserved with others, there is a warmth and dignity about her to which people respond favorably. She enjoys working with and through people and usually gets along with them. Occasionally, nevertheless, some people may be disconcerted by her somewhat unfeminine tendency to be forthright and outspoken when provoked.

On the job she prefers to set her own pace and be in control over her domain. Direction and criticism are used constructively, but she dislikes close supervision after assignments are outlined for her. She is most effective when allowed to participate in planning and decision making affecting her activities, given adequate authority for implementing them, and support when needed. Generally, she makes every effort to figure things out for herself before presenting suggestions or plans for discussion and approval.

Attitudes toward authority are favorable. She is appropriately deferent, cooperates fully, and complies and conforms as required to promote the organization's objectives. However, when directives or procedures don't make sense to her, she will raise questions and offer her views—tactfully but unequivocally. She needs superiors who are competent, strong, worthy of her esteem and who keep communication lines open. Above all, she needs to be dealt with honestly and fairly and to be given adequate recognition for whatever she contributes to the overall effort.

Her outstanding trait, perhaps, is her impelling drive for personal achievement and career progress. And her strongest asset is indicated potential for further growth. Thus, although she is young, her experience is not extensive, and the fact that she's a woman will make her sometimes less effective, she should be capable of getting the new unit started.

On the basis of her work record, the psychologist's assessment, and the knowledge that Hinton would be pleased to finally have a woman on his management team, Richardson selected Barrington for the job. In January 1967, she was named manager of chemical research and given full responsibility for setting up and staffing the lab.

Since fire laws prohibited the establishment of a laboratory in Peabody's headquarters, the research facility was located in a loft in a warehouse several blocks away. By March 1967, the laboratory was operational and Barrington hired a senior researcher, five assistant researchers, and a secretary. A year later, after a crash program involving close collaboration among the researchers, Peabody

Soap was able to patent a process for the manufacture of "Peabody's Super Sensitives," a line of hypoallergenic products matched product by product to the regular Peabody line.

The sales increase of 50 percent over the next two years was due, in great measure, to the introduction of the new products. In January 1970, the company went public to raise much-needed capital for future growth—with funds earmarked for expansion in international markets. No new domestic product research of any magnitude would be required to meet these objectives.

Soon after the development and patenting of the "Super Sensitives" process the research staff was cut in half with the remaining members moving into quality control and analysis of new raw materials. Barrington received a citation from the board of directors and won an industry award for her work—but the company was no longer interested in expanding product lines. Realizing that she was at a dead end in her present position, Barrington hired a management trainee in 1970, so that she could prepare someone to assume her position. A year later the trainee was offered a promotion to assistant manager of market research. (Since he would receive more pay in the new position, company policy prohibited Barrington from refusing to let him make the move.) The following year, a similar promotion was accepted by his replacement.

In June 1972, separate product divisions were established. The work of the marketing function was to be phased out to the divisions over the next two years. At the same time, Richardson was promoted to president. John Carlisle, a distribution manager who was nearing retirement, was named marketing director. While most phases of the marketing divisionalization were easily achieved, the lab posed a real problem. Divisions were not interested in the additional overhead of separate labs. Yet they all insisted that a company lab was necessary. Carlisle had little knowledge of the lab function and did not care to supervise the section. To deal with the situation, he held a meeting of all division managers to determine to whom the lab should report. They decided on the quality control division and sent Barrington a memo informing her of the new reporting relationship.

Equal Employment Opportunity at Peabody Soap

A family tradition of community involvement was a vital part of Peabody Soap's corporate policy. Joshua Peabody had a personal policy of donating one-quarter of his annual earnings to community organizations. His son-in-law, William Hinton, received nationwide recognition for his successful racial integration of the Peabody factory in the 1950s—long before such actions were required by law. It came as no surprise when, in 1967, George Hinton was appointed as one of six Presidential advisors on the blue ribbon committee "Minority Employment and the American Future."

Although laws requiring affirmative action for minorities were not promulgated until 1969, Hinton had set goals for the promotion and hiring of minority group members as early as 1966. By 1973, every Peabody plant had a work force that reflected the racial composition of its community.

Finding an effective equal employment opportunity (EEO) manager, however, had been a difficult task. After several men failed at the position, Richard Adams proved to have the necessary qualities for the job. Adams, thirty-five years old, had been a white activist in the civil rights movement in the early sixties. His understanding of the problem of minority employment, combined with his ability to establish good rapport with managers, led to his success in Peabody's personnel department.

Peabody's work force had always been about 50 percent female. While production jobs in some industries weren't considered "women's work," cosmetic soap manufacture was an acceptable industry for female workers. Peabody actually assessed potential plant sites based on labor surveys of the rate of female unemployment in the area. If the figure was high and other factors were favorable, the location was selected.

The precision involved in the work, clean working conditions, and low wages had also been cited as reasons why women were employed in the industry. Peabody Soap, like its competitors, had been slow in moving women into management. In 1972, Sarah Barrington was the highest-ranking woman in the company—and one of only four women in middle or upper management.

In 1971, federal legislation requiring additional affirmative action for women was in the wind. Hinton's own daughter was pressuring him to take a closer look at the underutilization of women and the related issues of day care and job restructuring. Hinton had an "open door" policy—any employee could come directly to him with a problem—and several women within the company had used it to point out areas for improvement.

As a result, Hinton asked the personnel department to add a woman to Adams's staff to handle female affirmative action. In fact, Hinton suggested his own secretary, twenty-seven-year-old Brenda Goldman, for the job. "She's been with us for five years now—she's bright, capable, and knows our management," Hinton explained to Adams, "and she's not one of those women's libbers. I hate to give her up, but I'd feel more comfortable with her in the job." Goldman became EEO assistant two weeks later. Announcement of her promotion included Hinton's policy statement regarding equal employment (Exhibit 2).

From the outset, rapport between Adams and Goldman was difficult.

EXHIBIT 2

To: All Employees   December 5, 1971
From: George Hinton

At Peabody Soap, we have always been concerned with developing our resources—in terms of both people and products. It has also been our philosophy that discrimination, in any form, will not be tolerated here. We now recognize that women, as well as minorities, have suffered the effects of employment prejudice in the past.

We are, therefore, establishing a program of Affirmative Action for Women. Brenda Goldman, who joined the company as a secretary in 1968, will move up to become EEO Assistant for Women reporting to our EEO Manager. Her responsibilities, aside from the implementation of the women's program, will include counseling, developing recruitment resources, and providing other supportive services.

In the year ahead we will intensify our efforts in the identification of promotable women.

At Peabody Soap EEO is a corporatewide policy. Every division, department, and facility is charged with the responsibility of setting goals, and every manager is evaluated on the action he or she takes to ensure that our commitment is met. Monitoring the program, providing support services, and ensuring that all personnel practices are equitable are the duties of our Equal Employment Section.

It is my sincerest hope that we will continue to direct our energies toward EEO for women with the same vigor and enthusiasm with which we approach all other pressing business problems.

GOLDMAN: Where do I get started with the women's program, Dick? Guess I should begin by getting an idea of how we're going to be working together.

ADAMS: I'm looking forward to getting this women's thing started, Brenda. But frankly, we're going to have to hold back on anything big for awhile. Right now minorities—blacks in particular—are our biggest problem. That doesn't mean we're going to forget about women. You know, we've already made real headway. Sarah Barrington's doing a great job . . . she's one of the top 20 managers in the company. Besides, we're letting Carla O'Day and Helen Coates go on half-time jobs because they want to spend time at home with their young children. We've sent ten women to that "Women in Management" course at company expense . . . we've liberalized our maternity leave policy.

GOLDMAN: You're right, we have taken some excellent steps and most of the innovation came from you, Dick. . . . You must admit, though, that we still have monstrous problems. Look at the statistics. Women have a worse problem at Peabody's than do minorities.

ADAMS: I disagree. Black men have always had a tougher time finding work than have women.

GOLDMAN Dick, we could go around in circles about this. I don't agree with you. Black men and women both have had a tough time . . . and, I hasten to add, so do the other minorities—you forget about Chicanos, Asians, and American Indians. All of these groups are considered "affected classes" by the law.

ADAMS: Look, we've made progress and we'll keep making it . . . but we have to see this thing in perspective.

The conflicts were, of course, private; the reports that reached Hinton showed progress. To his knowledge, the EEO function was being handled well, and the company's reputation continued to be virtually untarnished.

Another aspect of the EEO operation of which Hinton was unaware was Goldman's image in the company. She had been accepted neither by her "constituency" nor by management.

Barrington's Resignation

On January 15, 1973, George Hinton received this letter:

Dear Mr. Hinton:

It is with deep personal and professional regret that I must submit my resignation, effective February 1, 1973. While Peabody Soap has provided me with the opportunity to make an outstanding contribution in chemical research, I find no room for developing beyond this department.

The recent shift in reporting relationships in my section and the manner in which that shift was accomplished make it clear that my services to the organization are no longer of value. Furthermore, my ability to effect a promotion to other departments has been deliberately inhibited.

I suggest you personally audit your EEO Program for Women. Many problems with potential legal implications exist in the organization.

Thank you for your personal encouragement over the last five years.

Sincerely,
Sarah Barrington

Hinton, alarmed by the letter, called the personnel department and asked them to send up a copy of Barrington's latest review (Exhibit 3) immediately. After a quick reading of Barrington's review, Hinton confirmed his belief that Barrington was an above-average manager in all respects. Next, Hinton asked Richardson to come to his office.

The Hinton/Richardson conversation went as follows:

EXHIBIT 3

EMPLOYEE PERFORMANCE APPRAISAL

		REVIEW PERIOD	
	From (Mo./Yr.) December 1971	To (Mo./Yr.) December 1972	

Employee Name SARAH BARRINGTON	Position, Title MANAGER, PRODUCT RESEARCH	No. Months in Present Position 10	No. Months Supervised by Rater 6	Seniority Date FEB 5, 1967	Field Location ADJACENT LAB

Responsibilities Performed (To be Written by Employee)	Performance Appraisal (To be Written by Rater)
List agreed upon objectives under each responsibility	Evaluate employee's performance on each responsibility and related objective

Employee objectives:

1. Complete tests for all possible new materials and processes '72 - '73
2. Assist marketing group by notifying them of tests of all competitor's products
3. Supervise a staff of 4
4. Develop better exposure for lab to other functions
5. Maintain progress on X-22 project

Rater appraisal:

1. Excellent
2. Excellent
3. Sarah is a good supervisor
4. Sarah is progressing in this area
5. X-22 completed satisfactorily

OVERALL JOB PERFORMANCE

☐ Unsatisfactory ☐ Fair ☐ Competent ☐ Highly Competent ☒ Exceptional

COMMENTS:

ADVANCEMENT POTENTIAL

☐ Can Develop Further in Present Position ☐ Adequately Placed ☒ Ready for Advancement Now

COMMENTS:

Rater's Signature John Carlisle	Date 12/8/72
Employee's Signature Sarah Barrington	Date 12/5/72
Manager's Signature John Carlisle	Date

Describe Two or More of Employee's Strongest Points:

1. Successfully delegates authority.
2. Does an excellent job of training subordinates
3. Runs an efficient lab, needs little supervision
4. Very professional in her approach

List Two or More Areas That Could Profit From Improvement:

1. Sarah is sometimes aggressive... some of the managers she works with find this "puts them off." It may inhibit her job performance.
2. She could benefit from more involvement in managerial activities.

What Are This Employee's Career Goals?

For some time Sarah has indicated interest in progressing to another management position. Nothing is available at present.

Suggested and Agreed Upon Actions to be Taken for Self Improvement and Achievement of Career Goals

Sarah is our top female manager and therefore is a good candidate for promotion. To do so, she must have closer communication with other managers. She would benefit from a little "softening" too - being a bit more gentle in her approach.

CURRENT SALARY	Weekly 340		20
RECOMMENDED SALARY	Weekly 397 Eff. Date Jan 1, 1973	SALARY GRADE CURRENT SALARY	Min ___ Mid ___ Max ___

HINTON: Herb, did you know that Sarah Barrington resigned?

RICHARDSON: No, George, but I did know she was unhappy here . . . it doesn't surprise me. For the last two years she's wanted to get out of the lab . . . but there's nowhere for her to go. She doesn't know any other function . . . and the fact that she's located in that other building just hasn't given her any exposure.

HINTON: Do you think it's because she's a woman?

RICHARDSON: Oh, George, I just don't think that's a problem with Sarah. She's had an excellent job and makes good money for a woman.

HINTON: How have her raises been?

RICHARDSON: Well, since she's been in the same job all this time . . . and this wage freeze has been in effect. . . . Oh, she makes a little less than twenty grand.

HINTON: Well, where could she go?

RICHARDSON: George, I don't know.

HINTON: Well, what about her reviews?

RICHARDSON: They're great. She's good at what she does . . . we've been very pleased, as you know, with the contributions she's made in research.

HINTON: We've never really talked about her for a promotion, have we?

RICHARDSON: George, I don't think anyone's ready for her to take over a major function as yet. We considered her for that international job . . . but, they just didn't think a woman could do the job.

HINTON: Herb, off the record, what do the guys think of her?

RICHARDSON: That's a tough question. . . . Nobody really talks about her very much. . . . They respect her judgment . . . but we don't know much more about her. Her trouble is that she doesn't sell herself enough. She doesn't socialize. Frankly, George, I don't know what more we can do to keep her here.

HINTON: Thanks Herb, I appreciate your candor. Oh, one more question. . . . How do you think Brenda is doing in her new job? You're closer to the action around here than I am.

RICHARDSON: To tell you the truth, George, I've been meaning to speak to you about Brenda. Although the figures are up slightly, I haven't heard anything about an affirmative action program for women, and from what I have seen and heard I think Brenda may be having problems. Just what the cause of the difficulty is, I'm not sure; it may be the setup in that office, or it may be Brenda herself. Let me do some more probing and I'll get back to you.

HINTON: You really think Brenda may be at fault?

RICHARDSON: Well, it's possible. We just may have to move her out.

HINTON: Thanks, Herb. Let me know what you find out.

Hinton then called Barrington and asked her to come to his office. Traditionally brief at his meetings, Hinton decided to break the rule with Barrington to delve more deeply into her side of the story. The relationship between Barrington and Hinton had always been cordial and open.

HINTON: Sarah, I really don't want to accept your resignation. I'd like you to stay on. Tell me exactly why you've made this decision . . . and don't be afraid of chewing my ear.

BARRINGTON: I joined the Peabody Soap Company in 1967 because, as I stated on my application, I wanted the opportunity to grow with a growth company. In fact, I chose to go into industry because I hoped to move from strict chemical research into other related areas of the organization. The reasonableness of that goal is evident when one looks at the experience of the two trainees I've had. Both men hold degrees similar to mine. I hired them at Herb's urging. . . . "You can't get promoted until you have a replacement," he kept stressing. Both Simon and Roger were offered promotions to other parts of the company. They make almost as much as I do now, and their work experiences and the exposure they're getting will make them more valuable to the company.

So much for what might sound like jealousy . . . and if it does, I'm sorry. I'm proud of Simon and Roger because I hired and trained them in the beginning. I mention them only as examples. In fact, my secretary was promoted to a training position in the Soap Division last month—so your affirmative action program does work.

But, back to my problems. Although I've indicated to both Herb and my new supervisor that I want to progress beyond my present job, nothing has happened. Other managers have been promoted from technical to nontechnical jobs. Take Frank Everett, he was quality control manager and now he runs the "Super Sensitive" Division.

My reviews have been good and have indicated that I'm ready, but when top jobs open up, no one even thinks of me. There was a job open for a research director in the International Division—it would have meant a big promotion in grade, pay, and status. I wasn't even considered, as I found out later, because they "didn't think a woman could do the job." It involved travel and dealing with raw materials suppliers—I do those things in my job now. And I had all the requirements, too. No one thinks I'm "strong" enough to negotiate or wheel and deal.

When Herb left—I had thought that he was my real mentor—things got worse. Carlisle doesn't know me or what we do in the lab, and frankly, he doesn't care. I discussed my desire to be promoted and he simply said he'd get back to me on it; he hasn't.

You wonder why I haven't pursued it further? George, have you seen my last review?

(He indicated that he'd just read it.) Well, look at the strengths and weaknesses section. Carlisle listed aggressiveness as a weakness. If I come on too strong, I'm considered "brassy" or "pushy" . . . and unfeminine. If I'm the least bit reticent, they think I don't have the stuff managers are made of. No one seems to be able to cope with the idea of a woman manager.

Frankly, George, I've been discriminated against for the last few years. I've never been promoted; I've never had much of a raise; I've never received a stock option; I've never been invited to the annual management meeting . . . probably because it's held at the Downtown Club, where women aren't even allowed.

It's harder for people to level with me, too. Herb never gave me many pointers about improvement. I hardly got any feedback, negative or positive. The other men here won't treat me as an equal either and there aren't any other women even near my level in the organization . . . so I have no one to emulate or consult.

George, there really isn't anything you can do about these things, I know. I don't mean to sound melodramatic, but I'm honestly fed up with having to perform like I'm Superwoman . . . and being treated like someone's little sister.

HINTON: I'm glad you've been so frank with me, Sarah. Have you talked to anybody in Personnel about this?

BARRINGTON: Yes, I did give Brenda a call and we had lunch. We've known each other for a long time and I'd hoped she could give me some advice. She suggested talking it over with Herb. I did, but he didn't seem very concerned. . . . I think he's lost interest in me since his promotion.

George, Brenda's in an impossible situation. Adams hasn't given her any guidance in counseling; he's just made a statistician out of her. She cited two cases where she's afraid we're going to have sex discrimination suits—but she can't get anywhere with Adams. . . . He simply sees the women's program as a threat. Most of the women in the company don't even know who Brenda is. In fact, there's an independent women's group already holding meetings outside the company. It's common knowledge that Brenda is all but totally ineffectual.

At the close of their conversation, Hinton asked Barrington if she'd wait a few days before her final resignation. Barrington agreed and offered a handshake.

Hinton then began to consider his course of action.

The Sanmo Clinic (A)

Friday, November 16

Margaret Walton, billing supervisor for the Sanmo Clinic, closed her office door to ponder a personnel problem. Her 29 employees presented her with the usual range of minor problems: occasional tardiness and absenteeism, family problems requiring time off, and the infrequent personality clash with coworkers.

This problem seemed more serious and might even end in termination for a junior employee, Lisa Coop. Earlier today, Lisa was waving her arms in frustration at her inability to understand a problem she had encountered in her job. The setting was the billing office of the Sanmo Clinic, a large (150 physicians, 900 employees) clinic in Seattle. Lisa's position as biller involved processing patient medical accounts and responding to inquiries about the accounts from physicians, insurance companies, government agencies, and the patients themselves.

The position of biller is fairly complex. The biller must master the complexities of medical codes forwarded by attending physicians, as well as the paperwork requirements of state and federal agencies (for example, Medicare). (See Exhibit 1.)

The research and written case information were presented at a Case Research Symposium and were evaluated by the Case Research Association's Editorial Board. This case was prepared by C. Patrick Fleenor of the Albers School of Business, Seattle University, as a basis for class discussion.

Distributed by the Case Research Association. All rights reserved to the author and the Case Research Association. Permission to use the case should be obtained from the Case Research Association.

Alone now in her office, Margaret began to reconstruct the events of the past nine months.

In early February, Lisa had transferred from another department in the clinic. At that time, Margaret held the position of assistant supervisor. Before accepting Lisa as a transfer, Margaret and her supervisor had requested copies of Lisa's performance reviews. The first review (Exhibit 2), dated November 9 the preceding year, had stressed the need for improvement in critical areas of job performance. Her probationary period had been extended at that time, and a follow-up review had been conducted three months later. The second review (Exhibit 3) showed significant improvement. On the strength of the second review, Lisa had been accepted for transfer.

Lisa had requested transfer to the billing department a few weeks prior to Ms. Walton's promotion to billing department supervisor. While the transfer was being processed, Lisa's supervisor contacted Ms. Walton's superior, Carol Burd, to point out that Lisa had missed considerable time from work the previous year. Since it was the clinic's policy to place transfer employees on probationary status for three months in the new department, Ms. Walton's supervisor asked her to stress to Lisa the need for good attendance. Ms. Walton contacted Ms. Coop to express concern about her past use of sick time. She pointed out that if the problem continued after her transfer, it could create difficulty for her in successfully completing her three-month pro-

EXHIBIT 1
Sanmo Clinic organization chart

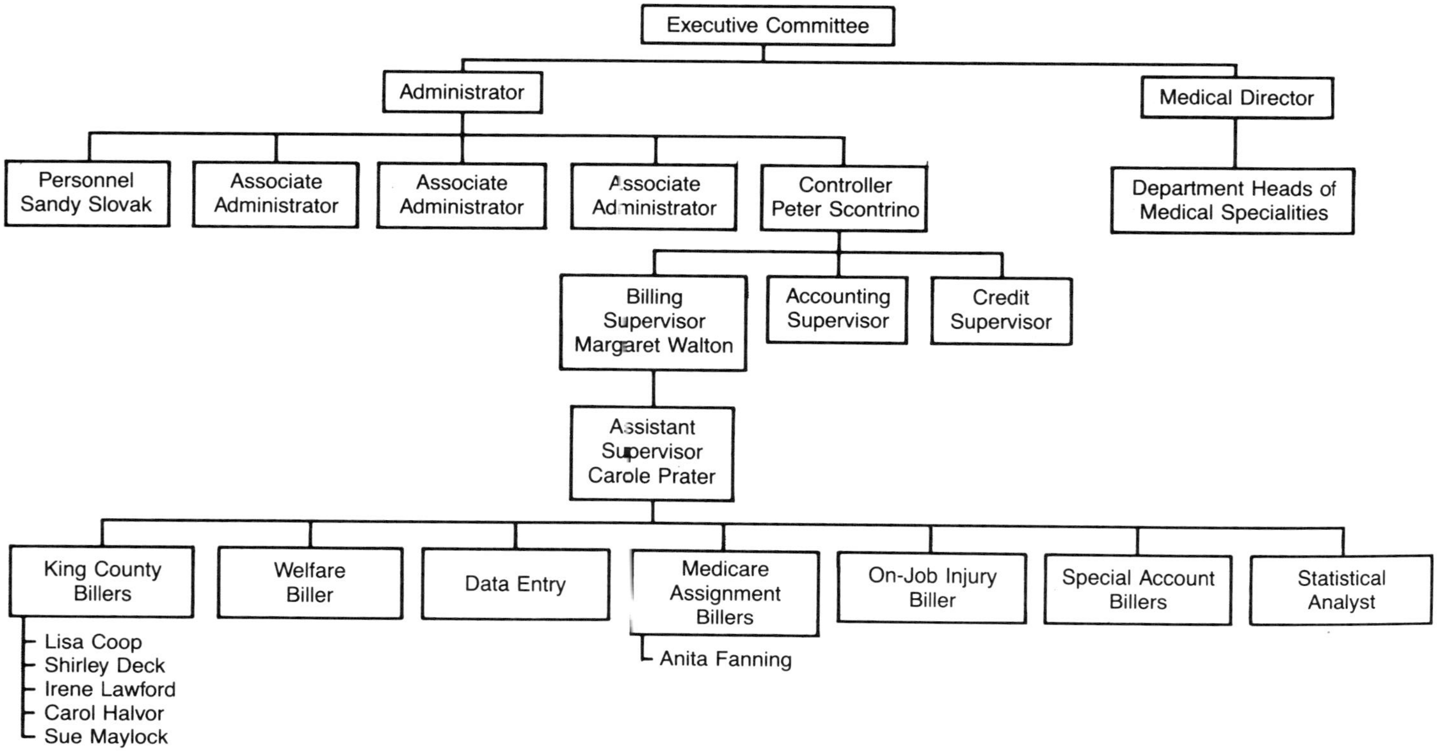

EXHIBIT 2

90-DAY REVIEW OF WORK PERFORMANCE

	Satisfactory	Needs Improvement

QUALITY OF WORK

	Satisfactory	Needs Improvement
Meets department standards		✓
Thoroughness		✓
Accuracy		✓

PRODUCTIVITY

	Satisfactory	Needs Improvement
Meets job requirements		✓
Proper use of own time		✓
Proper use of time of others		✓

DEPENDABILITY

	Satisfactory	Needs Improvement
Follows instructions		✓
Shows good judgment		✓
Demonstrates punctuality and good attendance	✓ *since this department*	

ATTITUDE

	Satisfactory	Needs Improvement
Cooperates with coworkers	✓	
Conducts self in businesslike manner	✓	

APPEARANCE

	Satisfactory	Needs Improvement
Dresses in manner fitting to position	✓	
Personal hygiene	✓	

COMMENTS:

I feel Lisa could show more interest in learning. Also she should learn to accept policies and procedures without constant complaining. Should learn to offer suggestions and constructive criticism. Must listen and follow instructions.

_____ Permanent employment
___✓___ Probation extended to (date) ____*Nov 9th*____

*Lisa Loop*   _*Maxine Anderstrom*_
Employee's signature   Department Head or Supervisor

EXHIBIT 3

90-DAY REVIEW OF WORK PERFORMANCE

	Satisfactory	Needs Improvement
QUALITY OF WORK		
Meets department standards	✓	
Thoroughness	✓	
Accuracy	✓	
PRODUCTIVITY		
Meets job requirements	✓	
Proper use of own time	✓	
Proper use of time of others	✓	
DEPENDABILITY		
Follows instructions	✓	
Shows good judgment	✓	
Demonstrates punctuality and good attendance	✓	
ATTITUDE		
Cooperates with coworkers	✓	
Conducts self in businesslike manner	✓	
APPEARANCE		
Dresses in manner fitting to position	✓	
Personal hygiene	✓	

COMMENTS:

Lisa has improved greatly in all aspects of her duties. She accepts responsibility for her position and has established good relations with patients and coworkers.

___✓___ Permanent employment
_____ Probation extended to (date) _____

Lisa Coop
Employee's signature

Maxine Anderstrom
Department Head or Supervisor

bationary period in the new department. She explained that Lisa still had the opportunity to remain in her present position with its status as a permanent employee; however, Ms. Coop indicated a desire to transfer and joined the billing department as scheduled. Lisa said, "Eventually, I want to become a physician's office assistant, and I need background in as many areas as possible."

From the first day on the new job in early February, Lisa seemed to have difficulty coping. The workload was high, and it was not uncommon for each biller to accrue several days' backlog on the desk. Lisa soon began falling even more behind than usual for a new employee, causing concern for Ms. Walton and the assistant supervisor, Carole Prater. As the days went by, Lisa's backlog continued to increase, and she began to express frustration in various ways. She began slamming record books, complaining loudly about the workload to all within hearing, became tardy regularly

(up to half an hour), and finally, on October 3, struck and damaged a microfilm viewer.

Margaret Walton met with Lisa the next day and expressed her concern about the tardiness and inappropriate behavior toward the job. During the interview, Lisa remained almost completely silent:

MARGARET: Lisa, we simply cannot accept the kind of outburst you made in the office yesterday.

LISA: (Silence)

MARGARET: If you need help, you know where to go for it, don't you?

LISA: Yeah

MARGARET: I've also noticed a pattern of tardiness developing. You know that the workday begins at 8:00, and we expect employees to be on time regularly.

LISA: (Silence)

After the meeting, Ms. Walton issued a memo to Ms. Coop (Exhibit 4), with a copy to the personnel department.

EXHIBIT 4

THE SANMO CLINIC

Interoffice Memo

DATE: October 12

TO: Lisa Coop   FROM: Margaret Walton

This is to reaffirm our meeting of last week when we discussed the necessity for improvement in your tardiness in arriving for work and the manner in which you express your frustrations on the job.

I know you understand that we consider these an important aspect of your job performance.

Now that you are aware of our concerns, we are confident that you will be able to make the necessary changes. Please feel free to talk with me if you feel I can assist you in any way.

Margaret

Lisa called in sick the next two days, during which time the workload on her desk was evaluated. Ms. Walton was astounded to find a backlog of itemization requests (requests from patients for itemized statements) extending more than two months. After Lisa's return, more discussions were held with her, and Ms. Walton requested a status sheet on Lisa's work. On October 16 and 17, several irate patients contacted the clinic to complain about delays in billing information. One patient had talked to Lisa several times over a two-month period but had not yet received the requested information. Ms. Walton decided to place Lisa on probation for six weeks and, after meeting with her, wrote the memo in Exhibit 5.

The situation seemed to stabilize for several weeks until today, November 16, when Lisa threw a tantrum in the office.

EXHIBIT 5

DATE: October 18, 19—

TO: Lisa Coop

FROM: Margaret Walton
            Billing Department Supervisor

Over the past two weeks, we have met with you on several occasions to discuss concerns that we had regarding your progress in the position of King County Biller.

Due to a patient inquiry, it has come to our attention that you have incurred a severe backlog in the itemization requests on your desk. This backlog extends as far back in date as 8/14/—, a two-month period. It includes reports to attorneys and insurance companies which had been requested for settlement of claims. We cannot stress enough the importance of the timely handling of these requests.

As you know, we have a report that you complete at the end of each month, the Status Report, on which you indicate any backlogs or areas where you need assistance. It is your responsibility to complete this report, which we have not received from you for two months. We also had a summer employee with us until September 29, whose primary job assignment was to give help with itemizations, charts, and batches to the King County billers. You had been advised to request her help whenever you needed it.

Because of your backlog, additional work is incurred by a variety of departments in the clinic including the physicians' office and Medical Records. It is also a problem for the Credit Office, who become involved with working an account that would have been cleared by insurance payment had the response been handled on time from our office. It also causes the patient unnecessary concern and frustration.

This problem with the handling of your desk functions, combined with our past discussions, causes us to seriously question your satisfactory progress in the handling of your job responsibilities.

For this reason, we are placing you on a probationary status until January 1, 19—. It is necessary that over this time period you demonstrate your ability to appear for work promptly at your starting time and change your attitude and handling of the functions and irritations that are part of your job on a daily basis. In order to successfully handle the position you must also develop a sense of work priorities and establish a work schedule so that all functions of your desk are handled routinely on a timely basis.

We feel that you have the ability to successfully meet these requirements. We would also like you to know that we will work with you in any way that you feel would assist you in developing the work habits you need.

Your progress toward meeting these requirements will be reviewed on January 2. A determination will be made regarding your continuing status as an employee in the Billing Office based on your progress.

Lisa Coop
(Attest to Reading Above)

Margaret Walton (Supervisor)

The outburst began when Lisa turned to the desk on her right and said to Shirley Deck, "Can you help me? There is a credit balance on this account, and I can't see where it came from."

SHIRLEY: Is it an insurance account?
LISA: Yes, King County Insurance.
SHIRLEY: Are there any personal payments?
LISA: (After glancing at the account sheet) No.
SHIRLEY: Then there must have been a duplicate payment from King County.
LISA: But I don't understand how that could happen.
SHIRLEY: It's not uncommon, but we have to straighten it out. We need copies of the billing register where the charges have gone to King County, then we can identify duplicate payments by matching them against the charges.

LISA: (Voice rising) How can I be expected to know that? I've never been trained on credit balances!
SHIRLEY: You have so; several of us, including me, have spent time with you. In fact, you've probably had more help than the other new people.
LISA: (Waving her arms, almost shouting) Margaret Walton has never tried to help me! No one trained me on credit balances for King County accounts.

Lisa then angrily struck the microfilm viewer and left the office. A few minutes later she returned and resumed work. Carole Prater cautioned Lisa about her outburst. Lisa made no response. Carole reported the incident to Margaret.

Margaret took no action, preferring to think the matter over until Monday.

Lisa was on Margaret's mind a great deal over the weekend. Because Margaret did not like to terminate employees, she decided to reprimand Lisa while giving her another chance to change her behavior. On Monday, Margaret discussed the incident with Lisa, stressed the seriousness of the problem and issued the letter shown in Exhibit 6.

Again, Lisa's behavior seemed to improve, although the work backlog on her desk did not

EXHIBIT 6

November 21, 19—

TO: Lisa Coop

FROM: Margaret Walton
         Billing Supervisor

On Friday, November 16, 19—, it was brought to my attention by Carole Prater, Assistant Supervisor, that your frustration over attempting to work credit balance accounts, in which you had not been trained, resulted in inappropriate behavior in the office. You were also rude to a fellow employee who had been attempting to help you because she saw your frustration mounting.

Approximately one week prior to this incident, we had discussed these accounts, and I told you not to try to work them without assistance. The agreement was that you would seek help from one of two experienced employees when you were ready to work them. In attempting to work these alone, you set yourself up for the anger and frustration that resulted in this show of temper.

As we stated to you on Friday, this kind of behavior is not acceptable and will not be tolerated in our office. Such behavior is threatening to other employees and is very destructive to the spirit of cooperation, which is so important to the team effort of which you are a part.

As you know, this sort of behavior was discussed with you earlier. Any repetition of this behavior may be cause for immediate termination.

I have read the above:

Margaret Walton
Margaret Walton, Supervisor

Lisa Coop
Lisa Coop

Carole Prater
Carole Prater, Asst. Supervisor

cc: Mr. Scontrino
Personnel File

I did not sign this report in agruement but to show I had read it.

appear to be shrinking. Margaret had met previously with Lisa to set work priorities, so felt that the most important items were being processed.

Then on January 4, an angry patient spoke with assistant supervisor Carole Prater about a billing problem. The patient, a Mrs. Selig, had talked to Lisa on three earlier occasions, requesting an itemized bill. Each time, Lisa assured her that the problem would be dealt with. After talking to the patient, Ms. Prater contacted Lisa, asked her to set aside her other work, prepare the itemization for Mrs. Selig, and put it in the afternoon mail.

On January 9, an insurance company employee called Ms. Walton regarding an account Lisa had been assigned to handle in November. The account was found in Lisa's file, unworked.

Two days later, Mrs. Selig called again, demanding her itemized statement. The statement was found lying on Lisa's desk. (See Exhibit 7.)

EXHIBIT 7

THE SANMO CLINIC

Interoffice Memo

TO: *Margaret Walton*   DATE: *Jan 15, 19—*

FROM: *Carole Prater, Asst. Supervisor – Billing Office*

On January 4, I received a call from Mrs. Laura Selig, clinic #325-776, who complained that she had requested an itemized statement from our office three times with no results. This was one of Lisa Coop's letters so I checked with her to see if she had a request pending in her file, which she did. I explained to Lisa that the patient was upset and asked her to set aside what she was doing and itemize Mrs. Selig's account so it would go out in that day's mail. Lisa said she would do this.

On January 11, I again received a call from Mrs. Selig, who was very irate because her statement still had not come. Upon checking with Lisa, I found that the itemization for Mrs. Selig was on her desk but had not been mailed out.

The Sanmo Clinic (B)

January 11

Margaret Walton concluded that Lisa Coop must be terminated immediately. Lisa had no comment when she was terminated with two weeks' pay.

On Wednesday, January 23, the personnel department informed Margaret that Lisa Coop had filed a grievance with the clinic about her termination.

Margaret expressed mild surprise, since Lisa had been so uncommunicative and passive in the several sessions leading up to

The research and written case information were presented at a Case Research Symposium and were evaluated by the Case Research Association's Editorial Board. This case was prepared by C. Patrick Fleenor of the Albers School of Business, Seattle University, as a basis for class discussion.

Distributed by the Case Research Association. All rights reserved to the author and the Case Research Association. Permission to use the case should be obtained from the Case Research Association.

her termination. The personnel representative said, "There's one real surprise in Lisa's complaint—she accuses you of racism."

MARGARET: How can she do that?

P. REP.: I know she doesn't look it, but she's black: her father is black.

MARGARET: But I didn't even know she was black—how can she charge me with racism?

P. REP.: She tried to file a complaint with the State Human Rights Commission. They told her to exhaust the internal grievance procedure first. We're going to have to be careful with this one. Write a summary of your documentation for the grievance committee. I'll send a copy of Lisa's grievance to you.

Margaret was disturbed by the allegations in the grievance (Exhibit 1) and thought carefully before framing her reply. After discussing the grievance with Carole Prater, Shirley Deck, and others, and reviewing the documentation, Margaret submitted her response (Exhibit 2.)

EXHIBIT 1

January 21, 19—

RE: Lisa L. Coop
        5262 N. W. 28th
        Seattle, WA 98105

Attention: SANMO CLINIC GRIEVANCE BOARD

On Friday, January 11, 19—, at approximately 4:30 P.M. I was terminated by my supervisor Margaret Walton for the following reasons:

I was informed that the work on my desk was behind, and when I pointed out to her that this was not so, she then informed me that I was just not reaching the goal of the job and that she felt I would do better in another area such as reception. At this point, I was given a check in the amount of $350 and told she would mail a final paycheck. She then told me that she realized my shift was over at 5:30, but that she preferred I leave right then.

On October 18, 19— Margaret Walton entered a report in my personnel file which I signed because Mrs. Walton told me that signing the report did not indicate that I agreed with it but that I had read the report. In this report she indicated that she had several discussions with me on my progress as a King County biller. In fact, we had only one meeting concerning my progress as a King County biller. The other discussions we had merely concerned the fact that I was from ten to fifteen minutes late to work, which was due to the fact that I was having great transportation problems and at the time just moved near the Seattle-Tacoma Airport.

The second paragraph concerns a backlog in itemization requests on my desk. I did indeed have a severe backlog in my itemizations but this was because I had never been taught priorities on my desk. I felt that the work which was most important was doing the actual billing, making sure that the clinic was being paid for their services, and answering letters from patients with complaints, etc. Considering the training I was given I was doing a good job at keeping those areas of my desk up to date. My itemizations were going to be done as soon as I had a break in the other areas of my desk.

The third paragraph concerns my monthly status reports and making use of our summer help. To my knowledge I turned in all status reports given to me. Our assistant supervisor is very strict about getting these reports in. If a status report is not turned in within a few days after it is given to us, we are reminded to get it in. Considering this, I don't see how there could be any way I could have neglected to turn in not only one, but two reports. As far as our summer help goes, I did ask Dianne to help me once, and she did all my itemizations. I really didn't know what I could have her help me with except itemization requests because I was fairly new in the office. The second report entered in my personnel file concerns an outburst I was said to have had in the office on November 16. I cannot express how strongly I disagree with this report. A few of the other new girls in the office and myself have not been trained on our credit balance accounts. On Friday, November 16, I had my desk in good order excluding my credit balance accounts. These were awfully far behind. All four of us had been asking for help but were not getting it. I decided that day that I would tackle them myself and just do the best job I could. I didn't get very far before I was having a problem. I asked one of the other employees, Shirley Deck, for help on these accounts. We worked on one single account for almost 30 minutes and were still making no progress. Rather than her just telling me that she simply didn't understand how to work the problem herself, she tossed the account to me and told me she wasn't going to do it for me and that I had been given just as much training as anyone else. I then made it very clear to her in a moderate but firm tone of voice that I did not want her to work the account for me but wanted her to show me how to work the account. I told her that I had not been trained at all on these accounts and I thought it wrong for her to speak to me the way she did. Our assistant supervisor, Carole Prater, heard what was going on due to the fact that she sits right in front of us, not because I was carrying on in such a manner as to catch her attention from another area of the office. I may be wrong, but in my eyes Mrs. Walton's report makes it sound as though I carried on so that I caught attention from employees in the office. It just didn't happen the way the report states.

I do know that Mrs. Walton and I have had a definite personality clash from the very beginning. I was hired into the department by Carol Burd, who was in Mrs. Walton's position at the time. I was to start in two weeks and there were no problems. Before my two weeks were even up, Mrs. Walton came to the insurance desk I was working on at the time and told me she was absolutely appalled at my absence record in the insurance department. These absences had already been excused as I had two surgeries that year and I was gone on leave of absence. She told me that she thought I should reconsider coming into her department because absences like this could not be tolerated. This was after Mrs. Burd had already hired me. I assured her there would be no problem and she then said we would try it. I feel that I had valid reason to have been gone from work for that time period.

I definitely came into the office at a bad time. They were shorthanded, and everyone was extremely busy and upset about being shorthanded. Irene Lawford, the regular trainer in the office, did start to train me. Again, because the office was shorthanded we would be constantly interrupted by phones and by Irene having to take care of one of her patient accounts. I would basically have to do the best I could and ask someone who might be free any questions I might have. I was learning from trial and error. Shortly after, Irene had an unfortunate health problem and needed immediate surgery. She was gone over a month. So there went my trainer. I would just ask questions when I could interrupt someone. This is how I was trained, which was no fault of anyone's, seeing that the office was in a bad position at the time. This was where I was getting behind in my itemization requests mentioned in the first report. But the rest of the desk was doing as good as could be expected. Certainly I was not happy with the position I was in but at that time there was nothing much that could be done until things got back to normal. After making it through that bad time in the office I began to do well at my desk not having to ask too many questions. The only problem again was credit balances. I finally did get help from two people in the office, but they turned out to be no help. There are some people, as you know, who are very good with explaining and teaching others. Carol Halvor was one who was assigned to me. The problem there was that by the time she would figure out how to work the problem herself, we would both have forgotten what the problem was. She would have me a little more mixed up than I was in the first place. Anita Fanning was asked to help me. She is good at her job but never ask her a question. She would state the problem, give the answer, and move to the next problem. She didn't have the patience to really explain what to look for and how to work the problem. Her method was zip right through, no questions asked, and if she could do it, so could you. I wasn't the only one who had a problem with her training methods. I made sure not to ask her for help again, as she did my credit balances for me one day to help out, and after the checks went out to the patients, I got many calls from patients who were refunded in error and wondering what was going on. One account was refunded $3,200 in error when it was so obvious the money should not have been refunded but should have been applied to another patient's account. So the check went to the wrong patient, and he cashed the check. The clinic then had to apply $3,200 of their money to the correct account as it was an error of one of their employees. So the clinic was out $6,400 and also had to pay for a lawyer to try to get the $3,200 back from the patient that was refunded in error.

With this in view, I think I have good reason for not going back to either one of these employees for help. It has really been a problem, and I finally decided that if I got behind on my credits it was not my fault because I had tried very hard and was getting no more help. The other newer girls had the same attitude as I about the credit balances. We all had tried.

It seemed like there was nothing I could do that would please Ms. Walton. Everything I did she would find something wrong with the way I handled it. There was a point there where we would not speak. If she wanted something done, she would write a note and I would answer in the same manner. There would be times I would be called into her office and I would be so sure that she was going to tell me she was pleased with my progress and she would do exactly the opposite, shooting me all the way down to the ground.

Just before my termination I was allowed to go on vacation. While on vacation, my billing cycle went out and it was a very large cycle. When I came back from vacation my desk had a week's worth of work to do plus a large cycle to work and get in the mail. Needless to say, I had a lot of work to be done. I got my cycle done and in the mail and I was working on the rest of the desk. Everything was fine. On the morning of my termination, I was advised by the assistant supervisor that Sue Maylock would be sitting with me for the whole day to train me on my credit balances, and hopefully she could get me in a position where I could work most of them myself. I was thrilled, mostly because Sue Maylock is a wonderful person, and I knew she would be very good at training.

We worked the accounts all day. I learned many things from Sue that day, but most important I was finally going to be able to work my credit balance accounts for the most part on my own thereafter.

At approximately 4:30 that afternoon, we were interrupted by the assistant supervisor and I was asked to step into Mrs. Walton's office. This time I was so sure I was finally going to get a good report, but instead was terminated. I asked no questions and said nothing. When she said what she had to say I knew I did not do a thing to deserve this and that she simply did not want me there. She never did.

My questions are:

1. Why have me trained, after my asking for training at least four months, on the day she's planning to terminate me?

2. Why was I not given the chance to transfer to another department, if I just could not work up to Mrs. Walton's standards, as I have seen happen with other employees?

3. Why was she allowed to handle it in the manner she did? Fire me on the spot and tell me she preferred I leave now rather than wait until my shift was over.

4. At the time I was terminated my desk was in no worse condition than any other King County biller's desk has been, or was in the same condition. I have talked since to the employee who took over my desk, and she said when she looked through my desk she could not believe I could have been terminated because of the condition of the desk.

I am (or was) working on three years' employment at the Sanmo Clinic. I started out in the medical records file section and then moved to several other areas of the medical records department including the first floor insurance desk. My goal has been office assistant for a doctor in the clinic. I wanted to move around to several areas in the clinic so that one day, when I became office assistant, I would know the functions of departments most questioned by your patients. I know from experience that many patients are misinformed by office assistants when given information about the business office, insurance department, medical release desk, Medicare, etc. I wanted to be a good assistant and be as helpful to the patients as I could. And it just made me feel good to know all I do about so many different areas in the clinic. After six months in the business office my plans were to apply for an office assistant position. When I started having problems with Mrs. Walton I knew I would have to stay longer. I would have to stay as long as it took to please her and leave me with at least a few good words. Now she has just taken all this away from me. I realize that I should have no problem finding another job, and I realize there are other hospitals to work at.

I don't want to work somewhere else. I love the Sanmo Clinic. I think there is a beautiful atmosphere there to work in. For the most part, all the employees there are very friendly, and I've made many friends there. I love the patients especially. I love the feeling I get when they need my help and I do what I can, and they walk away with a smile, pleased with my service. I've become friends with a few of the patients, especially the elderly. I've had two elderly women treat me to dinner. Please do what you have to do to see this for yourselves. Please don't allow an honest personality clash to ruin my plans for myself there at the Sanmo Clinic. I want more than anything to come back, preferably to a receptionist position. I have always worked full time there but I am in a position now in which I could survive on part-time hours and work into full time eventually. Whatever needs to be done to possibly let me come back to the clinic, I will do it. Watch every move I make, immediate termination if any problems arise. Whatever it takes, I can and will do it. I do need to hear something as soon as possible. I have been asked to go through your grievance board rather than the Human Rights Discrimination Board. I feel that since I can see no valid reason for my termination I am dealing with racial discrimination. I am doing as he asked so show some concern and give answers and help. If I can get no satisfactory help I will have to pursue the problem with the Board of Human Rights.

It has been very hard for me to get down on paper my side of the problems I had in Mrs. Walton's department. I just need someone there to understand that what has happened is wrong and I do not intend to let it slip by. I deserve the chance to prove her wrong and come back to the Sanmo Clinic.

If you would like to speak to me in person, please call me any time of the day or night at 524–7873. I'll leave a number to reach me any time I may leave the house, so please feel free to call me no matter where I am.

Sincerely,

Lisa L. Coop

EXHIBIT 2

January 31, 19—

TO: Sandy Slovak
        Director of Personnel Services

FROM: Margaret Walton
        Billing Department Supervisor

RE: TERMINATION OF EMPLOYEE – MISS LISA COOP

Prior to July 1 of last year, I was employed in the Billing Department as the Assistant Supervisor. During that period, Miss Coop applied for a position as a King County biller. She was interviewed by Mrs. Carole Burd, Billing Department Supervisor, and myself, and was offered the position. Within a few days, Miss Coop's then-current department supervisor approached Mrs. Burd and me with the fact that Miss Coop had missed extensive time from work during the previous year. It was Mrs. Burd's direct request that I contact Miss Coop and explain our concern about her past use of sick time. I was asked to point out that if it continued after her transfer, it could create great difficulty for her in successfully completing her three-month probationary period with our department. I explained she still had the opportunity to remain in her present position with its status as a permanent employee if she felt that was the best decision. She indicated she still wanted to transfer, and joined our department as scheduled. I would like to point out that a contact was made (1) at the request of my supervisor, (2) to ensure that Miss Coop was aware of the requirements of the probationary period, and (3) to ensure Miss Coop's awareness that she would be losing her status as permanent employee upon transfer.

I often communicate with the employees in the Billing Department through the use of notes. This is especially true in the King County or Medical Bureau Group because of the nature of their work schedule. It is extremely difficult to make contact with them without interrupting them during a call from a patient or problem research. Often my notes are used by the employees as documentation for action they take on an account. Also, my schedule requires me to be out of the office or in meetings on many occasions. It is not an indication of an attempt on my part to avoid contact with the employee but rather an attempt to save time for both of us by avoiding the wasted efforts of making contact that first and second time.

I would also like to point out that Miss Coop had been trained on all aspects of her desk, including the working of credit balances on the private accounts, as she indicates on her status reports of 10–18 and 1–10. The only remaining aspect still to be explained to her was the credits on the King County or Medical Bureau Accounts. The training on this type of credit balance is left until the employee has established good control over the other responsibilities of the desk. This is primarily because the employee must be able to work in the two accounting systems at the same time, the Private Accounts and the King County or Medical Bureau Accounts. This is often a difficult task or concept for the new employee, as it requires a solid understanding of how the Medical Bureau billing system works.

Most often these credits result from two major causes: (1) errors in adjustment into the Medical Bureau Billing System, made by the employee during her first few months of employment, which are not true credits; and (2) duplicate payments or processing at King County or one of the other Medical Bureaus.

During one of two discussions with Miss Coop in my office, around the first week of November, Mrs. Prater and I explained the difficulties involved with working the Medical Bureau credits and told her not to attempt to work these credits by herself. When she felt she was ready to work on them, she was asked to schedule a time with one of two senior employees so that she could get the assistance she would need. It was left in this manner because Miss Coop indicated she wanted to take care of some priority items on her desk before she worked the King County or Medical Bureau credits. I was very specific in stating at least twice during the meeting that Miss Coop would need assistance and should not attempt to work these credit accounts alone. I then spoke with the two senior employees to advise them that Miss Coop would be contacting them regarding scheduling a training session.

Despite my meeting with Miss Coop, she began working the Medical Bureau credits on November 16, without seeking assistance. Mrs. Deck, who sat next to Miss Coop, became aware that Miss Coop was having some difficulty. She attempted to assist her in working one of the accounts. Because our microfilm has the range of only three months at a time on each page, it is extremely difficult to follow the flow of an account that extends over many months. A much easier approach is the one suggested by Mrs. Deck to Miss Coop: making copies of the microfilm, which can be spliced together.

During the discussion that occurred between Miss Coop and Mrs. Deck, Miss Coop would not accept the suggestion for handling the research on the account. Mrs. Deck indicated she could not assist Miss Coop until the suggestion was followed. Miss Coop appeared to become extremely upset and began making statements regarding her views of her training in such a manner that it attracted the attention of the assistant supervisor, Mrs. Prater, and other employees in the area.

Prior to October 12, I had observed Miss Coop exhibit anger and frustration by slamming books on her desk and mishandling the microfilm viewer. I had also been advised by two of her fellow employees that they were hesitant to approach Miss Coop with problems or ask her for information when she was acting in this manner. At that time Mrs. Prater and I met with Miss Coop, outlined the problem, and explained why this behavior was not appropriate. We advised her that it was necessary to become more aware of the image she presented.

Because of our previous discussion outlining that a change in her manner of reacting when angry or frustrated was essential, and because of the fact that Miss Coop had been specifically requested to ask for assistance from two qualified employees before working the Medical Bureau credit accounts, we felt it was appropriate to advise her in writing that her behavior was unacceptable and could be the cause of termination if repeated.

Later follow-up with both senior employees indicated that Miss Coop never requested their assistance, even though after I checked with them the first time, I immediately spoke with Miss Coop and reminded her to contact them for a work session.

To respond specifically to Miss Coop's questions:

1. The training session was scheduled several days in advance with another employee when I had been advised that she could be shifted from her regular duties for a day later in the week. This was a very unusual luxury and only occurred because of the timing of year-end reports being prepared in Computer Services. My first thought was to use her in the King County or Medical Bureau area because that had been her previous job assignment, and we had several employees who could benefit from her assistance with problems. I gave Miss Coop priority because I was aware that she had not initiated contact for training.

2. I did not offer Miss Coop the opportunity for transfer because of my concern over her demonstrated inability to be a good representa-

tive of the clinic. I have never had an employee under my supervision who generated the number of telephone complaints that we have experienced with Miss Coop. The decision to place Miss Coop on probation as of October 18 and the later decision to terminate her status as an employee on January 11 were directly associated with telephone calls from her patients.

3. The decision was made to terminate Miss Coop's employment with the clinic on January 11. She was terminated at the end of that day and paid two weeks' pay in lieu of notice, as is the stated policy of the clinic. I did not feel it would serve any purpose to ask her to remain until 5:30.

4. I do not know which employee Miss Coop has spoken with in this office. At this time, the responsibilities of the desk are being shared by the employees of the King County Group.

I would like to state that my decision to terminate Miss Coop was based on her inability to handle routine responsibilities on a timely basis, thereby causing disgruntled patients to initiate contact with her supervisors. This, in turn, created a very poor image of the clinic. For example, on January 4, Mrs. Prater had a call from one of Miss Coop's patients, Mrs. Selig, who had called and spoken with Miss Coop on three previous occasions. During the January 4 conversation she stressed her irritation over the fact that, despite having spoken with Miss Coop on several occasions, she had yet to receive the itemization of her account that she had requested during each call. Mrs. Prater assured her the request would go out on January 4 as a priority. Miss Coop was asked to pull the request, which was found in her files, and make sure it was mailed by the end of the day. On January 11, Mrs. Prater was again contacted by Mrs. Selig, who demanded an explanation as to why she had still not received the itemization. Upon checking, Mrs. Prater found that the itemization was still lying on Miss Coop's desk. Miss Coop explained to Mrs. Prater that she must have forgotten about her request to handle it as a priority item.

Despite the amount of energy and training we had expended in an attempt to increase Miss Coop's ability and awareness of what was required, she was not performing at the same level as two other employees in the same group, who were hired one to two months after Miss Coop's transfer to the department. I feel our efforts to assist Miss Coop were handicapped by the fact that almost all of our meetings were carried out with total silence on her part. She never indicated she saw the smallest amount of merit in our concern over her progress. She also never indicated she saw any problems that needed to be resolved. My impression was that she did not harbor any willingness to attempt to change those patterns of her work habits that would have enabled her to make satisfactory progress in her position. The unwillingness to communicate or participate with us in what should have been a mutual goal, her success in the position, did not enable me to recommend her transfer to other departments within the clinic.

The status report she completed on January 9 was in direct contradiction to the actual status of the desk. None of the following areas of her responsibility were in a timely state:

Itemization Requests: there was a backlog with the oldest requested November 1. Miss Coop's status report of January 10 indicated all requests were current.

Correspondence: the oldest was dated December 4. Miss Coop's status report of January 10 indicated the oldest date was December 26.

Hard Cards: these had not been handled since November 8 per her list. She indicated on her status report of January 10 that she had 23 pending, which needed to be handled, and 20 awaiting reply. On her desk January 11 were 6 responses from patients, which were still in the envelopes, unworked.

Credit Balances: there were five refund checks on the desk which had been returned from July to September. These had not been researched, nor had the credits been applied back to the patient's account. Her status indicates on Medical Bureau credits that only December and January remained to be worked.

Charts: there were 10 charts on her desk that she had requested for problem research. The problems dated back to calls taken on November 30. Miss Coop had received the charts on December 8, but the problems were still unworked at the time of her termination.

At the time I terminated Miss Coop I did recommend that she not seek employment in a position that required extensive paperwork or follow-through on problems. I did suggest that I felt she would be good in a position where her main responsibilities were to greet people, such as a general receptionist or a switchboard operator. I also indicated that I thought she had strong skills in that area, and I would be willing to express such feelings to a prospective employer.

My overall assessment of the desk after reviewing it upon Miss Coop's termination is that unusual problems were filed away indefinitely, and follow-through on any other aspect of Miss Coop's responsibilities was spotty and incomplete.

The Sanmo Clinic (C)

The actual ruling of the grievance committee is shown in Exhibit 1.

The research and written case information were presented at a Case Research Symposium and were evaluated by the Case Re-

search Association's Editorial Board. This case was prepared by C. Patrick Fleenor of the Albers School of Business, Seattle University, as a basis for class discussion.

Distributed by the Case Research Association. All rights reserved to the author and the Case Research Association. Permission to use the case should be obtained from the Case Research Association.

EXHIBIT 1

THE SANMO CLINIC
(address)
(phone)

Administration:

. . . .
. . . .
. . . .

February 8, 19—

Lisa Coop
5262 N. W. 28th
Seattle, WA 98105

Dear Ms. Coop,

The Grievance Committee has had several meetings since our initial meeting with you on February 1 and has reached the following conclusions:

1. We can find no evidence to establish that there was any race discrimination involved in your termination from the Billing Department.

2. We find that you were dismissed with just cause. In comparing your job performance with two other employees of similar background and length of time as billing clerk, we found that your volume of work was significantly lower and the timeliness of work completed was significantly behind that of your coworkers. We further noted

that your sick leave frequency has remained consistently high during your employment at the clinic.

We have determined that you were sufficiently and adequately trained, counseled, warned, and disciplined. Because your performance did not significantly improve during your probationary period, Margaret Walton had no alternative but to remove you from your position and replace you with another employee. Doing otherwise would have jeopardized the work flow of the Billing Department.

However, in talking with the Director of Medical Records and your previous supervisor in Medical Records, they informed us that your performance in that department, with the exception of your attendance, was satisfactory. It is therefore our decision to offer you reinstatement in the Medical Records Department as a Medical Release Clerk. This will give you a chance to reestablish a good work record at the clinic, and if in six months your performance is found to be satisfactory, you may apply for other openings in the clinic.

Your termination will be converted to a leave of absence, and you will be placed on a three-month probationary period, as is the custom when being transferred from one position to another. We will place you at the entry level of Insurance Clerk, which is $700. When you successfully complete your three-month probationary period, you will be moved to the one-year level for that position, $736. The successful completion of your three-month probationary period will include not only performing your job duties in a satisfactory manner but additionally there must be no absenteeism. After your probationary period is successfully completed, your attendance record must fall within the policy for acceptable limits of absenteeism, which I have enclosed with a copy of your attendance record.

Please contact Sandy Slovak, Personnel Director, by Tuesday, February 12, and let her know if you would like to accept the position offered to you in the Medical Records Department. If you do decide to come back to the clinic, we hope your return will prove to be a successful one.

Sincerely,

R. E. Zackrison
Associate Administrator

REZ:ee

Birkenfield Furniture Manufacturing Company

Birkenfield Furniture Manufacturing Company, located in the coastal mountains of Washington, is in a unique position. For the first time in years sales are up, and there is a possibility that the company will break even this year. Yet the future of the firm is threatened by an economic turnaround. Prosperity, it seems, isn't always what it's cracked up to be.

Background

Mr. William McPherson, 52, president and chief stockholder of Birkenfield Furniture, came to Ilwaco, Washington, seven months ago. His background is unrelated to the furniture industry, though his father was a cabinetmaker in New Hampshire. Mr. McPherson attended two years of college at the University of New Hampshire where he studied electrical engineering and mathematics. He dropped out of college in 1942 and joined the Air Corps, and he was stationed in England and North Africa as a flight technician. After he was discharged in 1945, Mr. McPherson moved from New Hampshire to Chicago where he was employed in a large retail chain store. Advancing quickly, McPherson soon became a store manager in Seattle. In 1957, when he was 34 years old, Mr. McPherson purchased a

bankrupt plumbing supply company. He was quite successful, and he opened a second store in 1968. Mr. McPherson sold his business in 1974 because he no longer wished to live and work in a congested metropolitan area. For some time he had been looking for a quiet rural area in the Pacific Northwest where he could raise his family in a more natural, relaxed setting.

Ilwaco is a small and quietly conservative town of about 1,500 people. Located on the coast near the mouth of the Columbia River, it is about 150 miles southwest of Seattle. Life in Ilwaco is typical of many small coastal towns. Lumbering and fishing are the major occupations: the work is hard and the rewards are few. The area, though, is unsurpassed for ruggedness and beauty, and the lack of economic growth is sometimes viewed as an asset rather than a liability.

Birkenfield Furniture Manufacturing Company was founded in 1937 by Arvid Johannsen, son of Ilwaco's first mayor. Located in an abandoned salmon cannery, the company manufactured a narrow line of tables, chairs, and window sashes. The company grew until fire destroyed the old cannery in 1949. Relocated from the waterfront to an abandoned building several blocks away, Birkenfield continued to prosper, or so the company records seemed to indicate. When Mr. McPherson purchased the company he told a business associate, "I find it hard to believe that Birkenfield ever made a dime."

This case was prepared by Gerald Hampton and Bruce Mullins. Reprinted by permission of Professor Gerald M. Hampton, Albers School of Business, Seattle University.

Product Lines

Birkenfield Furniture is presently manufacturing a limited line of chairs and components for bookshelves, in addition to assorted small items such as cutting boards, macrame beads, wooden toys, and chess sets. A partial description of the product line is given in Exhibit 1. The unfinished products are sold primarily to several large furniture manufactures in the Seattle-Tacoma area, which take the assembled but unstained chairs and stain them to match the rest of their product lines. Birkenfield also sells to a chain of discount houses on the West Coast, which sell the unassembled goods directly to the customer. A more detailed income picture is shown in Exhibit 2. McPherson feels that new sources of revenue will be needed if Birkenfield is to get out of debt and prosper.

EXHIBIT 1
B.F.M.C. partial list of products

Chairs	Factory Cost	Factory Price
M.W. 0187–74	$10.54	$14.44
M.W. 0630–75	12.68	16.90
M.W. 1015–72	12.97	17.53
M.W. 1103–72	13.58	19.40
M.W. 1204–74	14.78	19.45
M.W. 0617–75	15.98	20.76
B.Z. 0401–75	$ 9.78	$12.07
B.Z. 0919–73	10.37	12.96
B.Z. 1115–74	10.78	13.15
B.Z. 0107–75	12.64	14.70
B.Z. 0804–75	12.64	15.09
Turned components*		
S.R. 1130–74	$ .61	$ .78
S.R. 0414–73	.72	1.04
S.R. 0911–74**	.83	1.10

*Turned components (lathed wooden table legs, bookcase components, etc.) are sold to other furniture manufacturers.
**The code numbers used indicate the customer, month, day, and year of the initial order.

EXHIBIT 2
B.F.M.C. comparative income statements
July–Dec. 1974; Jan.–June 1975

	July–Dec.	Jan–June
Revenue:		
Sales	$695,374	$749,605
G.B.H.*	732	449
Net income	$696,106	$750,054
Expenses:		
Cost of goods sold	$327,448	$335,851
Salaries and wages	224,909	235,900
Depreciation	775	1,200
Insurance	8,550	8,593
Utilities	12,400	12,960
Taxes	71,615	72,105
Interest	47,810	50,425
Misc.	4,753	4,915
Net expenses	$698,260	· $721,949
Increase to equity	$ (2,154)	$ 28,105

*Sales of woodchips

Labor Force

Birkenfield has several major advantages in the furniture manufacturing industry. Wages in Ilwaco are much lower than in such strongly unionized areas as Seattle or Portland. The low wages are crucial to Birkenfield because of its lower productivity and higher wastage. The wood supplies are purchased from G.B.H. Mills, a local sawmill that has supplied Birkenfield with reasonably priced raw materials since 1939.

McPherson believes that the labor force at Birkenfield is the company's most import asset. The typical worker at Birkenfield's is a

EXHIBIT 3
Hourly wage scales, furniture industry

	Ilwaco	Seattle*	Portland*
Ripsaw operator	$3.95	5.02	4.93
Gluers	$3.90	4.32	4.40
Sanders	$3.85	4.58	4.50
Maintenance	$3.48	5.07	5.00
Unskilled	$2.45	2.95	2.90

*Unionized rates

woman, middle-aged, loyal, and hardworking. Two of the foremen are male, as are the machinists in the repair shop (see Exhibit 4). Typically, housewives in Ilwaco take outside jobs to supplement the family income, and they have little inclination toward promotion and advancement within the firm. For many of Mr. McPherson's workers, the income derived from their jobs makes the difference between good times and bad in their families.

EXHIBIT 4
Organizational structure (Total: 53 full-time employees)

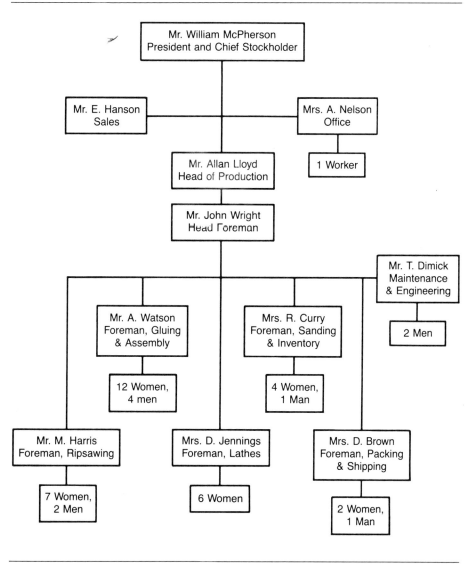

Production

The two primary disadvantages at Birkenfield are the random production schedules and the age of the building and equipment. The building housing Birkenfield is almost 50 years old, having been constructed in the late 1920s. The two-story wood frame building, typical of that era, houses an assemblage of woodworking equipment, the average age of which is 15 to 20 years. The oldest equipment in the shop still in use is a set of wooden gluing clamps that bear the initials "A. J.," obviously belonging to the founder of the company. The first floor of the building houses the ripsawing, sanding, gluing, and lathing departments. The upstairs is given over to storage of raw materials and finished goods inventory. The shipping and receiving dock is behind the main building and is connected to the upstairs storage by an outside freight elevator. The roof of the building was replaced in 1965 after leaking water had damaged finished goods and short-circuited the freight elevator several times. McPherson was amazed at how long and how well the equipment had performed. Much of the credit for the careful maintenance of the machines went to Tom Dimick, the head of the repair shop. McPherson knew that the company would be in a precarious position if something were to happen to Dimick.

A major fault of the present production system is the high percentage of wastage and short production runs. One of the first things McPherson noticed prior to purchasing Birkenfield in February, 1975, was three metal bins overflowing with chipped, cracked, or damaged wooden pieces. When McPherson inquired about these bins, he was told that they contained the week's rejects of glued or lathed pieces. These were fed into a wood chipper each week, and the chips were sent by truck back to G.B.H. Mills for reprocessing into various wood products. Birkenfield recovered very little money on these chips in com-parison with the original cost of the wood. It was McPherson's contention that most of this wastage was caused by worker or machine error, but a significant portion was caused by excessively warped, knotty, or split wood supplied to Birkenfield by G.B.H. Mills. Although Mr. McPherson felt that this situation should be remedied, he felt very reluctant to offend G.B.H. Mills because of the close ties between the two companies through the years. He was also uncertain where he would find an alternative source of wood at a price he could afford in Ilwaco, although one mill up the coast had indicated that they would consider supplying wood to Birkenfield at a cost of 5 percent more per board foot than what G.B.H. was charging.

The problem of short production runs was, in McPherson's opinion, one of the most significant that Birkenfield faced. As an example, McPherson gives this account:

Two days after I assumed control [of Birkenfield], I received a telephone call from one of the buyers of our biggest customer in Seattle. In short, he made it clear that he desperately needed 50 sets of our dining room chairs, model M.W. 1103–72, immediately. When I informed him that we had only 40 sets in stock, he told me in no uncertain terms that that was my problem and that he needed the 50 sets immediately; then he abruptly hung up. I immediately called in John Wright, my head foreman, and told him of the situation. I was obviously still shocked by the man's brashness because John informed me that this kind of thing wasn't new. This particular customer had done it often in the past whenever things got hectic in Seattle. I realized then how much we are at the mercy of the customers; they have us over a barrel! We can't afford to offend any of our customers.

McPherson ordered that all production be halted and shifted to the production of the M.W. 1103–72 order. This caused several other orders to be shunted aside and caused considerable wastage of materials and manpower. As McPherson noted:

In a company that is in our position, it is almost impossible to dictate terms to our customers. There are several other furniture manufacturers in Seattle that would love to handle our clients' business. Something has got to be done about it.

Present Operations

In an attempt to increase the efficiency of his machines and workers, Mr. McPherson brought to Birkenfield Mr. Allan Lloyd, a production and time-studies man. Lloyd came to Birkenfield very highly recommended, and McPherson felt fortunate to acquire his service. Mr. Lloyd, 31, was a graduate of the M.B.A. program at the University of Southern California and was previously employed as a consultant by a Seattle electronics firm. Having grown up in the Seattle area he was acquainted with Ilwaco, and he anticipated the challenge that Birkenfield offered. His ultimate plan, as McPherson understood, was to gain experience in a small town locale to further his consulting ambitions. His job was to supervise and direct production operations to maximize efficiency and reduce wastage. He reported to Mr. McPherson, and he supervised all line foremen. (See Exhibit 4.)

Mr. McPherson also brought two additional supervisory people: Mrs. Agnes Nelson to keep the books, and Mr. Erik Hanson, McPherson's son-in-law, to help in sales. Hanson had previously been employed at McPherson's Plumbing Company; he now handled, with McPherson, all sales. He was well liked by those who knew him, and Mr. McPherson hoped that one day he would take over the family business. Mrs. Nelson, a widow in her sixties, had previously been the bookkeeper for Mr. McPherson in the plumbing business. She knew exactly how McPherson liked his books kept and was al-

ways a cheery face in the office. Birkenfield's previous bookkeeper had left the books in such a sad state that Mrs. Nelson was forced to take home boxes of old records to sort out at night. Assisting her was Lynn McPherson, Mr. McPherson's college-age daughter. Together the two of them had spent the summer putting together financial statements that would hopefully aid McPherson in running the company. (See Exhibits 2 and 5.)

On Friday morning, August 15, Debby Jennings, the lathe department foreman, came rushing into Mr. McPherson's office. She was very upset and appeared to be near tears.

EXHIBIT 5
Birkenfield Furniture Company comparative balance statement 12-31-74; 6-30-75

	12-31-74	6-30-75
Assets:		
Current		
Accts. Rec. Trade	295,711	324,852
Cash	(1,312)	3,555
Accts. Rec. G.B.II.	732	751
Prepaid Insurance	1,201	1,250
Non-Current		
Machinery and Equip.	14,807	14,738
Land	30,000	30,000
Building	18,100	18,100
Accum. Dep.	98,105	99,305
Inventory Raw Mat.	3,987	1,787
Inventory Fin. Gs.	14,900	12,752
Total Assets	476,831	507,090
Liabilities:		
Current		
Accts. Pay. Trade	38,973	40,019
Taxes Pay.	171,615	173,777
Interest Pay.	7,770	5,214
Non-Current		
Contract Pay, W.F.N.B.*	73,700	67,497
Total Liabilities	292,058	286,507
Capital Stock	184,773	218,377
Retained Earnings	0	2,206
Total Stockholders Eq.	184,773	220,583
Total Equities	476,831	507,090

*A long-term bank debt secured in 1971

"Mr. McPherson," she started, "You've just got to do something about Mr. Lloyd! Everyone in my department is so upset, they're all about ready to walk out. I'm sorry to come and bother you like this, but you're his boss, maybe you can do something."

McPherson walked out on the floor with Mrs. Jennings. It was true, work had almost stopped in the lathe department; it looked as though the women were about ready to leave. McPherson, still not knowing what had upset the workers, invited the women into his office to talk things over. He surmised that Lloyd had probably said or done something that had irritated the employees.

"It's that damn Lloyd, Mr. McPherson!" one woman started. "He wants us to work overtime again tonight. That's the second time this week! Listen, I've got a husband and four kids to feed and clean up after. You tell me how I can do that if I have to keep working here in the evening. All of us are in the same situation, and there's no way I can keep this job if I have to work overtime every other night."

Mr. McPherson suddenly realized the seriousness of the situation. Birkenfield would go out with the next tide if all the workers walked out on him. McPherson explained to the women that the company was trying to expand sales and that this required building up the finished goods inventories, so some overtime was necessary. However, he promised that they wouldn't have to work overtime that night, and he said that he would make sure that they would be informed at least one shift in advance of any future overtime. The women workers seemed satisfied at this and left the office to eat lunch. Taking Mrs. Jennings to one side, Mr. McPherson asked why she hadn't informed him earlier about the labor troubles. In an exasperated voice she said:

"It's that Lloyd again! You told me to report directly to him so that you would have more time to devote to getting the rest of the company straightened out. Lloyd just sits on our complaints and never does anything about them. He's had a couple of good ideas, but he sure doesn't know how to get them across without getting everyone mad at him. A diplomat he's not."

McPherson remembered several instances that seemed to support what the women had told him. Lynn McPherson, who was working at the plant during the summer, had come to her father on several occasions to pass on tips and suggestions offered by workers. The workers seemed to feel more comfortable talking to Lynn rather than to Lloyd or one of the "bosses." This led McPherson to install a suggestion box next to the coffee machine just outside his office. The box, however, yielded fewer results than anticipated. The workers, it appeared, preferred to verbalize ideas rather than commit them to writing.

"I don't really see what they're so upset about," was Lloyd's reply to McPherson's queries. "They can't seem to realize that this business has to grow to get out of the rut it's in, and right now that requires some overtime from everyone. To increase profits we've got to show our customers that we can deliever the goods without delay; maybe then we have a chance. I've been working for six weeks trying to set up standards and improve the production figures, but as close as I've been able to figure it, production has only risen 5 percent. Most of that came from straightening out the gluing area. Everywhere else I've met nothing but a lot of hostility and resentment. I've never even heard of a worker situation like this before. You'd think these ladies would want the extra money that overtime puts into their paychecks."

McPherson had never considered employee morale low before. Now, however, as he walked from department to department, he saw that the workers weren't as talkative as he recalled they had been some time earlier. He figured that they had all heard of the incident in the lathe department and were in agreement about working overtime. McPherson was curious about why the gluing people had improved while the rest of the plant had apparently declined. McPherson called Alex Watson, foreman of the gluing department, and complimented him on the workers' performance. Watson replied, "Coming from you, Mr McPherson, that's a real compliment. It's good to feel like someone up front is taking an interest in us out on the floor."

When McPherson prodded him to elaborate on his department's achievements, Watson finally attributed them to a bright girl in his department, Margie Lewis.

"I don't know how she does it, Mr. McPherson, but Margie is just real good with stuff like that. My crew was pretty upset after Lloyd first came through giving orders and telling us all how to do our jobs. But Margie explained them to us, and they seemed more reasonable coming from her than from Lloyd."

Within the next week McPherson almost forgot about the incident of the previous Friday. The women had only worked one day of overtime, and on the surface things seemed to be back to normal. Thursday afternoon, August 21, McPherson found a telephone message waiting for him from the Washington State Labor Relations Board. When he returned the call he was informed that the board had received a complaint from a group of the workers at Birkenfield. The complaint contained allegations of management harassment, low wages, and poor working conditions. The workers had questioned the board about possible actions open to them, including establishing a union shop. McPherson was very disturbed at this revelation, especially since he was generally unaware of such a high level of discontent among his workers. He knew that the company could not afford unionization now; it just did not have the cash to pay higher wages or benefits.

Mr. McPherson realized that the future of Birkenfield was in jeopardy. The decisions that he would have to make now would be among the toughest of his career.

Seabrook Manufacturing Company

"All we need now is a strong man to complete the side show!" exclaimed Joe Larson, purchasing manager of the Seabrook Manufacturing Company, as he entered the office of Dale Wolff, personnel representative for the Purchasing Department.

"What do you mean, Joe?" asked Dale.

"You know that we have a lot of visitors and suppliers through here, and that old bag isn't doing much to doll up the area. These secretaries have a good deal to do with the impressions people get of our outfit, and they should be at least presentable! We spend thousands of dollars for carpeting and pictures and now this!"

"Whom are you talking about?"

"I don't know what her name is, but you know damn well whom I'm talking about! The Blimp! Take care of it, will you?"

The Purchasing Department of Seabrook Manufacturing Company occupied the major portion of the third floor of the headquarters building of the company. The main working force was located in a large open area at several rows of desks. Executives of the division, all of whom were under the control of Larson, were located in private offices that extended along the outer edge of the general working area.[1] The secretary for each executive was

situated at a desk directly in front of the office of the executive for whom she worked, but was separated from the rest of the workers by a wide aisle. This aisle was the main passage used by visitors and personnel from other divisions of the company to get from the reception lobby to the executives' offices. The secretaries' desks were finished with a walnut stain as contrasted with the lighter-colored finishes used on other desks in the open area, and the space between secretaries' desks was significantly greater than the space between other desks on the floor. The office layout of the Purchasing Department is shown in Exhibit 1.

Mary Lampson, the secretary in question, had just been promoted to her new position as Jack Henderson's secretary and had moved to her new location while Larson had been away on a business trip. After his former secretary had submitted her resignation, Jack Henderson had selected Mary Lampson as his new secretary after reviewing the personnel files and talking with several individuals currently employed in the department whom Dale Wolff had recommended as candidates for the position.

Mary Lampson was forty-eight years old, and had been with the Seabrook Manufacturing Company for seventeen years, ten in the Purchasing Department. She had started work at Seabrook shortly after her husband died. Prior to her assignment as Henderson's secretary, she had performed secretarial duties for

---

[1]Dale Wolff reported directly to Joe Larson.

EXHIBIT 1
Purchasing department office layout

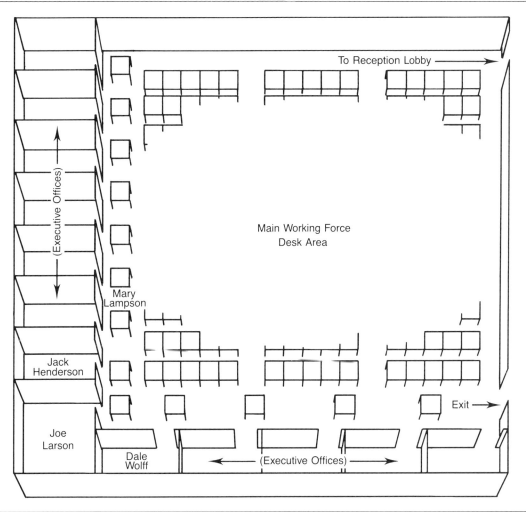

several units in the department but had always been located in the open area with the general employees of the division. She had two grown sons who had completed college and had moved to other parts of the country, and one other son, twenty years old, who was a sophomore at Eastern State University. Her record at Seabrook was unblemished. She had created favorable impressions wherever she had worked, and her former supervisors were unanimous in their praise of her abilities.

Mary Lampson was five feet four inches tall and weighed two hundred and twenty-five pounds. Although her weight had been a continuing problem for her, she was very pleased with her recent progress on a weight control program, and had lost sixty pounds in the last two years by following her doctor's orders very closely. She was enthusiastic about her new job, for she could use the increase in salary to help put her youngest son through college, and, as she put it, "keep the creditors a little farther from my door."

While not knowing quite how to "take care of it," Dale Wolff decided that his first step should be to talk with Jack Henderson, Mary's boss.

After Wolff related his conversation with Larson, Jack Henderson replied: "What a hell of a way to run a railroad! You do what you want to, Dale, but things are in pretty miserable shape when looks are more important than ability. I'm certainly not going to mention this to Mary!"

Michael Simpson

Michael Simpson is one of the most outstanding managers in the management consulting division of Avery McNeil and Co.[1] A highly qualified individual with a deep sense of responsibility, Simpson had obtained his M.B.A. two years ago from one of the leading northeastern schools. Before graduating from business school, Simpson had interviewed a number of consulting firms and decided that the consulting division of Avery McNeil offered the greatest potential for rapid advancement.

Simpson had recently been promoted to manager, making him the youngest individual at this level in the consulting group. Two years with the firm was an exceptionally short period of time in which to achieve this promotion. Although the promotions had been announced, Simpson had not yet been informed of his new salary. Despite the fact that his career had progressed well, he was concerned that his salary would be somewhat lower than the current market value that a headhunter had recently quoted him.

Simpson's wife, Diane, soon would be receiving her M.B.A. One night over dinner, Simpson was amazed to hear the salaries being offered to new M.B.A.'s. Simpson commented to Diane, "I certainly hope I get a substantial raise this time. I mean, it just wouldn't be fair to be making the same amount as recent graduates when I've been at the company now for over two years! I'd like to buy a house soon, but with housing costs rising and inflation following, that will depend on my pay raise."

Several days later, Simpson was working at his desk when Dave Barton, a friend and colleague, came across to Simpson's office. Barton had been hired at the same time as Simpson and had also been promoted recently. Barton told Simpson, "Hey Mike, look at this! I was walking past Jane's desk and saw this memo from the personnel manager lying there. She obviously forgot to put it away. Her boss would kill her if he found out!"

The memo showed the proposed salaries for all the individuals in the consulting group that year. Simpson looked at the list and was amazed by what he saw. He said "I can't believe this, Dave! Walt and Rich will be getting $2,000.00 more than I am."

Walt Gresham and Rich Watson had been hired within the past year. Before coming to Avery McNeil they had both worked one year at another consulting firm. Barton spoke angrily: "Mike, I knew the firm had to pay them an awful lot to attract them, but to pay them more than people above them is ridiculous!"

SIMPSON: You know if I hadn't seen Walt and Rich's salaries, I would think I was getting a reasonable raise. Hey, listen, Dave, let's get

---

[1] Avery McNeil is primarily an accounting firm that has two divisions besides accounting—tax and management consulting.

Reprinted from *Managing Organizations: Readings and Cases,* by David A. Nadler, Michael L. Tushman, and Nina G. Hatvany (Boston, MA: Little, Brown & Co., 1982): 489–490. Copyright © 1982 by David A. Nadler, Michael L. Tushman, Nina G. Hatvany. Used by permission.

out of here. I've had enough of this place for one day.

BARTON: Okay, Mike, just let me return this memo. Look, it's not that bad; after all, you are getting the largest raise.

On his way home, Simpson tried to think about the situation more objectively. He knew that there were a number of pressures on the compensation structure in the consulting division.

If the division wished to continue attracting M.B.A.'s from top schools, it would have to offer competitive salaries. Starting salaries had increased about $3,500 during the last two years. As a result, some of the less experienced M.B.A.'s were earning nearly the same amounts as others who had been with the firm several years but had come in at lower starting salaries, even though their pay had been gradually increasing over time.

Furthermore, because of expanding business, the division had found it necessary to hire consultants from other firms. In order to do so effectively, Avery McNeil had found it necessary to upgrade the salaries they offered.

The firm as a whole was having problems meeting the federally regulated Equal Employment Opportunity goals and was trying especially hard to recruit women and minorities.

One of Simpson's colleagues, Martha Lohman, had been working in the consulting division of Avery McNeil and Company until three months ago when she was offered a job at another consulting firm. She had become disappointed with her new job and on returning to her previous position at Avery McNeil was rehired at a salary considerably higher than her former level. Simpson had noticed on the memo that she was earning more than he was, even though she was not given nearly the same level of responsibility. Simpson also realized that the firm attempted to maintain some parity between salaries in the auditing and consulting divisions.

When Simpson arrived home, he discussed the situation with his wife: "Diane, I know I'm getting a good raise, but I am still earning below my market value—$3,000 less than that headhunter told me last week. And the fact that those two guys from the other consulting firm are getting more than I shows the firm is prepared to pay competitive rates."

DIANE: I know it's unfair Mike, but what can you do? You know your boss won't negotiate salaries after they have been approved by the compensation committee, but it wouldn't hurt to at least talk to him about your dissatisfaction. I don't think you should let a few thousand dollars a year bother you. You will catch up eventually, and the main thing is that you really enjoy what you are doing.

SIMPSON: Yes, I do enjoy what I'm doing, but that is not to say that I wouldn't enjoy it elsewhere. I really just have to sit down and think about all the pros and cons in my working for Avery McNeil. First of all, I took this job because I felt that I could work my way up quickly. I think that I have demonstrated this, and the firm has also shown that they are willing to help me achieve this goal. If I left this job for a better paying one, I might not get the opportunity to work on the exciting jobs that I am currently working on. Furthermore, this company has time and money invested in me. I'm the only one at Avery that can work on certain jobs, and the company has several lined up. If I left the company now, they would not only lose me, but they would probably lose some of their billings as well. I really don't know what to do at this point. Diane, I can either stay with Avery McNeil or look for a higher paying job elsewhere; however, there is no guarantee that my new job would be a "fast track" one like it is at Avery. One big plus at Avery is that the people there already know me and the kind of work I produce. If I went elsewhere, I'd essentially have to start all over again. What do you think I should do, Diane?

PART SEVEN
Special Issues in
Organizational Behavior

Rondell Data Corporation

"Goddamn it, he's done it again!"

Frank Forbus threw the stack of prints and specifications down on his desk in disgust. The Model 802 wide-band modulator, released for production the previous Thursday, had just come back to Frank's engineering services department with a caustic note that began, "This one can't be produced, either. . . ." It was the fourth time production had kicked the design back.

Frank Forbus, director of engineering for Rondell Data Corporation, was normally a quiet man. But the Model 802 was stretching his patience; it was beginning to look just like other new products that had hit delays and problems in the transition from design to production during the eight months Frank had worked for Rondell. These problems were nothing new at the sprawling old Rondell factory; Frank's predecessor in the engineering job had run afoul of them, too, and had finally been fired for protesting too vehemently about the other departments. But the Model 802 should have been different. Frank had met two months before with the firm's president, Bill Hunt, and with Factory Superintendent Dave Schwab to smooth the way for the new modulator design. He thought back to the meeting . . .

"Now we all know there's a tight deadline on the 802," Bill Hunt said, *"and Frank's done well to*

This case was prepared by Professor John A. Seeger, Bentley College. Copyright © 1981 by John A. Seeger. Used with permission.

ask us to talk about its introduction. I'm counting on both of you to find any snags in the system and to work together to get that first production run out by October 2. Can you do it?"

"We can do it in production if we get a clean design two weeks from now, as scheduled," answered Dave Schwab, the grizzled factory superintendent. *"Frank and I have already talked about that, of course. I'm setting aside time in the card room and the machine shop, and we'll be ready. If the design goes over schedule, though, I'll have to fill in with other runs, and it will cost us a bundle to break in for the 802. How does it look in Engineering, Frank?"*

"I've just reviewed the design for the second time," Frank replied. *"If Ron Porter can keep the salesmen out of our hair and avoid any more last-minute changes, we've got a shot. I've pulled the draftsmen off three other overdue jobs to get this one out. But, Dave, that means we can't spring engineers loose to confer with your production people on manufacturing problems."*

"Well, Frank, most of those problems are caused by the engineers, and we need them to resolve the difficulties. We've all agreed that production bugs come from both of us bowing to sales pressure and putting equipment into production before the designs are really ready. That's just what we're trying to avoid on the 802. But I can't have 500 people sitting on their hands waiting for an answer from your people. We'll have to have some engineering support."

Bill Hunt broke in, *"So long as you two can talk calmly about the problem I'm confident you can resolve it. What a relief it is, Frank, to hear the way you're approaching this. With Kilmann [the previous director of engineering] this con-*

versation would have been a shouting match. Right, Dave?" Dave nodded and smiled.

"Now there's one other thing you should both be aware of," Hunt continued. "Doc Reeves and I talked last night about a new filtering technique, one that might improve the signal-to-noise ratio of the 802 by a factor of two. There's a chance Doc can come up with it before the 802 reaches production, and if it's possible, I'd like to use the new filters. That would give us a real jump on the competition."

Four days after that meeting, Frank found that two of his key people on the 802 design had been called to production for emergency consultation on a bug found in final assembly: two halves of a new data transmission interface wouldn't fit together because recent changes in the front end required a different chassis design for the back end.

Another week later, Doc Reeves walked into Frank's office, proud as a new parent, with the new filter design. "This won't affect the other modules of the 802 much," Doc had said. "Look, it takes three new cards, a few connectors, some changes in the wiring harness, and some new shielding, and that's all."

Frank had tried to resist the last-minute design changes, but Bill Hunt had stood firm. With a lot of overtime by the engineers and draftsmen, engineering services should still be able to finish the prints in time.

Two engineers and three draftsmen went onto 12-hour days to get the 802 ready, but the prints were still five days late reaching Dave Schwab. Two days later, the prints came back to Frank, heavily annotated in red. Schwab had worked all day Saturday to review the job, and had found more than a dozen discrepancies in the prints—most of them caused by the new filter design and insufficient checking time before release. Correction of those design faults had brought on a new generation of discrepancies; Schwab's cover note on the second return of the prints indica-

ted he'd had to release the machine capacity he'd been holding for the 802. On the third iteration, Schwab committed his photo and plating capacity to another rush job. The 802 would be at least one month late getting into production. Ron Porter, vice president for sales, was furious. His customer needed 100 units *NOW*, he said. Rondell was the customer's only late supplier.

"Here we go again," thought Frank Forbus.

Company History

Rondell Data Corporation traced its lineage through several generations of electronics technology. Its original founder, Bob Rondell, had set the firm up in 1920 as "Rondell Equipment Company" to manufacture several electrical testing devices he had invented as an engineering faculty member at a large university. The firm branched into radio broadcasting equipment in 1947 and into data transmission equipment in the early 1960s. A well-established corps of direct-sales people, mostly engineers, called on industrial, scientific, and government accounts, but concentrated heavily on original equipment manufacturers. In this market, Rondell had a long-standing reputation as a source of high-quality, innovative designs. The firm's salespeople fed a continual stream of challenging problems into the engineering department, where the creative genius of Ed "Doc" Reeves and several dozen other engineers "converted problems to solutions" (as the sales brochure bragged). Product design formed the spearhead of Rondell's growth.

Rondell offered a wide range of products in its two major lines. Broadcast equipment sales had benefited from the growth of UHF TV and FM radio; it now accounted for 35 percent of company sales. Data transmission had blossomed, and in this field an increasing number of orders called for unique specifications, ranging from specialized display panels to entirely untried designs.

The company had grown from 100 employees in 1947 to over 800. (Exhibit 1 shows the current organization chart of key employees.) Bill Hunt, who had been a student of the company's founder, had presided over most of that growth, and took great pride in preserving the "family spirit" of the old organization. Informal relationships between Rondell's veteran employees formed the backbone of the firm's day-to-day operations; all the managers relied on personal contact, and Hunt often insisted that the absence of bureaucratic red tape was a key factor in recruiting outstanding engineering talent. The personal management approach extended throughout the factory. All exempt employees were paid on a straight salary plus a share of the profits. Rondell boasted an extremely loyal group of senior employees and very low turnover in nearly all areas of the company.

The highest turnover job in the firm was Frank Forbus's. Frank had joined Rondell seven months previously, replacing Jim Kilmann who had been director of engineering for only 10 months. Kilmann, in turn, had replaced Tom MacLeod, a talented engineer who had made a promising start but had taken to drink after a year in the job. MacLeod's predecessor had been a genial old-timer who retired at 70 after 30 years in charge of engineering. (Doc Reeves had refused the directorship in each of the recent changes, saying, "Hell, that's no promotion for a bench man like me. I'm no administrator.")

For several years, the firm had experienced a steadily increasing number of disputes between research, engineering, sales, and production people—disputes generally centered on the problem of new product introduction. Quarrels between departments became more numerous under MacLeod, Kilmann, and Forbus. Some managers associated those

disputes with the company's recent decline in profitability—a decline that, in spite of higher sales and gross revenues, was beginning to bother people. President Bill Hunt commented:

Better cooperation, I'm sure, could increase our output by 5–10 percent. I'd hoped Kilmann could solve the problems, but pretty obviously he was too young, too arrogant. People like him—that conflict type of personality—bother me. I don't like strife, and with him it seemed I spent all my time smoothing out arguments. Kilmann tried to tell everyone else how to run their departments, without having his own house in order. That approach just wouldn't work here at Rondell. Frank Forbus, now, seems much more in tune with our style of organization. I'm really hopeful now.

Still, we have just as many problems now as we did last year. Maybe even more. I hope Frank can get a handle on Engineering Services soon . . .

The Engineering Department: Research

According to the organization chart (see Exhibit 1), Frank Forbus was in charge of both research (really the product development function) and engineering services (which provided engineering support). To Forbus, however, the relationship with research was not so clear-cut:

Doc Reeves is one of the world's unique people, and none of us would have it any other way. He's a creative genius. Sure, the chart says he works for me, but we all know Doc does his own thing. He's not the least bit interested in management routines, and I can't count on him to take any responsibility in scheduling projects, or checking budgets, or what-have-you. But as long as Doc is director of research, you can bet this company will keep on leading the field. He has more ideas per hour than most people have per year, and he keeps the whole engineering staff fired up. Everybody loves Doc—and you can count me in on

EXHIBIT 1
Rondell Data Corporation's organization chart

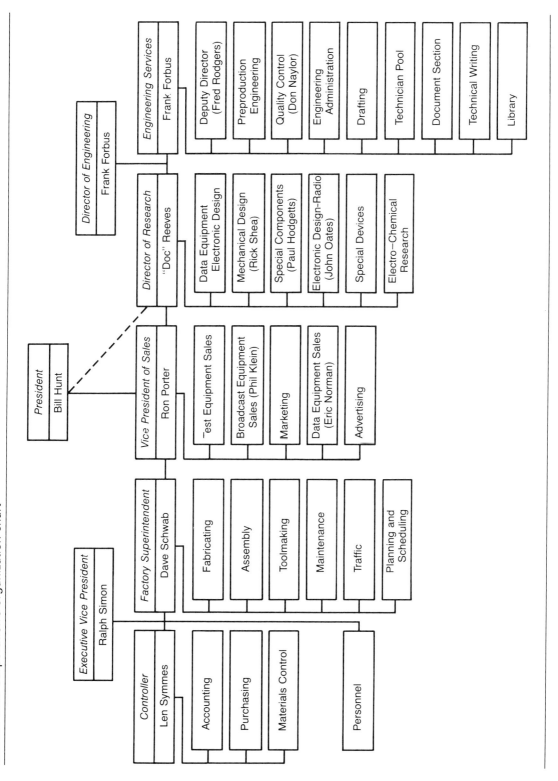

that, too. In a way, he works for me, sure. But that's not what's important.

"Doc" Reeves—unhurried, contemplative, casual, and candid—tipped his stool back against the wall of his research cubicle and talked about what *was* important:

Development engineering. That's where the company's future rests. Either we have it there, or we don't have it.

There's no kidding ourselves that we're anything but a bunch of Rube Goldbergs here. But that's where the biggest kicks come from—from solving development problems, and dreaming up new ways of doing things. That's why I so look forward to the special contracts we get involved in. We accept them not for the revenue they represent, but because they subsidize the basic development work which goes into all our basic products.

This is a fantastic place to work. I have a great crew and they can really deliver when the chips are down. Why, Bill Hunt and I [he gestured toward the neighboring cubicle, where the president's name hung over the door] are likely to find as many people here at work at 10:00 P.M. as at 3:00 in the afternoon. The important thing here is the relationships between people; they're based on mutual respect, not on policies and procedures. Administrative red tape is a pain. It takes away from development time.

Problems? Sure, there are problems now and then. There are power interests in production, where they sometimes resist change. But I'm not a fighting man, you know. I suppose if I were, I might go in there and push my weight around a little. But I'm an engineer, and can do more for Rondell sitting right here, or working with my own people. That's what brings results.

Other members of the research department echoed Doc's views and added some additional sources of satisfaction with their work. They were proud of the personal contacts they built up with customers' technical staffs—contacts that increasingly involved travel to the customers' factories to serve as expert advisors in preparation of overall system design specifications. The engineers were also delighted with the department's encouragement of their personal development, continuing education, and independence on the job.

But there were problems, too. Rick Shea, of the mechanical design section, noted:

In the old days I really enjoyed the work—and the people I work with. But now there's a lot of irritation. I don't like someone breathing down my neck. You can be hurried into jeopardizing the design.

John Oates, head of the radio electronic design section, was another designer with definite views:

Production engineering is almost nonexistent in this company. Very little is done by the preproduction section in engineering services. Frank Forbus has been trying to get preproduction into the picture, but he won't succeed because you can't start from such an ambiguous position. There have been three directors of engineering in three years. Frank can't hold his own against the others in the company. Kilmann was too aggressive. Perhaps no amount of tact would have succeeded.

Paul Hodgetts was head of special components in the R & D department. Like the rest of the department he valued bench work. But he complained of engineering services.

The services don't do things we want them to do. Instead, they tell us what they're going to do. I should probably go to Frank, but I don't get any decisions there. I know I should go through Frank, but this holds things up, so I often go direct.

The Engineering Department: Engineering Services

The engineering services department provided ancillary services to R & D and served as liaison between engineering and the other Rondell departments. Among its main functions were drafting; management of the central technicians' pool; scheduling and expediting engineering products; documentation and publication of parts lists and engineering orders; preproduction engineering (consisting of the final integration of individual design components into mechanically compatible packages); and quality control (which included inspection of incoming parts and materials, and final inspection of subassemblies and finished equipment). Top management's description of the department included the line, "ESD is responsible for maintaining cooperation with other departments, providing services to the development engineers, and freeing more valuable people in R & D from essential activities which are diversions from and beneath their main competence."

Many of Frank Forbus's 75 employees were located in other departments. Quality-control people were scattered through the manufacturing and receiving areas, and technicians worked primarily in the research area or the prototype fabrication room. The remaining ESD personnel were assigned to leftover nooks and crannies near production or engineering sections.

Frank Forbus described his position:

My biggest problem is getting acceptance from the people I work with. I've moved slowly rather than risk antagonism. I saw what happened to Kilmann, and I want to avoid that. But although his precipitate action had won over a few of the younger R & D people, he certainly didn't have the department's backing. Of course, it was the resentment of other departments which eventually caused his discharge. People have been slow accepting me here. There's nothing really overt, but I get a negative reaction to my ideas.

My role in the company has never been well defined, really. It's complicated by Doc's unique position, of course, and also by the fact that ESD sort of grew by itself over the years, as the de-

sign engineers concentrated more and more on the creative parts of product development. I wish I could be more involved in the technical side. That's been my training, and it's a lot of fun. But in our setup, the technical side is the least necessary for me to be involved in.

Schwab [production head] is hard to get along with. Before I came and after Kilmann left, there were six months intervening when no one was really doing any scheduling. No workloads were figured, and unrealistic promises were made about releases. This puts us in an awkward position. We've been scheduling way beyond our capacity to manufacture or engineer.

Certain people within R & D, for instance John Oates, head of the radio electronic design section, understand scheduling well and meet project deadlines, but this is not generally true of the rest of the R & D department, especially the mechanical engineers who won't commit themselves. Most of the complaints come from sales and production department heads because items—like the 802—are going to production before they are fully developed, under pressure from sales to get out the unit, and this snags the whole process. Somehow, engineering services should be able to intervene and resolve these complaints, but I haven't made much headway so far.

I should be able to go to Hunt for help, but he's too busy most of the time, and his major interest is the design side of engineering, where he got his own start. Sometimes he talks as though he's the engineering director as well as president. I have to put my foot down; there are problems here that the front office just doesn't understand.

Sales people were often observed taking their problems directly to designers, while production frequently threw designs back at R & D, claiming they could not be produced and demanding the prompt attention of particular design engineers. The latter were frequently observed in conference with production supervisors on the assembly floor. Frank went on:

The designers seem to feel they're losing something when one of us tries to help. They feel it's a reflection on them to have someone take over what they've been doing. They seem to want to carry a project right through to the final stages, particularly the mechanical people. Consequently, engineering services people are used below their capacity to contribute and our department is denied functions it should be performing. There's not as much use made of engineering services as there should be.

Frank Forbus's technician supervisor added his comments:

Production picks out the engineer who'll be the "bum of the month." They pick on every little detail instead of using their heads and making the minor changes that have to be made. The 15-to-20-year people shouldn't have to prove their ability any more, but they spend four hours defending themselves and four hours getting the job done. I have no one to go to when I need help. Frank Forbus is afraid. I'm trying to help him but he can't help me at this time. I'm responsible for 50 people and I've got to support them.

Fred Rodgers, whom Frank had brought with him to the company as an assistant, gave another view of the situation:

I try to get our people in preproduction to take responsibility but they're not used to it and people in other departments don't usually see them as best qualified to solve the problem. There's a real barrier for a newcomer here. Gaining people's confidence is hard. More and more, I'm wondering whether there really is a job for me here.

(Rodgers left Rondell a month later.) Another of Forbus's subordinates gave his view:

If Doc gets a new product idea you can't argue. But he's too optimistic. He judges that others can do what he does—but there's only one Doc Reeves. We've had 900 production change orders this year—they changed 2,500 drawings. If

I were in Frank's shoes I'd put my foot down on all this new development. I'd look at the reworking we're doing and get production set up the way I wanted it. Kilmann was fired when he was doing a good job. He was getting some system in the company's operations. Of course, it hurt some people. There is no denying that Doc is the most important person in the company. What gets overlooked is that Hunt is a close second, not just politically but in terms of what he contributes technically and in customer relations.

This subordinate explained that he sometimes went out into the production department but that Schwab, the production head, resented this. Personnel in production said that Kilmann had failed to show respect for oldtimers and was always meddling in other departments' business. This was why he had been fired, they contended.

Don Taylor was in charge of quality control. He commented:

I am now much more concerned with administration and less with work. It is one of the evils you get into. There is tremendous detail in this job. I listen to everyone's opinion. Everybody is important. There shouldn't be distinctions—distinctions between people. I'm not sure whether Frank has to be a fireball like Kilmann. I think the real question is whether Frank is getting the job done. I know my job is essential. I want to supply service to the more talented people and give them information so they can do their jobs better.

The Sales Department

Ron Porter was angry. His job was supposed to be selling, he said, but instead it had turned into settling disputes inside the plant and making excuses to waiting customers. He jabbed a finger toward his desk:

You see that telephone? I'm actually afraid nowadays to hear it ring. Three times out of five, it will be a customer who's hurting because we've failed to deliver on schedule. The other two calls will be from production or ESD, telling me some schedule has slipped again.

The Model 802 is typical. Absolutely typical. We padded the delivery date by six weeks, to allow for contingencies. Within two months the slack had evaporated. Now it looks like we'll be lucky to ship it before Christmas. (It was now November 28.) We're ruining our reputation in the market. Why, just last week one of our best customers—people we've worked with for 15 years—tried to hang a penalty clause on their latest order.

We shouldn't have to be after the engineers all the time. They should be able to see what problems they create without our telling them.

Phil Klein, head of broadcast sales under Porter, noted that many sales decisions were made by top management. Sales was understaffed, he thought, and had never really been able to get on top of the job.

We have grown further and further away from engineering. The director of engineering does not pass on the information that we give him. We need better relationships there. It is very difficult for us to talk to customers about development problems without technical help. We need each other. The whole of engineering is now too isolated from the outside world. The morale of ESD is very low. They're in a bad spot—they're not well organized.

People don't take much to outsiders here. Much of this is because the expectation is built up by top management that jobs will be filled from the bottom. So it's really tough when an outsider like Frank comes in.

Eric Norman, order and pricing coordinator for data equipment, talked about his own relationships with the production department:

Actually, I get along with them fairly well. Oh, things could be better, of course, if they were more cooperative generally. They always seem to say, "It's my bat and my ball, and we're playing by my rules." People are afraid to make production mad; there's a lot of power in there. But you've got to understand that production has its own set of problems. And nobody in Rondell is working any harder than Dave Schwab to try to straighten things out.

The Production Department

Dave Schwab had joined Rondell just after the Korean War, in which he had seen combat duty (at the Yalu River) and intelligence duty at Pyong Yang. Both experiences had been useful in his first year of civilian employment at Rondell's: the wartime factory superintendent and several middle managers had been, apparently, indulging in highly questionable side deals with Rondell's suppliers. Dave Schwab had gathered evidence, revealed the situation to Bill Hunt, and had stood by the president in the ensuing unsavory situation. Seven months after joining the company, Dave was named factory superintendent.

His first move had been to replace the fallen managers with a new team from outside. This group did not share the traditional Rondell emphasis on informality and friendly personal relationships, and had worked long and hard to install systematic manufacturing methods and procedures. Before the reorganization, production had controlled purchasing, stock control, and final quality control (where final assembly of products in cabinets was accomplished). Because of the wartime events, management decided on a check-and-balance system of organization and removed these three departments from production jurisdiction. The new production managers felt they had been unjustly penalized by this reorganization, particularly since they had uncovered the behavior that was detrimental to the company in the first place.

At present, the production department employed 500 people, of whom 60 percent worked in the assembly area—an unusually pleasant environment that had been commended by *Factory* magazine for its colorful decoration, cleanliness, and low noise level. An additional 30 percent of the work force, mostly skilled machinists, staffed the finishing and fabrication department. About 60 others performed scheduling, supervisory, and maintenance duties. Production workers were non-union, hourly paid, and participated in both the liberal profit-sharing program and the stock-purchase plan. Morale in production was traditionally high and turnover was extremely low.

Dave Schwab commented:

To be efficient, production has to be a self-contained department. We have to control what comes into the department and what goes out. That's why purchasing, inventory control, and quality ought to run out of this office. We'd eliminate a lot of problems with better control there. Why, even Don Naylor in QC would rather work for me than for ESD; he's said so himself. We understand his problems better.

The other departments should be self-contained, too. That's why I always avoid the underlings and go straight to the department heads with any questions. I always go down the line.

I have to protect my people from outside disturbances. Look what would happen if I let unfinished, half-baked designs in here—there would be chaos. The bugs have to be found before the drawings go into the shop, and it seems I'm the one who has to find them. Look at the 802, for example. [Dave had spent most of Thanksgiving Day (it was now November 28) red-pencilling the latest set of prints.] ESD should have found every one of those discrepancies. They just don't check drawings properly. They change most of the things I flag, but then they fail to trace through the impact of those changes on the rest of the design. I shouldn't have to do that.

And those engineers are tolerance crazy. They want everything to a millionth of an inch. I'm the only one in the company who has had any experience with actually machining things to a millionth of an inch. We make sure that the

things that engineers say on their drawings actually have to be that way and whether they're obtainable from the kind of raw material we buy.

That shouldn't be production's responsibility, but I have to do it. Accepting bad prints wouldn't let us ship the order any quicker. We'd only make a lot of junk that had to be reworked. And that would take even longer.

This way, I get to be known as the bad guy, but I guess that's just part of the job. [He paused with a wry smile.] Of course, what really gets them is that I don't even have a degree.

Dave had fewer bones to pick with the sales department because, he said, they trusted him.

When we give Ron Porter a shipping date, he knows the equipment will be shipped then.

You've got to recognize, though, that all of our new product problems stem from sales making absurd commitments on equipment that hasn't been fully developed. That always means trouble. Unfortunately, Hunt always backs sales up, even when they're wrong. He always favors them over us.

Ralph Simon, age 65, executive vice-president of the company, had direct responsibility for Rondell's production department. He said:

There shouldn't really be a dividing of departments among top management in the company. The president should be czar over all. The production people ask me to do something for them, and I really can't do it. It creates bad feelings between engineering and production, this special attention that they [R & D] get from Bill. But then Hunt likes to dabble in design. Schwab feels that production is treated like a poor relation.

The Executive Committee

At the executive committee meeting of December 6, it was duly recorded that Dave Schwab had accepted the prints and specifications for the Model 802 modulator and had set

Friday, December 29, as the shipping date for the first 10 pieces. Bill Hunt, in the chairperson's role, shook his head and changed the subject quickly when Frank tried to open the agenda to a discussion of interdepartmental coordination.

The executive committee itself was a brainchild of Rondell's controller, Len Symmes, who was well aware of the disputes that plagued the company. Symmes had convinced Bill Hunt and Ralph Simon to meet every two weeks with their department heads, and the meetings were formalized with Hunt, Simon, Ron Porter, Dave Schwab, Frank Forbus, Doc Reeves, Symmes, and the personnel director attending. Symmes explained his intent and the results:

> Doing things collectively and informally just doesn't work as well as it used to. Things have been gradually getting worse for at least two years now. We had to start thinking in terms of formal organization relationships. I did the first organization chart, and the executive committee was my idea, too—but neither idea is contributing much help, I'm afraid. It takes top management to make an organization click. The rest of us can't act much differently until the top people see the need for us to change.
>
> I had hoped the committee especially would help get the department managers into a constructive planning process. It hasn't worked out that way because Mr. Hunt really doesn't see the need for it. He uses the meetings as a place to pass on routine information.

Merry Christmas

"Frank, I didn't know whether to tell you now, or after the holiday." It was Friday, December 22, and Frank Forbus was standing awkwardly in front of Bill Hunt's desk.

"But, I figured you'd work right through Christmas Day if we didn't have this talk, and that just wouldn't have been fair to you. I can't understand why we have such poor luck in the engineering director's job lately. And I don't think it's entirely your fault. But . . ."

Frank only heard half of Hunt's words, and said nothing in response. He'd be paid through February 28 . . . He should use the time for searching . . . Hunt would help all he could . . . Jim Kilmann was supposed to be doing well at his own new job, and might need more help . . .

Frank cleaned out his desk, and numbly started home. The electronic carillon near his house was playing a Christmas carol. Frank thought again of Hunt's rationale: conflict still plagued Rondell—and Frank had not made it go away. Maybe somebody else could do it.

"And what did Santa Claus bring you, Frankie?" he asked himself.

"The sack. Only the empty sack."

Construction Equipment International, AG (A)

C onstruction Equipment International, AG, with headquarters in Zürich, is a wholly owned subsidiary of Road Machinery of America, Inc., the headquarters of which are in Detroit, Michigan, U.S.A. For many years, the parent company has been one of the leading manufacturers in the U.S. of material handling equipment, lifts and hoists, concrete mixing machinery, and heavy asphalt processing machines used in highway construction.

In the past ten years, there was a rapid increase in the foreign operations of RMA, first in terms of sales to independent distributors in Europe, South America, Australia, and the Far East and later in terms of manufacturing plants abroad. At first, all the selling was managed from the parent company's Detroit headquarters—that is, sales representatives were trained and stationed throughout the world, the market potential by country was estimated, customer orders were received from dealers, and shipments were made from the U.S.

The Establishment of Overseas Companies

Concurrent with the rapid growth of foreign sales, RMA top management took two important organizational steps. They set up manu-

This case was prepared by Professor Charles E. Summer as a basis for class discussion rather than to illustrate either effective or ineffective handling of an administrative situation. Copyright by IMEDE (International Management Development Institute), Lausanne, Switzerland. Reproduced by permission.

facturing plants in certain countries under subsidiary companies (i.e., RMA Belgium with two thousand employees today, twenty of whom are U.S. nationals, and RMA U.K., with four thousand employees today, twelve of whom are U.S. nationals). These companies report to the manufacturing department in Detroit. Second, they set up a company in Zürich to sell company products all over the world, except in the U.S., Canada, and South America.

Somewhat over 40 percent of all RMA sales volume worldwide, including domestic sales in the U.S., results from sales made outside the United States. RMA, therefore, might be categorized as multinational company, and CEIAG has become a principal selling arm, for all countries except the U.S., Canada, and South America.

CEIAG has changed markedly in the last six years. Six years ago there were about fifty employees in the Zürich headquarters: twenty-seven U.S. nationals acting as managers and sales representatives, and twenty-three non-U.S. nationals, serving in such clerical capacities as order handling, bookkeeping, and secretarial work. In addition, there were about forty sales representatives, serving territories from Bombay and Johannesburg to Salzburg. All these representatives were U.S. nationals, hired and trained in the U.S.

One year later—five years ago—there were 220 people in the Zürich headquarters, and the number of direct representatives throughout the world was increasing rapidly. Today the Zürich headquarters employs 330 people. There are seven major departments and department heads. With the exception of the manager of employee relations, all these managers are U.S. nationals, hired and trained in the U.S. In addition, there are forty-four members of middle management—division managers and assistant division managers within the seven major departments. Of these, thirty-six are U.S. citizens hired in the U.S., and eight are "local hires." The term "local hire" is used to denote employees hired by CEIAG, under the policies of the latter, rather than those hired by RMA under its policies. All these eight are heads of inside work divisions, office management, or accounting.

In addition, as of the time of writing of this case, the field force worldwide has increased to sixty-three sales representatives throughout the world, fifty-three of whom are U.S. foreign service employees, and ten of whom are "local hires."

In summary, in the short time since Michel Mottier, a young French clerical worker in Zürich, was sent to Detroit for training five years ago, the number of non-U.S. sales representatives worldwide has increased from zero to ten out of sixty-three; and the number of division middle managers of non-U.S. origin has increased to eight out of forty-four. However, all top management (the managing director and seven major department managers) are U.S. citizens except one.

Michel Mottier

Michel Mottier was employed by CEIAG on August 13, five years ago. At that time he had been employed by a Swiss firm. He speaks four languages—French, English, German, and Italian. At the time of employment, Mr. Hans Giorgetti, Personnel Director, explained to him the employment rules that were then explained to all "local hires." Among other things, Mr. Giorgetti told him "frankly, Mr. Mottier, there is not much chance that men who have not been trained in the United States will be transferred to the position of sales representative. This is a United States company, manufacturing and selling products primarily made in the U.S. We have no sales representatives who are not from the United States. However, we can offer you exceptional work, we think, in the Zürich office." At that time, it was the opinion of many executives in Detroit, and in Zürich, that selling methods and managerial methods in the United States required that both sales representative and managerial positions could best be filled by men who had been brought up in the United States, trained in the American educational system, and trained in the sales and managerial organization of RMA in the U.S. For example, there was one instance in Zürich in which a young man came to the personnel director and said that unless he could be assured of promotions beyond his present job, he would have to leave. The man's department manager, in this case, felt that the man in question was competent in his present job but that he should be allowed to leave, "since I can replace him with an engineer trained in the U.S.—it is much easier to work with men who, through training and experience, think like I do."

But in the case of Mottier, the head of the Parts Sales Department, William Brown, to whom he reported, responded differently when Mottier inquired of his own chances for advancement. Brown assessed that Mottier was as qualified as anyone he knew (including Americans) to advance as an outside parts sales representative. He wrote to the head of the RMA Parts Sales Department in Detroit, saying, "there is no point in this man sitting here doing internal administrative work when he has all of the potential qualities of a line sales representative—language, intelligence, energy, and personal skills." Brown requested that Mottier be sent to Detroit for a two-year training program operated for college graduates about his own age and training.

Mottier was soon sent to Detroit and spent eight months in the college training program of RMA. During his stay there, he attracted the attention of some of the executives in line sales management. They judged that he would be a valuable sales representative selling in the United States and informed the Zürich company of this fact, asking if he could be released. At this point, the Zürich personnel director, together with the manager of Parts Sales of CEIAG, reasoned "if he is good enough for selling the U.S., we would like to have him selling back here." Mottier became the first non-U.S. national to become a parts sales representative for CEIAG.

Training, Placement, and Compensation of Graduates

According to Mr. Giorgetti, Personnel Director, CEIAG, with its growing sales of technical equipment to large dealers in many countries, has an acute problem in finding enough qualified sales engineers to handle the business in its many and diverse sales territories. In the first place, all companies in the industrialized world have need for this type of person. This is as true in West Germany and the U.K. as it is in the United States. But for an international company like CEIAG, the supply of talent is even tighter. Applicants not only must know mechanical engineering, but they must know both the culture and the language of the territory to which they are assigned. Mr. Giorgetti gives the example of a recently placed sales representative in Lagos. This man was called upon to help the leader solve a technical problem with his employee-mechanics, who were attempting to respond to an important customer requirement for repairing and adjusting equipment. In this case, the representative was able to spend time with the mechanics, on the shop floor, conversing with them in French, and gaining their acceptance of his ideas. As a third important qualification, which adds to recruiting difficulty in a tight labor market, the men chosen should have a knowledge of English for integrating well into the parent company environment, and of still a third language. This last qualification is necessary in a multinational company for two reasons—to enable transfer and promotion earlier in the career and to provide for higher management talent later in the career.

Finally, there is a qualification that the applicant have the personal and human characteristics necessary for dealing with many customers. This, as is well-known in all countries, is a difficult combination to find, especially if the person must also have a good engineering education.

All these reasons, according to Mr. Giorgetti, contribute to a shortage of qualified people on the demand side. But management is faced with other necessities on the supply side. One of these is to maintain good relations with the professors of engineering at better technical schools, in order that they will call CEIAG to the attention of their graduates and, at the same time, inform the company of prospective trainees. For example, the company has at times been pressed to raise starting salaries for trainees as a means of attracting qualified people. In Switzerland, there are a few such schools and professors that are important, among which are the Polytechnic Federal High School in Zürich and the Ecole Polytechnique of the University of Lausanne. Currently, the company is offering trainees Swiss francs 1,600 to 2,000 per month ($368–$460). This range is slightly higher than the average for Swiss firms. Mr. Giorgetti states that if U.S. companies went substantially higher than this, professors and department heads, many of whom maintain excellent relationships with Swiss companies, which also are in need for talent, would react unfavorably.

It is therefore the company policy on compensation to pay people who are employed locally approximately the range paid by local employers.

> Not only does this keep our company in better relationship with people in the various countries, including other industrialists and governments—we cannot afford to disrupt the local economies—but it also makes sense competitively and economically. For example, if we are hiring a sales engineer in Scotland, the going rate for graduates of the best universities might be payment in pounds in the equivalent of U.S. $1,600, whereas the same average rate in universities in the U.S. is perhaps $8,000. If Detroit were to try to establish a single rate for hiring mechanical engineers all over the world, it would not work for the company or for other industrial companies in the countries concerned.
>
> We are very careful, however, to pay people who are hired in one country certain added benefits if they are assigned to a foreign post. These added benefits take the form of post allowances, quarters allowances, education allowances, and foreign service allowances, including periodic returns home for extended vacations.

Mr. Giorgetti further stated that "the formulation and administration of personnel policies in a multinational company is sometimes a difficult thing. We are sometimes faced with particular problems that require a great deal of thought." As an example, Mr. Giorgetti cited one such problem that arose this year.

Hans Buhler and Richard Steadman

Hans Buhler and Richard Steadman are two men who have been working in Zürich for a little over one year. Both of them were hired directly out of college, Buhler from the Eidgenossische Technische Hochschule in Zürich and Steadman from Purdue University in the U.S. Both were hired to go through a college training program lasting about two years, which was set up by RMA management in Detroit. In this program, men are given about five months' orientation and formal classroom-type work in Detroit, and this is followed by two on-the-job assignments lasting about twelve to eighteen months. Buhler and Steadman are now residing in Zürich and have been assigned on-the-job training positions in the area of dealer training operations. Both men have substantially the same training in mechanical engineering at their respective colleges. Both men are married but have not yet had children; Buhler is twenty-six and Steadman is twenty-seven. Buhler was hired by CEIAG and Steadman by RMA.

One of the projects to which the men have been assigned is the development of a one-week course designed to train the salesmen of one of CEIAG's largest dealers, Société pour Machines Industrielles S.A. This latter company, located in Paris, has six hundred employees engaged in large machine shops, maintenance shops, and service shops, as well as twenty salesmen who sell RMA products all over France. The director of Sales Training in Zürich decided on the need for this program, and SMI management in Paris has received it enthusiastically. It was also decided that this course should be held in Geneva and conducted in French so that the salesmen of SMI could easily understand and so that there would be a smoother working relationship between instructors and CEIAG personnel on the one hand and SMI salesmen and sales managers on the other.

Buhler and Steadman worked very hard on their assignments. First, they studied the new equipment to be covered in the program, sought out engineering specifications from many sources, and prepared and presented lecture-discussions, which were received with high compliment by the SMI salesmen. They also planned the mechanics of the conference, hotel arrangements, transportation arrangements, and such matters as coffee socials and the final dinner.

At a social hour preceding the final dinner, two of the salesmen from France, together with a member of management in the Paris customer-firm, paid a high compliment to Buhler. Several members of CEIAG top management were present at this dinner. Mr. Giorgetti was almost always invited to such meetings because of his facility in speaking with customers in French, English, and German. At this particular time, Buhler and Giorgetti were standing by the fireplace in the restaurant when the three men from Paris came over. One of them said to Giorgetti: "Hans, this has been an excellent conference. Not only have we improved our own knowledge of sales engineering, but we have respected Steadman and Buhler for their ability to arrange a conference without a flaw. Buhler, here, speaks French as well as we do and is quick on his feet with answers to our questions. Steadman is a fine engineer and will make a good sales engineer."

After the three men parted, Giorgetti said to Buhler, in German, "they really think a lot of you and Dick Steadman. And I might say that our company management is happy that you two do such good work."

Hans Buhler answered, laughing in a good-natured way, "Well, we surely worked hard, and I'm happy that you and the men from Paris think of us this way. I enjoy working with CEIAG people, especially with Dick Steadman. Everything would really be fine if some day you would pay us the same as our friends."

Mr. Giorgetti states that he and Buhler continued to have a pleasant conversation and pleasant visits with men from the French company. However, the remark of Buhler stuck in his mind.

Management faces some difficult problems in formulating policies for compensation, worldwide. Let me explain to you what I think Hans Buhler meant.

Buhler was hired here at Sfr. 2,000 per month, equivalent to U.S. $464. We raised him to the equivalent of $500 a month after six months, when he went to Detroit for training. In the U.S. he is entitled to the standard 20 percent foreign service allowance (equivalent to $100) and to a housing allowance that is worth an equivalent of about $150. This brings him to a total "take home" payment of about $750 while he was living in Detroit. This was definitely in line with the going rates being paid to his fellow trainees (about $750 in salary) who were hired in the U.S. universities, including his fellow worker here, Dick Steadman.

At the completion of training in the U.S., Hans was brought back to Zürich with a raise, and then given a second raise, to the point where he is making Sfr. 2,800, the equivalent of $644 per month. However, he no longer receives foreign service or housing allowances. He is treated under CEIAG policy as a person hired in his native country and permanently working here. This policy, as I have already explained, is necessary to keep from jeopardizing the local economy and the company economics.

Now let us look at Dick Steadman's salary history. He was hired at approximately the same time by Detroit as Buhler was by Zürich. According to the competitive market for graduate engineers in the U.S., he was started at $750 per month. At the conclusion of his U.S. training, he was assigned to Zürich as a U.S. foreign service employee, at a salary of $850 a month (he had one raise in the U.S. to $800). In Zürich, he is entitled to the standard 20 percent foreign service allowance ($170) and to the post allowance, which amounts to about $176—this is designed to cover the difference in cost of living (excluding housing) between Zürich and Washington, D.C.

Thus, Steadman's base pay plus allowances comes to about $1,196 a month while he lives in Zürich.

Our management in both Detroit and Zürich is constantly on the alert to compensation prob-

lems such as this, and particularly when we are dealing with talented young men who are productive like these. At the same time, you can see that salary administration in a big international company like RMA, and a large international subsidiary like CEIAG, is not an easy job. I would be interested in what you think about this example.

NOTE:

This case was written, edited, and submitted to Mr. Giorgetti and Mr. Kermit Hansen, Managing Director (President) of CEIAG for their approval. After making some minor corrections of fact, Mr. Hansen said:

"I agree completely with the statement made by Hans Giorgetti in the last paragraph. It seems to me that the obvious solution is to equalize pay between the two. However, opposed to this is the absolute necessity for maintaining salary levels in line with local practices. This is what makes the problem such a tough one."

Construction Equipment International, AG (B)

Construction Equipment International, AG, with headquarters in Zürich, is a wholly owned subsidiary of Road Machinery of America, Inc., the headquarters of which are in Detroit, Michigan, U.S.A. For many years, the latter company has been a leading manufacturer of material handling equipment, lifts and hoists, concrete mixing machinery, and allied products. Information on company operations, and on personnel policies, is to be found in Construction Equipment International, AG (A).

This case has to do with the thoughts and reactions of Willi Studer, thirty years old, toward his career, his employment by CEIAG, his training in Detroit, U.S.A., and his work in the Zürich headquarters of CEIAG. At the time of writing of this case (the same as CEIAG A) Willi Studer has been in Zürich for sixteen months in a sales engineering assignment in which he does certain sales planning work, helps to plan and conduct (lecturing) presentations to train dealer salesmen on technical qualities of the company's lift and hoist machinery, and sometimes travels with dealer salesmen in countries such as France, Germany, or Switzerland. This latter function involves direct help to final customers and training of dealer salesmen at the same time. For example, in traveling with a salesman,

Studer faces such customer questions as "What kind of a machine do I need to charge a brick stone oven with a narrow and low clearance?" Drawing on his knowledge of company products, plus his training as a mechanical engineer, Willi is an important link in the company's relations to its large dealers (the one in Paris has six hundred employees), their salesmen, and the final customer.

At the opening of the interview, the case writer stated that all that is needed for a good case is to describe facts and opinions about career and employment and suggested that "we start by simply asking what your career was before joining CEIAG, and how you happened to come to work for this company."

Incidentally, the interview was conducted in good English, with a slight accent. Most of the words below are those used by Willi Studer.

I joined CEIAG after I saw an advertisement for employment in a newspaper while I was waiting in the railroad station at Chur. I guess there are a lot of reasons why I chose this. I was born in a small town in the Bernese Oberland and later moved to Lucerne with my family. My first connection with Americans was when I was about eight years old. This was after World War II, and the American soldiers came here on vacation, in uniform. I knew how to ask for chewing gum, and it was a thrill to ask for it. I somehow got the impression that the Americans are nice, and even then I thought something like "they have a high standard of living, and they don't seem narrow minded, and someday you will make better money working for an American business."

Anyway, I went to primary school until I was thirteen, then middle school until sixteen. Having decided to be a mechanical engineer, I took an apprenticeship for four years, until twenty. You see, there are two ways to be an engineer in Switzerland. One way is apprenticeship, and then three years of engineering school. The other way is to go to the Eidgenossische Technische Hochschule (ETH, Zürich) for eight semesters or four years. After the apprenticeship, I was in the Swiss Army for almost a year, and then went to the Central Swiss Technical School (ZTL) for three years. I was then twenty-four.

After that, I got a job with a big American oil company, took a training program in their research center in England, and was assigned as a sales engineer on technical problems—giving schools and presentations to salesmen about company products, their uses and applications. Sometimes the job involved going to factories and helping solve complaints. I started there at Sfr. 1,100 per month when I was hired, and was making Sfr. 1,800[1] when I resigned three years later. Actually, I enjoyed the work, but the longer term prospects weren't too good for advancement. Switzerland is a smaller country, and it is impossible to have a company with all chiefs and no Indians; also, there were too many young people ahead of me. Maybe in twenty years I could have been a product manager or technical manager. They wanted to send me to a six-months training program in their research laboratories in the U.S. My wife and I both wanted to know and learn about the U.S. first hand, but under company policy my wife couldn't go (I couldn't afford to pay for her stay myself).

So I resigned after I saw that advertisement in Chur and after being interviewed at CEIAG by several people, even though the new job paid slightly less money. In the interviews, the main thing they looked at was how well I speak English and other languages. You know, it is not too easy to find good engineers who also have good knowledge of languages. All the way through school, some people are good at things like languages and others are good at things like arithmetic or physics. CEIAG told me what I will do for three years, including training for two years, which is spent in the company headquarters in the U.S. They also told me what I'd earn and that the trend in the company is to give over more and more of the management of overseas business to people who are native to the countries where the factories and markets are. Maybe even some day the whole overseas company will be managed by Europeans. My starting salary was Sfr. 1,600 as compared with my previous salary of Sfr. 1,800 plus a car. Maybe today I'd be getting Sfr. 2,500 if I had stayed with the old job. The really big thing was the long training stay in the U.S. and an opportunity to learn how people live over there and how they think, as well as how to speak the language really well.

At this point, Willi Studer gave an example of what he meant by an opportunity "to know how people live," and why this is important. He said that it is just as important for him to know how people in the U.S. live, as it is for U.S. nationals to know how people in other countries live.

Take for instance one time when my boss here at CEIAG asked me to conduct a study of how French agency companies (our potential customers) finance their purchase of machinery for their own sales operations. Our management needs this kind of information to plan our own capital requirements. We needed to know, among other things, whether the French businessman pays cash for his equipment, how much credit he gets, what kinds of interest rates he pays, where he gets his money (from manufacturers such as RMA?) and so on. Well, I could understand how our management needs to know this, but I knew we could not put these kinds of questions on a questionnaire or ask them in an interview. You can't go to a French businessman and say "Do you pay cash for your machinery"—he would consider this a serious invasion of his privacy, even more than in the U.S. And yet, that was one of the proposed questions on the form.

[1]At the time this case was written, one Swiss franc equaled twenty-three U.S. cents. One U.S. dollar equaled 4.30 Swiss francs.

The conversation then turned to the type of work experiences Willi Studer has had with CEIAG and, in a training capacity, with RMA in the U.S. Shortly after being hired in Zürich, Willi went with his wife to Detroit for a formal classroom-type training program combined with rotation to various jobs for direct on-the-job training. The length of this training in the United States was about two years.

The first five months were spent in study of teaching materials, in lectures, and in discussions on a wide range of information about RMA—its products, its engineering, its finance, etc. This gave us a real grounding in both the technical aspects of the company and its management. I think we got very much out of this, and at times we (the trainees) were assigned as group coordinators for conducting discussions. That was good training, too, and it gave us satisfaction.

This was followed by six months of sales engineering on-the-job training. I'll give you one example of what we did. Dealers all over the United States would contact us, either by letter or telephone, asking such questions as: "I have this certain metal plate that was used on the old model machine, number 58, and I wonder if it can be used successfully on the new machine, number 62. If I do use it, what modifications in the machine, and the plate, must be made?" or "I have a complaint from customers that such-and-such machine makes too much noise. What can be done to reduce the noise?"

From there, I went on to the construction department. After that, I spent four months in the used equipment section, and six months in dealer training. In the first, we acted as consultants to dealers at their places of business. In the second, we conducted training programs for dealer salesmen all over the nation who would come to Detroit. There, we explained the technical characteristics of products, the various uses and applications of products, and any other questions that these salesmen wanted to raise.

At this point, the case writer stated that there were two other subjects he wanted to explore: how Willi feels about working in a U.S. company, and how he feels about his own status and position in comparison to the status and position of U.S. citizens working for CEIAG in Zürich. Particularly, the case writer was interested in working conditions and pay.

Well, I like working for this company. In comparison to European companies, I think I can speak up and have somebody listen, and I think I can get more interesting work and get moved up faster. For the past sixteen months I've been doing sales planning work, dealer training work in Zürich, and some traveling with dealer salesmen. The salesmen learn from me, and I learn about company product applications from them.

There are at least eight Americans here in Zürich who got out of the Detroit training program about the same time (within two months) as I did. I know for certain that they are making more money than I am, partly because the pay rate for mechanical engineers hired in the U.S. is more than here, and partly because they are being paid foreign service allowances. Of course, I am now in my home country, and not getting such allowances.

My wife and I do notice the difference in the way an American here lives with his wife and the way we live. They spend a lot more money. For them, it is somewhat like being on vacation. They travel to Paris and Rome, and they go all over. If they see an antique or something, and its price is reasonable, they buy it. We all give parties and have people to dinner, but I know we have to be more careful about how much we spend on this.

I know they (the company) cannot pay the same salaries. It's just a question of demand and supply. If they can hire mechanical engineers at a given price, why should they pay more? When I got back from Detroit, and had been in Zürich a while, I did think I was getting too little. I went in and raised the question, and found that a raise from 2,000 to Sfr. 2,400 was already in the mill.

Since then, I've gotten two raises, up to Sfr. 3,240, and this represents a hell of an improvement. I know this isn't as much as the Americans, but it's probably more than I would be getting from a Swiss company.

From an employee standpoint it's simple. You can look at it in two ways. If you look at it as a Swiss, working in a Swiss company, you're happy. If you look at it as a mechanical engineer working in an international company and see that, because of language, you are sometimes doing a little more for the company than people without this qualification, you're unhappy.

The case writer then said that the interview was almost over and commented that, on the whole, Willi Studer seemed to be competent in his job and to have good prospects ahead. He wondered out loud if, in this employment situation, there were any other matters that ever made Willi feel unhappy.

Well, two or three years ago, people came into Zürich after the training in Detroit, stayed maybe a month, and then got a field assignment. That's the thing I have looked forward to all along. You get a territory, you have a lot of room to produce on your own, you are looked upon by the company as a full professional employee, and you begin to feel responsible for what happens. Now we are staying here (the others and I) for fifteen or sixteen months already, and I don't see the possibility of getting assigned in the immediate future. The percentage of details in our job means that there just simply isn't enough responsibility to justify our training!

Understand this, though, this is not a real gripe. I know I am going to make it and be successful, the question is only when.

Construction Equipment International, AG (C)

Construction Equipment International, AG (CEIAG), with headquarters in Zürich, is a wholly owned subsidiary of Road Machinery of America, Inc. (RMA), the headquarters of which are in Detroit, Michigan, U.S.A. For many years, the parent company has been one of the leading manufacturers in the U.S. of material handling equipment, lifts and hoists, concrete mixing machinery, and heavy asphalt processing machines used in highway construction. Measured by sales volume, the company would be in the top five corporations in the U.S. engaged in the production of these products.

This case concerns information about the employment and subsequent career, in both CEIAG and RMA, of Jonathan Cook, a British engineer. This information is related by Mr. Hans Giorgetti, manager of personnel and employee relations at CEIAG headquarters in Zürich. Particularly, this case reports on the compensation, placement, and transfer of Cook from the company viewpoint and the career moves and location moves of Cook from his own standpoint.

Jonathan Cook is a graduate of St. Andrews University, Scotland, which is regarded in academic circles as one of the top universities in science in the U.K. Eleven years ago, Cook was employed as a sales engineer, at the age

This case was prepared by Professor Charles E. Summer as a basis for class discussion rather than to illustrate either effective or ineffective handling of an administrative situation. Copyright by IMEDE (International Management Development Institute), Lausanne, Switzerland. Reproduced by permission.

of thirty-two, by Construction Equipment Ltd., a wholly owned subsidiary of RMA. This subsidiary has both manufacturing plants and a selling organization in the U.K. Cook was employed at a salary of £2,000 per year, equivalent approximately to Swiss francs 2,000 per month or U.S. $460 per month. Stationed at Edinburgh, Scotland, he was judged by his superiors (as revealed by company appraisal forms) to be a very competent sales engineer, interested in company products, and successful in his work with dealers throughout England and Scotland. He remained in this position for five years, until he was thirty-eight, receiving four salary raises during this period. Each time the sales manager in the U.K. reported to him that he had earned increases through hard work and competence.

About six years ago, Construction Equipment International, AG, which is the selling arm of RMA throughout most of the world, except for Canada, the U.S., and South America, badly needed a highly competent sales engineer in Delhi, India. This position seemed to the CEIAG Sales Manager for Asia and the Middle East (the Central Division) to be especially important and difficult to fill. First, there was at the time a shortage of trained engineers who also had the personalities to become good sales representatives. This was difficult enough. But the Indian representative would have unusual demands made on him. There is one very important equipment dealer in Delhi who has a large organization, selling machines all over India. This organization would be helped greatly by a good engineer to train its salesmen in technical applications of the company's products. In the words of Hans Giorgetti, "This is a helluva complicated job—import regulations, relations with the Indian Government, financing of machinery, Agency for Economic Development projects, and the works. Whoever has the job is the official link between sales, engineering, and management of both CEIAG and the customer-dealer. During the three years Jonathan Cook was there, he did an excellent job. In the annual reviews of performance with the Sales Manager of the Central (Asian) division, he was given high ratings."

Mr. Giorgetti also recalled how Jonathan Cook happened to get the job in India.

At a company meeting in Zürich, the sales manager for Asia, Jack King, met the sales manager for the U.K., Brian Quinn. As is customary at these meetings, managers frequently informally exchange information on personnel. In the course of conversation, King asks Quinn who are his best salesmen in the United Kingdom. Quinn describes a few people in great detail and seems enthusiastic about what a good group he has working in England and Scotland. He is particularly vivid in describing Cook. A few months later, when King had the difficult job of finding a man for New Delhi, he searched at several places in the CEIAG organization but had not found a man he thought qualified. Then he remembered the name Jonathan Cook and some of the description Quinn had given him. Because Construction Equipment Ltd. is a separate subsidiary within RMA, King had to check with the proper officials in England and then ask Mr. Giorgetti to handle the official employment transfer for CEIAG in Zürich. This was duly accomplished, and Cook was moved to New Delhi at a salary of Sfr. 3,100 ($713) a month.

Since he was doing a good job, he got good raises while there. At the time he left, his base salary was good—Sfr. 4,000 per month, or the

equivalent of $920. But his total compensation was even better. Under CEIAG compensation policy, he was getting 20 percent foreign service allowance (Sfr. 800), a 10 percent hardship location allowance (Sfr. 400) and a housing allowance equivalent to Sfr. 1,120 a month. All of this gave him a total of Sfr. 6,320 or U.S. $1,450 a month.

It is the company policy not to keep a man in India for more than three years. And so, the Asian Sales Manager contacted various people here in Zürich after Cook had spent two and one-half years there. He said that Cook had done a fine job. In addition to me, he contacted the head of the Product Development Division and the head of the Sales Training Department, here in Zürich. He probably also contacted other people, as well as sales managers he knows in other parts of the world. These contacts were for the purpose of locating a good transfer for Cook—a position where he could have responsibilities commensurate with his experience and level and a salary fitting for a man making what his salary was at that time.

None of these inquiries produced a spot, and so we discussed the situation here in Zürich among our management. It was decided that, no such position being immediately available in CEIAG, the best thing might be to consider the possibilities in the U.S., in the parent company RMA. After all, their organization is bigger than ours, and the salaries there are higher for sales positions. It was further decided that the General Sales Manager of CEIAG would recommend him to the head of the sales organization of RMA in Detroit. This was done, complete with the qualifications and past performance of Jonathan Cook.

RMA management responded with a position of Sales Representative in Toronto, Canada. This was three years ago, when Cook was forty-one, and he seemed very enthusiastic to get the job. In deciding what to pay him, RMA personnel people in Detroit, with information supplied by me, took note of the fact that he was making a total of Sfr. 6,320, including foreign service, hardship, and housing allowances. They were also aware that if Cook were hired by RMA, rather than CEIAG, he would be considered a "local hire"—a man hired by the domestic company to work domestic territory. Since he would no longer be an employee of the Zürich company, he would not therefore be considered as doing "foreign service." Rather, he would be just like any other domestic employee (the domestic area is considered to cover the U.S. and Canada). Therefore, to be equitable, it was decided that he should have at least the equivalent of what he was making in Delhi but without the housing allowance. So they took the Sfr. 6,320 total remuneration in Delhi, subtracted out the Sfr. 1,120 he was getting for housing, and reasoned that he was getting Sfr. 5,200 compensation for services. This is equal to about $1,200 a month. Therefore, RMA offered him the equivalent of U.S. $1,200 a month in Toronto, all payable as salary. This seemed acceptable to Cook. I am guessing that, while the amount in Toronto was exactly the same he had been getting in Delhi for his services, it appealed to him that his base salary increase was from $920 to $1,200. In other words, this is something permanent—and it raises a man's status in the company—whereas the difference, $280, which had been paid in the form of foreign service and hardship, operating out of the Zürich company, might someday be taken away and does not classify a man in such a high salary scale.

Well, Jonathan Cook stayed in Toronto three years, from ages forty-one to forty-four. Like his other positions, he did well in the job, produced a good amount of business and goodwill for the company, and got high recommendations from the manager above him. In fact, he did well enough that some of the top sales managers in Detroit judged him highly. He was brought to Detroit in a sales management position, at a salary of $1,600 per month. I was glad that he was a foreign national who had been promoted through ranks of CEIAG to a managerial position in the parent company.

After two months in Detroit, Cook asked for an appointment to see the executive in whose department he worked, his line manager. He said that he and his wife had been discussing the difficulties of living in the U.S. and particu-

larly the cost of living and the cost of trips back to their native Scotland, where both of them had strong ties. Cook said that he felt rather deeply the need for some additional compensation. As one means of granting such compensation, he wondered if the company might give him an educational allowance for his children—similar to the allowances available to certain RMA foreign service personnel under RMA policies, and to certain CEIAG foreign service personnel, under CEIAG policies.

In the judgment of RMA management, even though they regarded Cook highly, this simply was not possible. Some stable policies on compensation are absolutely necessary to maintain equity between people, and the policy was clear. RMA has its own policies for people it hires, and, under these, those people who are hired by RMA for a domestic position accept the practices of all domestic RMA personnel. To grant Cook any foreign service allowances would look discriminatory to other managers in the Detroit headquarters. Cook also pointed out that he felt he should be given an extended home leave every two years, to his native country, like other foreign nationals. But company policy clearly classified him as an employee hired by RMA for employment in RMA's domestic territory of operations. This he knew when he took the job.

In due time, Cook apparently became more and more dissatisfied with the situation. His immediate superior and the personnel management people in Detroit knew it. Knowing that Jonathan Cook was a very capable employee and that he had very valuable experience in both the Detroit company and the Zürich company, they talked with him several times about his career with the company. Together, they reached a solution. RMA management contacted the management of Construction Equipment Ltd. in England, and they were glad to have such a man return to the company from which he started. Everyone seemed satisfied. Cook was transferred back to England (employed by Construction International Ltd.) at a salary of £3,500 a year, or about $812 a month. The management in both Detroit and London recognized that this was less than the $1,600 he had been getting in

Detroit, but they also judged his job in the U.K. to be one of similar interest and prestige, and the salary to be one that is fully in line with this kind of job in the U.K. Jonathan Cook was in on these discussions, and he too, said that the salary was acceptable.

About a month after Cook reported to work in London and just about his forty-third birthday, he resigned from Construction Equipment Ltd. and took a job with a large company in England.

Mr. Giorgetti completed the information on Jonathan Cook's career in RMA—CEILtd.—CEIAG by stating that Cook's case, though a unique one in many ways, represents the kind of tough problem faced by a complex of companies operating over national borders and in a variety of cultures.

The case writer concluded the interview by observing that RMA seemed to him to have some characteristics of a multinational company. He recalled that somewhere near 45 percent of all RMA sales are made outside of the United States and Canada. He said that, while RMA does not seem to be as international in its operations as some of the multinational companies, such as Unilever in London, or Nestlé in Switzerland, it certainly has some of the same characteristics.

Moosajees, Limited

The management group of Moosajees, Limited of Ceylon* was concerned with increasing the company's production of combed or hackled coconut fiber for export. A major problem, as the company saw it, was not to increase the number of employees, for space limitations prevented this. Rather, the management believed ways should be devised to secure increased productivity from individual workers. However, the attitude of Ceylonese employees raised certain difficulties, and conventional methods of stimulating productivity had not proved successful.

Coconuts are stripped of their husks, split, and dried into copra, which is shipped abroad to be processed into oil; this export is one of Ceylon's major foreign exchange sources. In recent years, other coconut products, such as fibers, have found expanding markets. Increased demand for fibers had led to Moosajees' concern with worker productivity.

Moosajees was one of Ceylon's major exporters of fiber. The company had a processing plant in Colombo, the country's capital. Recovery of fiber from the husks of coconuts was done at various mills, mainly situated to the north and northeast of Colombo in the coconut producing areas. The fiber was delivered to Moosajees, which, as shippers, stored, sorted, graded, baled, and exported the commodity. The company received two kinds of fibers: mattress and bristle. The latter type, distinguished by its longer staple, could be further processed by combing or hackling. It was then tied into bundles and was used in the production of fiber brushes.

For the purpose of combing or hackling brush fiber, it had been customary in Ceylon to use women. Moosajees employed more than 300 women for this purpose. The women were paid on a piece rate, on the basis of a hundred-weight (112 pounds) of fiber hackled. Rates varied according to the quality hackled but had risen in recent years from Rupees[1] 5/50 to Rupees 8/50 per hundredweight for the upper quality limit.

As payment was on a piece-rate basis and because of local customs and attitudes, Moosajees had never kept a strict check on attendance or on the exact number of hours worked each day by women employees. Many women living in the neighborhood of the warehouse came to work in their spare time. They worked as long as they felt like it, returning home to prepare meals or attend to their children, or when they were bored with the rather unpleasant and tiring hackling process.

Under the demand situation that prevailed for a long period, the company had been content to accept these conditions for work for its female operatives. Although production could

[1]At the time this case was written, $1 equalled 4.70 rupees, approximately.

not be effectively organized, this had not been particularly significant. Hackling was a hand operation not involving machinery. Normal daylight was adequate for the combers and hacklers, weather conditions in Colombo required little more than a roof on the hackling building, and the irregular output of the women actually made checking their production fairly simple, since it combined to produce a fairly steady, if limited, yield. No timekeeping records were necessary; normal security precautions for the entire warehouse were sufficient; and everybody seemed satisfied.

However, two things occurred that made increased production important. The first of these was an increase in foreign demand for hackled fibers, which Moosajees was anxious to meet since the company's management was considerably more profit-oriented than were its women employees. Secondly, a continuing decline in Ceylon's foreign exchange position had concerned the government and led it to encourage those companies in the export trade to do what they could to expand sales abroad. Moosajees had, therefore, both economic and patriotic reasons for producing more hackled fiber.

The most obvious way to increase output was to hire more employees. Since Ceylon has a chronic unemployment problem, it was not difficult to find women who were willing to work. However, limitations of space prevented any significant expansion in the company's labor force. Moreover, the country's labor laws prohibited the use of female workers in a night shift, so that operating two or three shifts was impossible. If, as an alternative, the company displaced less productive workers in favor of new ones who might be more productive, the result was likely to be difficulties with the government department of labor or with labor organizers. Since the company had never developed production norms that it could enforce, dismissal of an employee for what Moosajees

might consider low production would not necessarily be accepted as adequate cause.

The company recognized that one solution might be to work toward the development of production standards and that this should be prefaced by enforcement of attendance and of working hours. An attempt to do this, however, merely led to strong resentment and expressions of annoyance. Any effort to attract women outside normal working hours seemed also destined to failure, since most of the female work force were married and occupied with home duties at those times.

The next step taken was to increase payment for fiber hackled, in the hope that this would lead to greater output. Somewhat to the surprise of the Moosajees management, however, the result was not increased production but poor attendance. Apparently, while Moosajees had not established production norms or tasks for the workers, they themselves had developed earnings objectives of their own. When this objective was reached, the employee merely failed to report for work. If an increase in the piece rate made it possible to secure the objective in less time, then the employee saw little reason to put in more time to earn more than she wanted.

Moosajees management was considering what it might do. Better enforcement of hours and attendance records was a long-run objective and pretty clearly one that could not be implemented at this time. As the consumption level of the Ceylonese rose, it seemed reasonable to assume that increased consumer goods wants would be developed and that the desire to meet these wants would lead to an interest in higher earnings, but this, too, was in the future. Appeals to produce more goods because of the country's situation and the requirement of higher export sales were suggested; however, the management doubted that the typical female worker would be very moved by patriotism. Ceylon had been independent only since 1948, and national fervor was strongest among intellectuals and government employees. Such workers as

Moosajees employed were concerned with little more than food, shelter, clothing, and some relatively simple pleasures.

Acme Aircraft Corporation

George Bruster took an engineering job with the Acme Aircraft Corporation soon after his graduation from State Engineering College. He was initially assigned the responsibility of supervising a group of engineers and engineering aides involved in conducting experimental test programs on various models of airplanes and airplane components.

Prior to his graduation, Bruster had spent several summers working for Acme Aircraft and had worked part-time for this organization for a period while attending school. At the time of his permanent employment, he had held every position in the testing group other than that of crew chief. Because of his previous experience, he was assigned the position of crew chief—an unusual assignment for a "new" engineer.

The average size of a testing crew was seven to ten individuals, of whom five were usually graduate engineers and the remainder engineering aides and technical assistants. The responsibilities of the crew chief included the overall planning and coordinating of the test programs with which his group was involved. Approximately half of the crew chief's responsibilities were administrative rather than technical; because of the nature of his responsibilities, the crew chief often was not the engineer on the crew who had the most experience or the greatest technical knowledge.

Often older engineers, specialists in electronics or design, for example, would be working on crews headed by younger, less experienced engineers. This type of arrangement had rarely created friction in the past—especially as the older specialists were usually not interested in accepting responsibility for anything but their particular part of a testing series. In addition, crew membership was constantly changing as crews were disbanded and reformed as tests were completed and new tests undertaken.

Exhibit 1 shows the organization of a typical testing unit.

On November 1, about four months after he had taken the full time job with Acme, George Bruster's group was assigned the project of testing a new model component for an experimental aircraft which Acme was developing. It was only the second major assignment that George's group had had since he took over as crew chief. This particular test series was of prime importance, for the results of the tests would be instrumental in providing data upon which Acme would base its design proposal to government representatives. If the company could provide an acceptable design, it would be in a favorable position eventually to gain a large—and profitable—production contract.

The unit supervisor stressed the importance of this particular series of tests to George and informed him that the entire testing group was under considerable pressure from top management to get quick and accu-

EXHIBIT 1
Organization chart of a testing unit

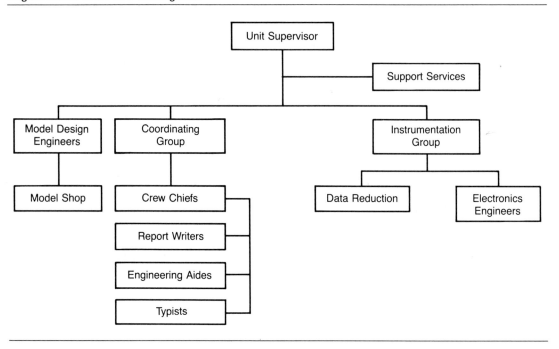

rate results. Top men from the model design and instrumentation groups, as well as one of the best report writers in the coordinating group, had been assigned to the tests.

Because of scheduling problems regarding the test facilities available at the Bristol plant of Acme—the home office of the test group headed by Bruster—arrangements were made for the current series of tests to be conducted at the Culver City facilities of Acme. Culver City was located approximately 900 miles from Bristol; while the Culver City operations were organized in the same manner as those at Bristol, the operations were run autonomously because of the physical distance between the two facilities. Thus, while Bruster and his crew would actually conduct the tests, they would be using the equipment and facilities of the Culver City operation.

George Bruster arrived at the Culver City test facility on November 7 to coordinate with the people there and make final test arrangements. After determining that the test was scheduled for December 1 and that his crew would receive the full cooperation of the local facility, he went to the data reduction group to arrange for the computer processing of data that would result from the test. The head of the data reduction unit, Gil Harmon, introduced George to the chief programmer, Dick Jones, with whom he was to work throughout the data reduction process.

George explained the importance of the test and showed Dick the type of information that would be required as final data from the digital computers.

After studying the information for a few minutes, Dick said, "I'll have to write a new program in order to give you the information you want. None of our present standard programs are capable of handling this job.''

''How long will it take to write a new program?'' George asked.

''Oh, I could probably have it finished by the fifth of December. That's the last day of your test, so it will be done in time to reduce your data.''

''That won't do!'' George exclaimed. ''We must have data from day to day all during the test. This proposal is red hot, and we must analyze our data on a day-by-day basis. That's the only way we can be sure we are taking the right approach in our test program. Each day's testing will be dependent on the data from the day before. So, what do you think? Can you have your program finished by the first?''

''Well I dunno,'' mumbled Dick. ''I might be able to finish by the first if there are no hitches in the program, but things seldom go that smoothly.''

''But it is possible to finish by the first?'' insisted George.

''It's possible, but I have other important programs to work on. Everything would have to work properly the first time.''

''This project is so important it just has to be done on time. We don't have any choice but to plan it for the first of the month.''

''Okay, I'll give it all the effort I can. With a little luck it will probably be ready for the first.''

''Swell,'' concluded George. ''I'll count on it.''

After concluding all pretest arrangements, George returned to Bristol. During the remainder of November he was in frequent telephone communication with Culver City. All preparations were progressing satisfactorily and Dick Jones assured George that the program would be finished by the last day of November.

On November 30, George and his crew arrived at Culver City. The test was to begin the next day.

George found everything in readiness for his test, except that the data program was not quite finished. He went to Dick Jones and asked what the holdup was.

''No holdup,'' Dick replied. ''The program will be completed by the end of the day, and we can check it out on the computer first thing in the morning. If everything checks out okay, we will be able to run your data from the first day's testing sometime tomorrow night. So you'll have your data the next day, just as you requested.''

''What happens if everything doesn't check out?'' asked George.

''It'll take a little while to iron out any bugs that may show up. But it shouldn't hold us up much; a few hours maybe.''

''Will you be able to work overtime on this if it becomes necessary?''

''I think so. We should be able to get your data for you one way or another, so don't worry. We'll let you know if we run into any major problems.''

George was reassured and returned to his hotel satisfied that all was in readiness for the start of his test the following day.

The testing groups existed as staff units. As such, they conducted tests at the request of line and project groups who were in need of the particular information. It was the usual practice for the group requesting a test to send along a representative to make whatever decisions regarding the test program that might come under the jurisdiction of the line organization.

The requesting group for this test had sent along their senior project engineer, Richard Wallen, because of the importance of the test. Wallen was a fairly new supervisor but was well qualified technically. He was a "driver," who worked his subordinates hard during rush programs such as this and had a reputation of sometimes "rubbing people the wrong way" in order to achieve an immediate goal.

Wallen was directly responsible to the division general manager for the success of the program. One of his major concerns was whether the final data would be ready on a day-to-day basis. He asked George about it the night before the test.

George replied, "Dick Jones told me everything would be ready on time. The odds are real slim that anything would go wrong; and if something went wrong, it would only slow us down a couple of hours."

The following day the data from the first shift of testing was turned over to Jones for processing. However, the program did not check out properly and Jones was unable to give George his data the following day.

The same situation occurred the next two days of testing, with Jones unable to make his program work despite working several hours overtime each day.

On the fourth day, the results were no better. Three hours after the testing shift was completed, Wallen and Bruster went to see Jones. When they found that Jones had gone home, Wallen "blew his top" and told George Bruster to telephone Jones at his home and demand to know why he wasn't at the office working on the programming problem.

A few minutes later, Gil Harmon, head of the data reduction unit, received a worried phone call from Jones, who quoted George as saying "If you don't get down here and start working on this program, it may cost you your job!"

Harmon passed on this information to Conners Simpson, who was instrumentation su-

pervisor at Culver City. Simpson was shocked and angered at the attitude the visiting group was taking toward one of his men. He immediately phoned Wallen and demanded an explanation. He told him in no uncertain terms to "lay off" his men and also told Wallen to follow the proper chain of command and notify him first the next time there was a problem. In addition, Simpson stated that he "had no intention of letting Jones come down and work on your damn program. Jones has been working twelve hours a day for the past week and has several other problems to deal with also. Besides, it's too late to salvage much of the data."

Before he hung up the phone, Simpson told Wallen, "This thing has gone too far. I'm going to take it to the boss and get it ironed out first thing in the morning. I want you and your crew chief to meet me, Jones, and Harmon in the boss's office at eight o'clock tomorrow morning."

The meeting was held, but the test series was considered unsatisfactory by all involved. The group had failed to get the desired information, and additional tests would have to be rescheduled at considerable cost in time and money.

The meeting proved to be a unique experience for George Bruster. Wallen denied outright that he had told George to use the strong language in speaking to Jones that had upset everyone so badly.

George could only reply that he thought that such language was Wallen's intent. George subsequently left the meeting shaking his head unhappily and trying to understand how the whole affair had deteriorated into such a mess.

Dick Spencer

After the usual banter when old friends meet for cocktails, the conversation between a couple of university professors and Dick Spencer, a former student who was now a successful businessman, turned to Dick's life as a vice-president of a large manufacturing firm.

"I've made a lot of mistakes, most of which I could live with, but this one series of incidents was so frustrating that I could have cried at the time," Dick said in response to a question. "I really have to laugh at how ridiculous it is now, but at the time I blew my cork."

Spencer was plant manager of Modrow Company, a Canadian branch of the Tri-American Corporation. Tri-American was a major producer of primary aluminum with integrated operations ranging from the mining of bauxite through the processing to fabrication of aluminum into a variety of products. The company also made and sold refractories and industrial chemicals. The parent company had wholly-owned subsidiaries in five separate United States locations and had foreign affiliates in 15 different countries.

Tri-American mined bauxite in the Jamaican West Indies and shipped the raw material by commercial vessels to two plants in Louisiana where it was processed into alumina. The alumina was then shipped to reduction plants in one of three locations for conversion into primary aluminum. Most of the primary aluminum was then moved to the company's fabricating plants for further processing. Fabricated aluminum items included sheet, flat, coil, and corrugated products; siding; and roofing.

Tri-American employed approximately 22,000 employees in the total organization. The company was governed by a board of directors which included the chairman, vice-chairman, president, and twelve vice-presidents. However, each of the subsidiaries and branches functioned as independent units. The board set general policy, which was then interpreted and applied by the various plant managers. In a sense, the various plants competed with one another as though they were independent companies. This decentralization in organizational structure increased the freedom and authority of the plant managers but also increased the pressure for profitability.

The Modrow branch was located in a border town in Canada. The total work force in Modrow was 1,000. This Canadian subsidiary was primarily a fabricating unit. Its main products were foil and building products such as roofing and siding. Aluminum products were gaining in importance in architectural plans, and increased sales were predicted for this branch. Its location and its stable work force were the most important advantages it possessed.

This case was developed and prepared by Professor Margaret E. Fenn, Graduate School of Business Administration, University of Washington. Reprinted by permission.

In anticipation of estimated increases in building product sales, Modrow had recently completed a modernization and expansion project. At the same time, their research and art departments combined talents in developing a series of twelve new patterns of siding which were being introduced to the market. Modernization and pattern development had been costly undertakings, but the expected return on investment made the project feasible. However, the plant manager, who was a Tri-American vice-president, had instituted a campaign to cut expenses wherever possible. In his introductory notice of the campaign, he emphasized that cost reduction would be the personal aim of every employee at Modrow.

Salesman

The plant manager of Modrow, Dick Spencer, was an American who had been transferred to this Canadian branch two years previously, after the start of the modernization plan. Dick had been with the Tri-American Company for 14 years, and his progress within the organization was considered spectacular by those who knew him well. Dick had received a Master's degree in Business Administration from a well-known university at the age of 22. Upon graduation he had accepted a job as salesman for Tri-American. During his first year as a salesman, he succeeded in landing a single, large contract that put him near the top of sales-volume leaders. In discussing his phenomenal rise in the sales volume, several of his fellow salesmen concluded that his looks, charm, and ability on the golf course contributed as much to his success as his knowledge of the business or his ability to sell the products.

The second year of his sales career, he continued to set a fast pace. Although his record set difficult goals for the other salesmen, he was considered a "regular guy" by them, and both he and they seemed to enjoy the few occasions when they socialized. However, by the end of the second year of constant traveling and selling, Dick began to experience some doubt about his future.

His constant involvement in business affairs disrupted his marital life, and his wife divorced him during the second year with Tri-American. Dick resented her action at first, but gradually seemed to recognize that his career at present depended on his freedom to travel unencumbered. During that second year, he ranged far and wide in his sales territory and successfully closed several large contracts. None of them was as large as his first year's major sale, but in total volume he again was well up near the top of salesmen for the year. Dick's name became well known in the corporate headquarters, and he was spoken of as "the boy to watch."

During his first year as salesman Dick had met the president of Tri-American at a company conference. After three days of golfing and socializing they developed a relaxed camaraderie considered unusual by those who observed the developing friendship. Although their contacts were infrequent after the conference, their easy relationship seemed to blossom the few times they did meet. Dick's friends kidded him about his ability to make use of his new friendship to promote himself in the company, but Dick brushed aside their gibes and insisted that he'd make it on his own abilities, not someone's coattail.

By the time he was 25, Dick began to suspect that he did not look forward to a life as a salesman for the rest of his career. He talked about his unrest with his friends, and they suggested that he groom himself for sales manager. "You won't make the kind of money you're making from commissions," he was told, "but you will have a foot in the door from an administrative standpoint, and you won't have to travel quite as much as you do now."

Dick took their suggestions lightly, and continued to sell the product, but was aware that he felt dissatisfied and did not seem to get the satisfaction out of his job that he had once enjoyed.

By the end of his third year with the company Dick was convinced that he wanted a change in direction. As usual, he and the president spent quite a bit of time on the golf course during the annual company sales conference. After their match one day, the president kidded Dick about his game. The conversation drifted back to business, and the president, who seemed to be in a jovial mood, started to kid Dick about his sales ability. In a joking way, he implied that anyone could sell a product as good as Tri-American's, but that it took real "guts and know-how" to make the products. The conversation drifted to other things, but this remark stuck with Dick.

Sometime later, Dick approached the president formally with a request for a transfer out of the sales division. The president was surprised and hesitant about this change in career direction for Dick. He recognized the superior sales ability that Dick seemed to possess, but was unsure that Dick was willing or able to assume responsibilities in any other division of the organization. Dick sensed the hesitancy but continued to push his request. He later remarked that it seemed that the initial hesitancy of the president convinced Dick that he needed an opportunity to prove himself in a field other than sales.

Trouble Shooter

Dick was finally transferred back to the home office of the organization and indoctrinated into productive and administrative roles in the company as a special assistant to the senior vice-president of production. As a special assistant, Dick was assigned several trouble-shooting jobs. He acquitted himself well in this role, but in the process succeeded in gaining a reputation as a ruthless headhunter among the branches where he had performed a series of amputations. His reputation as an amiable, genial, easy-going guy from the sales department was the antithesis of the reputation of a cold, calculating headhunter which he earned in his trouble-shooting role. The vice-president, who was Dick's boss, was aware of the reputation that Dick had earned but was pleased with the results that were obtained. The faltering departments that Dick had worked in seemed to bloom with new life and energy after Dick's recommended amputations. As a result, the vice-president began to sing Dick's praises, and the president began to accept Dick in his new role in the company.

Management Responsibility

About three years after Dick's switch from sales, he was given an assignment as assistant plant manager of an English branch of the company. Dick, who had remarried, moved his wife and family to London, and they attempted to adapt to their new routine. The plant manager was English, as were most of the other employees. Dick and his family were accepted with reservations into the community life as well as into the plant life. The difference between British and American philosophy and performance within the plant was marked for Dick, who was imbued with modern managerial concepts and methods. Dick's directives from headquarters were to update and upgrade performance in this branch. However, his power and authority were less than those of his superior, so he constantly found himself in the position of having to soft-pedal or withhold suggestions that he would have liked to make, or innovations that he would have liked to introduce. After a frustrating year and a half, Dick was suddenly made plant manager of an old British company which had just been purchased by Tri-American. He left his first English assignment with mixed feelings and moved from London to Birmingham.

As the new plant manager, Dick operated much as he had in his trouble-shooting job for the first couple of years of his change from sales to administration. Training and reeducation programs were instituted for all supervisors and managers who survived the initial purge. Methods were studied and simplified or redesigned whenever possible, and new attention was directed toward production that better met the needs of the sales organization. A strong controller helped to straighten out the profit picture through stringent cost control; and, by the end of the third year, the company showed a small profit for the first time in many years. Because he felt that this battle was won, Dick requested transfer back to the United States. This request was partially granted when, nine months later, he was awarded a junior vice-president title and was made manager of a subsidiary Canadian plant, Modrow.

Modrow Manager

Prior to Dick's appointment as plant manager at Modrow, extensive plans for plant expansion and improvement had been approved and started. Although he had not been in on the original discussions and plans, he inherited all the problems that accompany large-scale changes in any organization. Construction was slower in completion than originally planned, equipment arrived before the building was finished, employees were upset about the extent of change expected in their work routines with the installation of additional machinery and, in general, morale was at a low ebb.

Various versions of Dick's former activities had preceded him, and on his arrival he was viewed with dubious eyes. The first few months after his arrival were spent in a frenzy of catching up. This entailed attending con-

stant conferences and meetings, reading volumes of past reports, becoming acquainted with the civic leaders of the area, and sending a plethora of dispatches to and from the home office. Costs continued to climb unabated.

By the end of his first year at Modrow, the building program had been completed, although behind schedule, the new equipment had been installed, and some revamping of cost procedures had been incorporated. The financial picture at this time showed a substantial loss, but since it had been budgeted as a loss, this was not surprising. All managers of the various divisions had worked closely with their supervisors and accountants in planning the budget for the coming year, and Dick began to emphasize his personal interest in cost reduction.

As he worked through his first year as plant manager, Dick developed the habit of strolling around the organization. He was apt to leave his office and appear anywhere on the plant floor, in the design offices, at the desk of a purchasing agent or accountant, in the plant cafeteria rather than the executive dining room, or wherever there was activity concerned with Modrow. During his strolls he looked, listened, and became acquainted. If he observed activities which he wanted to talk about, or heard remarks that gave him clues to future action, he did not reveal these at the time. Rather he had a nod, a wave, a smile, for the people near him, but a mental note to talk to his supervisors, managers, and foremen in the future. At first his presence disturbed those who noted him coming and going, but after several exposures to him without any noticeable effect, the workers came to accept his presence and continue their usual activities. Supervisors, managers, and foremen, however, did not feel as comfortable when they saw him in the area.

Their feelings were aptly expressed by the manager of the siding department one day when he was talking to one of his foremen: "I wish to hell he'd stay up in the front office where he belongs. Whoever heard of a plant manager who had time to wander around the plant all the time? Why doesn't he tend to his paperwork and let us tend to our business?"

"Don't let him get you down," joked the foreman. "Nothing ever comes of his visits. Maybe he's just lonesome and looking for a friend. You know how these Americans are."

"Well, you may feel that nothing ever comes of his visits, but I don't. I've been called into his office three separate times within the last two months. The heat must really be on from the head office. You know these conferences we have every month where he reviews our financial progress, our building progress, our design progress, and so on? Well, we're not really progressing as fast as we should be. If you ask me, we're in for continuing trouble."

In recalling his first year at Modrow, Dick had felt constantly pressured and badgered. Ho always sensed that the Canadians he worked with resented his presence since he was brought in over the heads of the operating staff. At the same time he felt this subtle resistance from his Canadian work force, he believed that the president and his friends in the home office were constantly on the alert, waiting for Dick to prove himself, or fall flat on his face. Because of the constant pressures and demands of the work, he had literally dumped his family into a new community and had withdrawn into the plant. In the process, he built up a wall of resistance towards the demands of his wife and children who, in turn, felt as though he was abandoning them.

During the course of the conversation with his university friends, he began to recall a series of incidents that probably had resulted from the conflicting pressures. When describing some of these incidents, he continued to emphasize the fact that his attempt to be relaxed and casual had backfired. Laughingly,

Dick said, "As you know, both human relations and accounting were my weakest subjects during the Master's program, and yet they are two fields I felt needed the most at Modrow at this time." He described some of the cost procedures that he would have liked to incorporate. However, without the support and knowledge furnished by his former controller, he busied himself with details that were unnecessary. One day, as he describes it, he overheard a conversation between two of the accounting staff members with whom he had been working very closely. One of them commented to the other, "For a guy who's a vice-president, he sure spends a lot of time breathing down our necks. Why doesn't he simply tell us the kind of systems he would like to try, and let us do the experimenting and work out the budget?" Without commenting on the conversation he overheard, Dick then described himself as attempting to spend less time and be less directive in the accounting department.

Another incident he described which apparently had real meaning for him was one in which he had called a staff conference with his top-level managers. They had been going "hammer and tongs" for better than an hour in his private office, and in the process of heated conversation had loosened ties, taken off coats, and really rolled up their sleeves. Dick himself had slipped out of his shoes. In the midst of this, his secretary reminded him of an appointment with public officials. Dick had rapidly finished up his conference with his managers, straightened his tie, donned his coat, and wandered out into the main office in his stocking feet.

Dick fully described several incidents when he had disappointed, frustrated, or confused his wife and family by forgetting birthdays, appointments, dinner engagements, and so forth. He seemed to be describing a pattern of behavior which resulted from continuing pressure and frustration. He was setting the scene to describe his baffling and humiliating position in the siding department. In looking back and recalling his activities during this first year, Dick commented on the fact that his frequent wanderings throughout the plant had resulted in a nodding acquaintance with the workers, but probably had also resulted in foremen and supervisors spending more time getting ready for his visits and reading meaning into them afterwards than attending to their specific duties. His attempts to know in detail the accounting procedures being used required long hours of concentration and detailed conversations with the accounting staff, which were time-consuming and very frustrating for him, as well as for them. His lack of attention to his family life resulted in continued pressure from both wife and family.

The Siding Department Incident

Siding was a product which had been budgeted as a large profit item of Modrow. Aluminum siding was gaining in popularity among architects and builders because of its possibilities in both decorative and practical uses. Panel sheets of siding were shipped in standard sizes on order; large sheets of the coated siding were cut to specifications in the trim department, packed and shipped. The trim shop was located near the loading platforms, and Dick often cut through the trim shop on his wanderings through the plant. On one of his frequent trips through the area, he suddenly became aware of the fact that several workers responsible for the disposal function were spending countless hours at high-speed saws cutting scraps into specified lengths to fit into scrap barrels. The narrow bands of scrap which resulted from the trim process varied in length from 7 to 27 feet and had to be reduced in size to fit into the disposal barrels. Dick, in his concentration on cost reduction, picked up

one of the thin strips, bent it several times and fitted it into the barrel. He tried this with another piece, and it bent very easily. After assuring himself that bending was possible, he walked over to a worker at the saw and asked why he was using the saw when material could easily be bent and fitted into the barrels, resulting in saving time and equipment. The worker's response was, "We've never done it that way, sir. We've always cut it."

Following his plan of not commenting or discussing matters on the floor, but distressed by the reply, Dick returned to his office and asked the manager of the siding department if he could speak to the foreman of the scrap division. The manager said, "Of course, I'll send him up to you in just a minute."

After a short time, the foreman, very agitated at being called to the plant manager's office, appeared. Dick began questioning him about the scrap disposal process and received the standard answer. "We've always done it that way." Dick then proceeded to review cost-cutting objectives. He talked about the pliability of the strips of scrap. He called for a few pieces of scrap to demonstrate the ease with which it could be bent, and ended what he thought was a satisfactory conversation by requesting the foreman to order heavy-duty gloves for his workers and use the bending process for a trial period of two weeks to check the cost saving possible.

The foreman listened throughout most of this hour's conference, offered several reasons why it wouldn't work, raised some questions about the record-keeping process for cost purposes, and finally left the office with the forced agreement to try the suggested new method of bending, rather than cutting, for disposal. Although Dick was immersed in many other problems, his request was forcibly brought home one day as he cut through the scrap area. The workers were using power saws to cut scraps. He called the manager of the siding department and questioned him about the process. The manager explained that each foreman was responsible for his own processes, and since Dick had already talked to the foreman, perhaps he had better talk to him again. When the foreman arrived, Dick began to question him. He received a series of excuses, and some explanations of the kinds of problems they were meeting by attempting to bend the scrap material. "I don't care what the problems are," Dick nearly shouted, "when I request a cost-reduction program instituted, I want to see it carried through."

Dick was furious. When the foreman left, he phoned the maintenance department and ordered the removal of the power saws from the scrap area immediately. A short time later the foreman of the scrap department knocked on Dick's door reporting his astonishment at having maintenance men step into his area and physically remove the saws. Dick reminded the foreman of his request for a trial at cost reduction to no avail, and ended the conversation by saying that the power saws were gone and would not be returned, and the foreman had damned well better learn to get along without them. After a stormy exit by the foreman, Dick congratulated himself on having solved a problem and turned his attention to other matters.

A few days later Dick cut through the trim department and literally stopped to stare. As he described it, he was completely nonplussed to discover gloved workmen using hand shears to cut each piece of scrap.